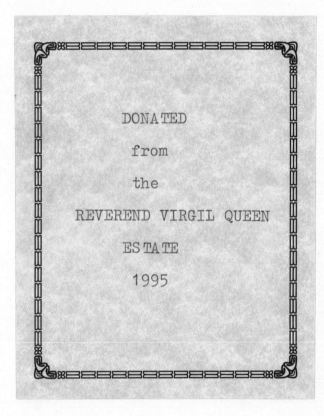

HUGH BOURNE
1772–1852

HUGH BOURNE

From the painting in the Library, Hartley Victoria College, Manchester.

[Frontispiece

HUGH BOURNE
1772–1852

BY

John T. Wilkinson
M.A., B.D., F.R.Hist.S.
Ranmoor Tutor of Church History
Hartley Victoria College, Manchester

LONDON · THE EPWORTH PRESS

Published by
THE EPWORTH PRESS
(FRANK H. CUMBERS)

25–35 City Road, London, E.C.1

New York · *Toronto*
Melbourne · *Cape Town*

PRINTED AND BOUND IN ENGLAND BY
HAZELL WATSON AND VINEY LTD
AYLESBURY AND LONDON

In Grateful Remembrance of

ARTHUR SAMUEL PEAKE
1865–1929
SCHOLAR
TEACHER
FRIEND

PREFACE

No servant of Christ every laboured more ardently for the spread of the Gospel than did Hugh Bourne, one of the founders of Primitive Methodism. It is therefore fitting that, in this, the centenary year of his death, some record should be made of his unceasing toil. His contribution to English Methodism ought not to be forgotten.

The main source of information concerning him is his own manuscript journal, which he kept almost daily for half a century, though unfortunately a considerable portion of this remarkable document seems to be irretrievably lost. In addition, there is a manuscript autobiography covering his early years, the first draft of which he wrote when he was seventy-two years of age. These manuscript sources, which are in the Library of Hartley Victoria College, Manchester, have been minutely examined in preparation for the present work.

Of printed sources, *The Memoirs of the Life and Labours of the late Venerable Hugh Bourne* (2 vols., 1855 and 1857), by John Walford, Bourne's nephew, are the most valuable, despite the strictures of contemporary criticism (e.g. *The Christian Ambassador* (1858), p. 220). The biography by Antliff (1872), based on Walford, and its revision by McKechnie (1892), though not without value, are of secondary importance. This is also true of the large amount of periodical material, mostly of later date.

I have been greatly privileged, as Librarian of the College, in having access to these Bourne MSS, and I am grateful to the Principal (the Rev. Dr H. G. Meecham), for permission to reproduce the 'Buckley' portrait of Hugh Bourne, which hangs in the College Library. I am also indebted to the Rev. Frank Cumbers, B.A., B.D., for allowing me to work through the Conference MS Journals, which are in the archives of City Road, London.

I desire to say how much I owe to the late Dr W. Lansdell Wardle, a former Principal of the College, with whom I discussed the project not long before his lamented death in 1946, and who urged me to undertake the work.

In addition, I should like to record my thanks to Mr Herbert

Hawthorne, of Bucknall, Stoke-on-Trent, who has shown me much kindness, as also to the many correspondents who have so willingly answered my inquiries.

I trust that this centenary study of Hugh Bourne may bring inspiration to many who labour for the cause of Christ in this generation.

J. T. W.

MANCHESTER
1952

CONTENTS

ABBREVIATIONS

Antliff
  The Life of the Venerable Hugh Bourne. W. Antliff, D.D. 1872.

Bourne *HPM* (1823)
  History of the Primitive Methodists (1823 edn.).

Bourne MSS (Auto.)
  The MS Autobiography of Hugh Bourne. A, B, and C Texts.

Bourne MSS (Jour.)
  The MS Journals of Hugh Bourne.

Clowes *Jour.* (1844)
  The Journals of William Clowes (1844).

Clowes MSS
  The MS Note-books of William Clowes.

Conf. MS Jour.
  MS Journals of the Primitive Methodist Conference from
  1827.

Gen. Mins.
  General Minutes of the Conference of the Primitive Methodist Connexion. From 1820.

Herod
  Biographical Sketches. G. Herod. n.d.

Kendall
  The Origin and History of the Primitive Methodist Church. H. B.
  Kendall. 2 Vols. n.d.

Mins. of Conf.
  Minutes of the Methodist Conference. From 1744.

MM
  Methodist Magazine. 1798–1835.

NHM
  A New History of Methodism. W. J. Townsend, H. B. Workman,
  and G. Eayrs. 2 Vols. 1919.

Petty
  *The History of the Primitive Methodist Connexion from its origin to
  the Conference of 1859.* Petty, J. 1860.

PML
> *Primitive Methodist Leader.* 1905–29.

PMM
> *Primitive Methodist Magazine.* From 1819.

PMQR
> *Primitive Methodist Quarterly Review.* 1879–1910.

PMW
> *Primitive Methodist World.* 1883–1907.

Walford
> *The Memoirs of the Life and Labours of the late Venerable Hugh Bourne.* J. Walford. 1855–7.

WHS Proceedings
> *Proceedings of the Wesley Historical Society.*

CHAPTER ONE

THE FORMATIVE YEARS (1772–88)

I

THE ANCESTORS of the Bourne family, according to Walford, were of Norman origin, and came into England in the reign of William the Conqueror, settling in North Staffordshire, where they obtained estates which long since have passed into other hands. Their descendants were numerous, and the name is to be found frequently in the earliest records of local parish registers, which date from the late sixteenth century. The line may be traced with reasonable certainty as far back as the beginning of the seventeenth century, and we find that an earlier Hugh Bourne was baptized in the parish of Norton-le-Moors in 1612.[1]

John Bourne,[2] the grandfather of Hugh, lived at the Abbey Farm in this parish, and was the father of eight children, the eldest, Joseph,[3] being born in 1733, and the youngest, Hugh,[4] at Burslem, eleven years later, the family having then moved to Bridge End. In addition to farming, John Bourne carried on the trades of wheelwright and timbering. He was a man of great industry, and being thrifty and prudent in the management of his affairs he accumulated some wealth, which enabled him to place his sons on farms or in trades, equal to those of the respectable yeomen of the neighbourhood.

His eldest son, Joseph Bourne, married Ellen Steele, the daughter of a farmer at Hatchley, near Cheadle, at Burslem parish church, on 24th January 1763,[5] by special licence. At the time of their marriage new developments were taking place in the pottery industry, in and around Burslem, owing to the new scientific methods of Josiah Wedgwood and the brothers Adams, who were master-potters. This meant a large extension

---

[1] *Par. Reg.*, loc. cit. 11th December 1612. Hughe Bourne f [ilius] Wm.

[2] *Norton Par. Reg.* 27th March 1697. bap. John, s. of William and Mary Bourne. He was buried 29th August 1763 at Burslem (*Burslem Par. Reg.*, loc. cit.).

[3] ibid. 21st April 1733. bap. Joseph, s. of John and Mary Bourne.

[4] *Burslem Par. Reg.* 27th September 1744. bap. Hugh, son of John and Mary Bourne, of Bridge End.

[5] ibid. Joseph Bourne of B[urslem], Wheelwright, and Ellen x Steele, of Chedale sp. lic. Wits. Thomas Steele & Hugh Bourne.

of trade in distant places, and many farmers' sons in the neighbourhood were induced to become sellers of pottery in regions previously untouched. One such was Joseph Bourne, who, with his wife, turned his face northward, embarked at Liverpool and sailed for Greenock. This must have been not long after their marriage, for their first child, whom they named John after his grandfather, was born there toward the end of 1763.[6] The sojourn in Scotland was remunerative; they made money and returned to the Abbey Farm, probably in 1767, bringing with them a second son, bearing his father's name, Joseph.

Not long after their return, Joseph and Ellen Bourne took the Ford Hays Farm, in the Stoke parish, some two miles distant. After the manner of his father, Joseph Bourne commenced business as a wheelwright and dealer in timber, in addition to his farming. The family remained at Ford Hays for twenty-two years, during which time three daughters, Mary, Hannah, and Ellen, and three sons, Hugh, William, and James, were added to the household.[7]

Joseph Bourne, the father of Hugh, seems to have been a man of extremes. It was generally believed that his sojourn in Scotland was responsible for the creation of a fondness for strong drink, a desire which unfortunately remained with him through the years, to the intense grief of his wife and the dread of his children. A man of violent temper, he was nevertheless a professed Churchman; he insisted on his children learning the Church services, and would not allow them to use improper language. He was destitute, however, of the realities of religion, and opposed every community that dissented from the Church. He lived to within a few months of his hundredth year.

Ellen Bourne was a woman of fine character. The tribute of her son is significant: 'My mother was a woman of such prudence, management, industry, and economy, that could not be surpassed, if equalled.' Brought up from childhood in strict adherence to the worship of the Church of England, she sought to train her own children in the fear of God. Their early

[6] John Bourne was buried at Norton, 28th May 1849, having lived to the age of eighty-five. Bourne MSS (Jour.), loc. cit.

[7] *Bucknall Par. Regs.* give the following details: Mary, bap. 6th March 1768, d. 1781 or 1782; Hannah, bap. 16th March 1770; Hugh, b. 3rd April 1772, bap. 19th April; William (probably baptized at Norton, but entries in that register only reach 1751) emigrated to America (Bourne MSS (Jour.) February 1811); Ellen, bap. 23rd January 1775; James, bap. at Stoke (*Par. Reg.*), b. February 1781, bap. 11th March 1781.

education was almost entirely in her hand. Whilst spinning at her wheel she taught her children to read. Soon after the conversion of her son, Hugh, in 1799, she entered into a deeper experience of religion—'she learned a more excellent way'—and united with him in the fellowship of the Methodist society at Ridgway, a hamlet about half a mile from Bemersley. Her joy was increased by the conversion of her younger son, James, shortly afterwards. Despite the domestic affliction she continued to be 'a mother in Israel' to the rising cause, and concerning her closing years one wrote: 'Her soul was as the garden of the Lord, blooming with life and immortality.'

The call which came to her sons to become preachers of the Gospel touched her deeply, and in her closing days her solemn charge to them forms a moving scene.

Stand firm and unshaken by the infant cause: fan the holy flame, follow the openings of Divine providence, and when I am no more with you, the God of Abraham will be your guide. And thou, my beloved Hugh, son of my right hand, let not my affliction and death prevent thee from fulfilling thy appointments. Go, my son, preach the Gospel.[8]

That was on Friday, 25th July 1817. For Hugh it was a final farewell, for at the time of her death he was in the region of Belper, in Derbyshire, as the following entries in his Journal show:

Thursday, 7th August. At Windley, abroad. [My mother died tonight.] [9]
Friday, 15th August. Came home: my mother died on Thursday, 7th August, and was buried on Sunday, 10th August 1817. My mother has been pious for a long time. She was quite worn down with old age. She has had a rough road through life, a very rough road, but she has weathered the storm. On Friday, 1st August, she broke through all, and praised God almost the whole day. . . . In the same way she proceeded till the Thursday night following when, about 6 o'clock, she fell asleep in the Lord. Well, from her, I received my first religious impressions and to her care I owe a great deal. Her industry and labours in the things of this life have been great and continued. We were a large family, and my father a very drinking, violent, passionate man. But my mother's industry and great labours kept the family from want. . . . Now she rests from her labours. . . . I was out labouring in the ministry when she died and

[8] Walford, p. 7.
[9] These words seem to be a later insertion, probably made at the time of writing the entry for the following Friday, the script being similar.

they did not think it necessary to send for me. When I first knew of her death, I was filled with sorrow, but this was mixed with joy, when my brother James gave me an account of her death. O Lord, prepare me to follow her.

Both Joseph and Ellen Bourne were buried in the church-yard of Norton-le-Moors. She was in her eighty-fifth year.

II

Hugh Bourne, the third son and fifth child of his parents, was born on 3rd April 1772 at Ford Hays farm, in the parish of Stoke-on-Trent. The farmstead is still standing, though it has been raised and the roof is no longer thatched. As a residence there could hardly be anything more bleak, desolate, and soli-tary. Of it Bourne writes: [10]

Our neighbourhood consisted of three rather small farm-houses and there was no other house, nor school, nor place of worship . . . neither public road nor foot-road near our house. At times we would hardly see a stranger the month round. . . . So I grew up in a state of timidity and bashfulness seldom equalled, and this timidity con-tinued heavy upon me till I was more than thirty years of age.

This moorland origin left its ineffaceable mark on Bourne: his early environment became reflected in his strong, silent, and rugged nature.

As we have seen, Bourne's mother taught him to read and write, and under her care he made some progress in the first stages of arithmetic. Later, despite bad roads and the distance from any school, his father sent him to a school fully two miles away, at Werrington, in Caverswell parish. It was in the charge of Mr Samuel Cooper, who not only taught his pupils, but had some care for their moral and religious welfare, regularly pray-ing with them at the close of each day's session.

I well remember writing '1779' in my copy-book as the year of our Lord, so that I was then only seven years of age. . . . Here I had to tug at arithmetic and at the grammar and dictionary: and learn-ing the explanation of words in the dictionary took my fancy considerably.[11]

Bourne notes the somewhat strange design of his father in this new venture:

[10] Bourne MSS (Auto.), A and C Texts.
[11] Bourne MSS (Auto.), C Text, f. 4.

When my father's expensive habits are considered, his putting me to school may be thought extraordinary: but the hand of God was in it. An aged man, who was occasionally at my father's house, was very pressing for me to be brought up for a parson, and others took the same notion.[12]

After some time Hugh was removed to the endowed Church school at Bucknall, in Stoke parish, under the care of one, Mr Harrison, who was not to be so highly esteemed, however, as was the former master. His successor, a Mr Bennison, proved an excellent teacher, and his pupil made rapid progress, quickly becoming head of the school. Of Mr Bennison, Bourne always spoke with gratitude. Reading, English, grammar, arithmetic, and the first steps of mensuration, together with the rudiments of Latin, formed his studies.

It would seem, however, that his father's patience soon became exhausted, for Hugh was removed from school probably before he had reached the age of twelve[13] in order to take up work on the farm and in the wheelwright's shop. Yet he did not cease from study.

When quite taken from school my zeal for reading and study was intense. I went through arithmetic afresh, with geometry. I also paid attention to astronomy and natural philosophy, and made progress in history and geography: but my chief study was the Bible and religion . . . my lot was severe, for after the hard day's work, I frequently sat up till near midnight, reading. I gladly embraced it.[14]

When Hugh was sixteen years of age, the family moved to a larger farm at Bemersley,[15] some six miles north, in the parish of Norton-le-Moors. Joseph Bourne now gave up the trade of wheelwright and timbering, and this caused a change in the life of young Bourne, to which we shall come presently.

[12] Walford, p. 19.
[13] He could not have been more than twelve or thirteen years of age, as he learned the trade of wheelwright before the family let Ford Hays farm in 1788 (Walford, p. 21).
[14] Bourne MSS (Auto.), A and C Texts.
[15] The time of removal of farmers in North Staffordshire was May Day, which would be a little more than a month after Hugh's birthday.

CHAPTER TWO

SEEKING THE LIGHT (1788–1800)

I

As a small boy, Hugh Bourne occasionally listened to preaching in the small Methodist chapel at Ash, less than two miles from his home: the services were held on the Sunday afternoons alternate to the Bucknall parish church services, and certain members of the latter congregation went occasionally to the chapel and took him with them. He perceived the zeal of the Methodist preaching, but failed to understand much of it.

An early sense of his own sinfulness was entirely from an inward source and not prompted by external influence.

> My being convinced of sin had nothing to do with the Methodists, as I did not then know what Methodism was: that conviction was a matter between God and myself: no human being knew of it, neither durst I speak of it to anyone. I could then work a little, and it took place between me and the Lord when I was working in my little way in one of my father's fields.[1]

When the family removed to Bemersley in 1788, there was a small Methodist society at Ridgway, a hamlet about half a mile distant, the service being held in the Stanley Fields farm-house, the owner of which was named Birchenough,[2] but the parish services were more frequent, and therefore his association with the Methodists was very slight indeed.

It is fortunate that we have a personal record of Bourne's spiritual experience in early childhood, preserved in what we shall call his *Self-review*.[3] From this document we must now quote at some length:

> The Lord began to work upon me when I was a child. The very first thoughts that ever I can recollect were thoughts of God, and I

---

[1] Bourne MSS (Auto.), A Text, f. 10.
[2] A print is in Kendall (I.14).
[3] Bourne MSS (*Self-review*). This priceless and moving document, bearing the date, 'Bemersley, Aug[us]t 17, 1800', was written in the hope of drawing Thomas Maxfield into the same experience of conversion to which Bourne had recently attained. See *infra.*, p. 29. Walford (I.56) refers to the document as being (in 1855) in his possession.

think at this time I had as clear ideas of God as it was possible for anyone to have at that age. When I was about four or five my thoughts were that God was an everlasting and eternal Being, that He dwelt above the skies, that He created heaven and earth, and all things seen and unseen, that He was able to destroy all things, or to alter the form of everything, that He was present everywhere, that He knew the thoughts of everyone. I thought that heaven was a place of happiness, and those that were righteous and kept God's commandments were admitted thither, and could see God (which I thought the greatest happiness) and were happy for ever and ever: and that hell was a place of torments, and all that did wickedly and broke God's commandments were sent thither to be tormented by the devil and his angels in blue, flaming brimstone for ever and ever. These views made me very intent upon keeping what I thought to be God's commandments. I was delighted to know His will; I delighted in His name; I was eager to know how to please Him. . . .

I soon learned to read, and greatly delighted to read the Bible and religious books, and learned Morning and Evening Prayer (that is used in the Church) off by rote,[4] and a good many of Watts's hymns; and having read in one of them this line:

> Jehovah rides upon a cloud
> And thunders through the world,

I thought I should see Him when it thundered and accordingly I would be out-of-doors at such times, and my mother could not keep me in the house; having looked a good many times, and could not see Him, I asked my mother about it, and she told me that He was invisible; however, I still got out-of-doors when it thundered, for I thought that the Lord was there, and I would be as near Him as possible, for my soul was filled with love to Him and I thought that I was greatly beloved by Him also. . . . This I looked upon as an extraordinary work of grace, but whether I should have obtained the new birth at that time, if anyone had taught me the nature and necessity of it, I cannot tell: but, however, there passed a few years that I can look upon with pleasure.

When I arrived at about seven years of age, by constant reading and studying, I began to understand the nature and spirituality of the commandments.[5] . . . Now a new scene opened. I was not able to keep the law, so now I fell under the curse of a broken law. I now felt the terrors of the Lord come upon me. . . . I soon began to

---

[4] Bourne records: 'At my father's instance I committed to memory the course of morning and evening prayer in the Church prayer-book, with the *Te Deum*, Litany, and other matters. And in this labour I took much delight' (Bourne MSS (Auto.), C Text, f. 4).

[5] Walford (I.14–15) records an incident relating to this period and which indicates Bourne's early spiritual sensitiveness. A load of coals for the house being dropped on the far side of a brook, crossed only by a narrow plank, Hugh pleaded to help in the carrying, despite the danger. After much entreaty he was allowed to assist, and did it successfully, having secretly besought the help of God, and having promised in return that 'all the family should worship Him'. Afterwards the extent of his promise seemed beyond realization, and he came under deep self-reproach that 'he had lied unto God'. The experience was one of profound inward sorrow.

despair of ever getting to heaven, as I found in the Scriptures that the soul that sinneth it shall die, and without holiness no man shall see the Lord: these Scriptures . . . did rend my very soul . . . and I had no one that I could open my mind unto . . . for all the people I met with seemed as if they cared for none of these things, so I was left to struggle alone. . . . I wished thousands of times that I had been a bird, or beast, or anything but a man.[6]

Sometimes I found a little comfort in prayer, but was generally very dark, and harassed with a thousand temptations. I made constant resolutions against sin, but as they were made in my own strength, they were always swept away with the first wind of temptation.[7] . . . I continued in this dreadful state till the spring of the year 1799.

Bourne states that he sought to understand the meaning of 'justification by faith', as discovered by him in the *Prayer Book*, and that he 'read many books' in the hope of illumination, amongst them being *The Whole Duty of Man*[8] and *The Practice of Piety*,[9] together with treatises on the Commandments. 'I likewise heard many sermons at Bucknall chapel for that purpose . . . but miserable comforts were they all. . . . They did but lay out an excellent train of good works and moral duties.' He was seeking for the knowledge that 'true repentance' is 'the gift of God'.

I could not find out what Saint Paul meant by being enlightened and tasting of the heavenly gift, and being made partaker of the Holy Spirit. . . . I knew that there were things that I had not experienced.

These inward happenings occurred when Bourne was 'about twelve or thirteen years of age'.

To deflect his mind from this spiritual problem he now 'began to study the arts and sciences', resolving 'for the present' to be 'as circumspect' as he could.

Thus I began in a measure to fight against God, and endeavoured to stifle the convictions of His Spirit; and I now wonder that the Lord did not then cut me off . . . but such was His goodness and mercy toward me, that He not only spared me, but the conviction of sin never left me.

[6] cf. Clowes (*Jour.*, p. 17): 'Sometimes I used to walk in solitary and unfrequented places, wishing that I was a bird or beast or anything else that was not accountable to the tribunal of heaven.'

[7] Bourne compares his experience with that of St Paul in Romans 8, but adds: 'The 25th verse I could not apply to myself.'

[8] [R. Allestree.] (Pub. 1657.) Bourne refers to it as 'new', and this probably indicates that he found it in the London edition of 1735.

[9] Lewis Bayley, Bishop of Bangor. *The Practice of Piety* (1630) was a devotional guide for three generations.

Bourne steadily progressed in learning, now entering into the study of 'natural philosophy, mechanics, hydrostatics, hydraulics, pneumatics, and many other things'; yet, he adds: 'It was the one thing needful that I wanted, and without it I should have been always miserable.'

Certain prejudices against the Methodists seem to have arisen about this time: 'A few that had come under my observation did not adorn their profession.' The persons concerned, however, had been excluded from the society, a fact of which Bourne was unaware at the time, hence his hesitancy.

II

At this point we must recall the change that took place in Bourne's circumstances not long after the removal of the family to Bemersley. His father's sister had married one William Sherratt, who was now in occupation of the Abbey Farm, some three miles to the south of Bemersley. He was a celebrated engineer and millwright, and Hugh was now transferred to his uncle's trade, in which his scientific studies, now to be applied to windmills and watermills, were to prove invaluable. It was also more congenial to him than his previous work had been on his father's estate. 'I was never fond of wheelwrighting though I learned it: it was at my father's instance, not my own choice.' His uncle's business was extensive, and this furnished Hugh with opportunities of going farther afield: it should be remembered that there were no railways at this time, and so much travel had to be accomplished on foot. These journeyings with fellow-workmen brought occasions of temptation, particularly to intoxication, as for example in a distant part of Cheshire, whilst erecting a mill to crush bark for a tanner. But Bourne became resolute against it, and long afterwards declared: 'For more than forty years I had to bear the reproach of being as it was said, like nobody else.' [10]

His travels also brought other experiences. Returning on one occasion through Macclesfield, he noticed people wending their way down the street, as if on common purpose: asking the reason, he was told that they were going to the Methodist chapel. Time did not allow Bourne to join them, but a certain impression was left. 'My eye was upon the people, and it was impressed upon my mind, these have real religion: this startled

[10] 'I was intoxicated twice . . . in my nineteenth year: and I dreaded intoxication ever after' (Bourne MSS (Auto.), C Text, f. 8).

me from head to foot.' [11] This impression was never wholly effaced, though Bourne returned again to 'the old uncertainty', which continued for some years.

Then a new occasion arose, with the building of a windmill at Hanley, in the Potteries, upon which Bourne was engaged. He had understood that the clerk of works was a Methodist, and so he anticipated some opportunity for insight into 'the perfection of Methodism', as a kind of commentary upon his earlier Macclesfield experience. Unfortunately he had been misinformed, but assuming he was right, he was sorely distressed, as the overseer proved to be of doubtful morality. 'This I lay down as the worst accident that befel me. . . . I concluded there was no religion amongst the Methodists . . . because he was reckoned an honest man.' The result was a growth of carelessness in Bourne as to religion; doing business on the sabbath day lessened attendance at the parish services and, instead, he joined in sports. 'I sinned against light and knowledge to a high degree.'

Yet he was not left alone.

All this time the Spirit of the Lord followed me with convictions, but I endeavoured to put them from me, and to make myself easy, but all in vain: they still followed me and made my life miserable.[12]

The experience at Hanley, however, had not been wholly in vain for, in the house of the one who had so sorely disappointed him, Bourne picked up a copy of the *Arminian Magazine* for the year 1795.

I was interested with Bruce's 'Travels', and also noticed a religious letter, written by a female and dated 'Bristol October 22, 1771': this letter took my attention, and caused me to wonder who the Arminians were and where they lived.[13]

Bourne had also read other books on religion, 'of different denominations, Quakers and others; and some very old ones'. Amongst the latter was a treatise by the Puritan, Thomas Goodwin, entitled *A Child of Light walking in Darkness* (16 ?).[14] But the full light was not yet.

---

[11] Bourne MSS, A Text, f. 14. In his *Self-review* (f. 11) he refers to the incident: 'I observed a solemn awe rest upon the young people, that it gave me a great check . . . my mind was very tender to them ever after.'
[12] Bourne MSS, *Self-review*, ff. 12–13.
[13] Bourne MSS (Auto.), A Text, f. 15.
[14] *The Works of Thomas Goodwin, D.D.* (1861 edn)., III.227–350.

Not long afterwards Bourne's mother was in Burslem, and she asked one, Mr J. Mayer, a Methodist, to lend her a religious book for her own reading. He put into her hands 'a book as thick as a Bible, containing biographies, treatises, sermons, and tracts bound up together. In it was the *Life of John Fletcher*, sermons by John Wesley, Jane Cooper's *Letters*,[15] the auto-biographies of two Methodist preachers, Thomas Taylor [16] and John Haime; [17] also Alleine's *Alarm* [18] and Richard Baxter's *Call to the Unconverted*; a treatise on the Articles and Homilies of the Church of England.' All these were new to Bourne, and much illumination resulted from his reading of them.

In particular, a sermon by Wesley, 'On the Trinity',[19] deeply impressed him: he had for a long time been seeking for some 'right religious society' to which he could turn for guidance and fellowship. One passage in the sermon arrested him.

Whatsoever the generality of people may think, it is certain that opinion is not religion; no, not right opinion; assent to one, or to ten thousand truths. There is a wide difference between them. Even right opinion is as distant from religion as the east is from the west. People may be quite right in their opinions, and yet have no religion at all, and, on the other hand, persons may be truly religious, who hold many wrong opinions.

Bourne wrote:

The reading of these things cleared my way. It was like light rising in darkness: and it opened my mind . . . and gave me more light and information than any book I had ever before read. . . . It gave me to see that I might join any really religious society without under-valuing others, and might profit by all.[20]

There was still hesitancy, however, regarding joining the Methodists, partly because the unfortunate experience at Hanley lingered in his mind, and partly because the society at Ridgway met in a farm-house, 'which some thought not worthy'. The Methodist preaching was held at Stanley Fields, the farm-stead of John Birchenough, and on one occasion Bourne was asked to deliver a message at this farm. During conversation he

[15] *Letters wrote by Jane Cooper* . . . (1764). See Green, *Bibliography*, No. 225. Wesley described her as 'that lovely saint'.
[16] See *Arminian Magazine* (1780), III.367–85: also portrait, pp. 420–41.
[17] ibid., pp. 207–17, 265–73.
[18] Joseph Alleine (1634–68), *An Alarm to the Unconverted* (1672). The work to which Baxter had written the Preface was often bound up with the Baxter volume.
[19] *Sermons*, Std. edn., Vol. I, Sermon LV.
[20] Bourne MSS (Auto.), A Text, f. 19.

noticed a book in the window of the room: he found it to be
another copy of the *Arminian Magazine* for 1795, which he had
first seen at Hanley, and for the further reading of which he had
planned to return there. He asked Birchenough for the loan of
it. The immediate reply was: 'You are as welcome as the
flowers in May: and I have several more volumes and you shall
read them all.' It was in this further reading that Bourne discovered that the Arminians were the Methodists: his views
were changed. Were the Arminians of the West of England
different from the Methodists of Staffordshire? If the latter were
faulty, perhaps the others were not!

Another incident occurred about this time, whilst he was
working at Werrington for one who was a Quaker, and who
lent him 'large volumes containing the annals of the first race of
Quakers'.[21] Bourne became deeply impressed.

Having been delivered from laying stress on opinions, I found that
the religion of the heart was alike in all. The first race of the
Quakers were (*sic*) endued with the spirit of martyrs to a most extraordinary degree. And they exhibited examples of faith, patience, and
sufferings not often equalled ... many went through afflictions and
imprisonments to crowns of life, even in the most dreadful of
persecutions; their zeal for open-air worship was great: it could not
be conquered.[22]

Probably here is one of the first springs of Bourne's later commitment to open-air preaching and praying.

John Birchenough also lent him Coke and Moore's *Life of
Wesley* (1702): 'This gave me assistance.' Still more important
was the discovery of John Fletcher's *Letters on the Spiritual
Manifestation of the Son of God*,[23] which he found printed in the
Methodist Magazine for 1793, probably also loaned to him by
Birchenough; but the full impact of this was not yet, though
many years later Bourne wrote:

I got a clear view of the manifestations of Jesus Christ: of justification by faith; of being born again. And I felt a degree of satisfaction
in contemplating religion. But, alas, such a flood of evil thoughts
poured into my mind that ... I put off seeking religion to a future
time. ... To the present day the awfulness of that putting off almost
causes me to tremble.[24]

---

[21] Probably *A Collection of the Sufferings of the People called Quakers*, J. Besse, 2 Vols.
(London, 1753).
[22] Bourne MSS (Auto.), A Text, ff. 21–2.
[23] Bourne afterwards printed these letters in *PMM* (1822).
[24] Bourne MSS (Auto.), A Text, f. 23.

A strange impulse of fear was also somewhat decisive at this period. By chance, Bourne came across the story of a sea-captain named Barnaby (belonging to the reign of Charles the Second), who, with about thirty of his men, went ashore on Stromboli, where they saw a man in grey run into the crater of the volcano. The captain said that the man was his next-door neighbour—a Mr Booty, a pawnbroker in London. 'All concluded that he had died and was running into hell.' [25] The following morning Bourne narrated the story to his fellow-workmen at the Werrington mill, and as he did so he was possessed by the fear that similarly he might suffer final perdition. 'If I go into that burning mountain, I must never come out again.' Bourne adds:

My mind was made up in an instant: I must cut off everything that hindered. I must seek the Lord with my whole heart. . . . I must flee from the wrath to come. . . . I had sinned against the light. . . . But in a few days I felt a degree of comfort in prayer: and this established me fully to believe that the Lord had not fully forsaken me.[26]

Listening to a sermon on Luke xiii: 24 ('Strive to enter in at the strait gate'), preached probably by a local preacher at the Methodist Society at Ridgway,[27] Bourne found an exact description of his own spiritual condition, and this determination was deepened.

I now was resolved to obtain the like blessings. . . . I now agonized in prayer . . . and pleaded the promises. I told the Lord that I was ruined and undone, and confessed my inability to help myself . . . and begged Him to manifest Himself to me in the manner that He doth not unto the world; and, glory be to His High and Holy Name, in a few weeks He set my soul at liberty from the burden and guilt of sin, and brought me into the liberty of the children of God.[28]

[25] See *Arminian Magazine* (1783), VI.43–4. 'An account of Mr Booty: extracted from Captain Spink's Journal and from the Court of King's Bench.' On returning to London, Captain Barnaby told the news, and the pawnbroker's widow had him arrested. She claimed a thousand pounds for slander, and asserted that her husband had died in London. The thirty sailors appeared as witnesses in court, and the judge, believing that so many could not be deceived, gave verdict against the widow, and the captain was cleared.

[26] Bourne MSS (Auto.), A Text, ff. 23–7.

[27] Unfortunately a leaf (ff. 15–16) is missing from the MS of Bourne's *Self-review* at this point. It is therefore not possible to identify the preacher, but in what remains of the account Bourne describes him as one 'who did not appear to be a man of great abilities, and often used the vulgar language', but he was convinced by the marks of his personal religion. 'I thought that these things must be fulfilled in him.'

[28] Bourne MSS (*Self-review*.)

This deliverance came in the spring of the year 1799. His own words alone suffice to tell the story of it—the climax of nearly twenty years of seeking and striving.

One Sunday morning I was reading and meditating and praying and endeavouring to believe. Suddenly the Lord was manifested to me, as filling the universe with His Presence, and I heard an inward voice proclaim twice: 'Thy iniquity is forgiven, and thy sin is covered.' Light, life and liberty and happiness flowed into my soul, and such rapturous joy that I could scarce tell whether I was in the body or not. When I could articulate anything it was: 'My Father, my loving Father! My God, my reconciled God! My hope, my heaven and my all!' I now felt that I was able to believe in Christ with my heart unto righteousness, and with my mouth make confession to salvation: the burden of my sin was quite gone. . . . I now felt the love of God shed abroad in my heart by the Holy Ghost given unto me, enabling me to love every child of man, and ardently desired that all might come to the knowledge of salvation, and taste the happiness that I had experienced, and be everlastingly saved.

When this rapturous joy had a little subsided, I felt a calm, settled peace upon my mind. . . . All my desires were after God and holiness. I was as if brought into another world; creation wore a fresh aspect; the Scriptures were opened unto me and I read the Bible with new eyes, and every line was full of rich promises. I now began to live a new life, and everything seemed to rejoice with me. . . . Everything led me to God. I could contemplate everything in the universe and say, these are the works of God, and not only the works of God, but the work of my God and my loving Father.

I now delighted in the ordinances and eagerly longed for the return of another sabbath. I found life and liberty in all the means of grace, and could testify that the Lord was among us of a truth.[29]

Although the new experience filled Bourne 'with all joy and peace', there were days of shadow. Was all this but fancy? Might he not fall from grace? But he counted this as 'a suggestion of the enemy of souls to weaken faith', yet he found in it 'a humbling before God'. At this season he attended a quarterly 'meeting' of the Quakers at Leek, some seven or eight miles from Bemersley, at which a 'friend' spoke 'of the readiness of Christ to build up again those that had backslidden'. 'I felt the word applied to my heart by the Spirit, and was restored to peace again.'

Looking back upon the spiritual pilgrimage of 'these twenty sorrowful years', Bourne declared: 'Like Bunyan's pilgrim I had to make my way alone.'

[29] It should be remembered that the *Self-review*, dated 17th August 1800, was written some eighteen months after the experience of spiritual release, following which he had joined the Methodist society.

III

Now arose the problem of associating with some particular Christian community. Bourne had considerable affinity with the Quakers, having been 'much edified' in the reading of their history, but he was not certain as to the depth of their evangelical experience as compared with his own recent illumination; neither did he observe any practice of family worship in the home of his Quaker friend at Werrington. There were Methodists meeting in society at the Ridgway farmstead, but he had uneasiness about seeking to join this fellowship because one member of the household was 'of unhappy note' in the neighbourhood, and unscrupulous people set this one forth 'as being the best Methodist among them'. In this dilemma Bourne resolved to seek the guidance of God.

I determined to consult no man ... but wait until the Lord should make known His holy will ... and to attend diligently the means of grace.[30] ... I waited for some weeks for an answer.

The final decision came in the following manner. In June 1799 John Birchenough told Bourne of a love-feast to be held in the Methodist chapel at Burslem, toward the end of the month, and urged him to attend. On a previous Sunday morning the travelling preacher, being present at the Stanley Fields farm, was preparing tickets of membership, and asked Bourne his name, the latter having come over by Birchenough's invitation. Bourne replied: 'I am not one of you!' But Birchenough indicated the necessity of a ticket for admission to the love-feast, and Bourne, willing to attend, accepted the suggestion of the preacher, 'little thinking that receiving the ticket constituted me a member'. Bourne accompanied Birchenough to the Burslem meeting, and of this he afterwards wrote:

This love-feast I shall ever remember. In it the Lord manifested to me that it was His will for me to be a Methodist; and notwithstanding my timidity, I was near rising up to speak, and at the close I was heart and hand a Methodist.[31]

The next Sabbath morning he was present at the Ridgway class—which now had been removed to another house—and he records:

[30] The Bourne family had been accustomed to attend morning service at the parish church, whether at Ford Hays or Bemersley; but since Hugh's reading of the *Arminian Magazine*, he, his mother, and his brother James, had attended the Methodist preaching in the afternoons at the Stanley Fields farm.

[31] Bourne MSS (Auto.), A Text, f. 40; cf. *Self-review*, f. 22. 'I found it good to be there, and determined that this people should be my people.'

My beloved mother joined: our leaders were four Burslem
Methodist, planned to come in turn . . . and their kind attention to
us was great.[32]

Although there was preaching at Stanley Fields each Sabbath
afternoon, Bourne thought 'the public means of grace were
scanty', and so began to attend a meeting for prayer in Burslem
on Sunday mornings, and, later, preaching, at Tunstall, some
three miles west of Bemersley, and at Burslem, some three and
a half miles away. 'The satisfaction of being sure to hear
sermons made all amends', and Bourne adds: 'I grew most in
grace at preachings.'

Bourne now gave diligent study to religious truth. He found
in the magazines 'treasures of experience', more of Wesley's
sermons, and his *Notes on the New Testament*, and to these Bourne
added Fletcher's *Checks to Antinomianism*.

By the good hand of God upon me, I got a more clear and extensive knowledge of the Scripture, of Christian experience, and an
enlarged acquaintance with the doctrine of Christ.[33]

Although now a Methodist, Bourne had wide sympathies. 'I
was happy in not undervaluing other religious communities . . .
but I loved my own.' He seized any occasion for edification,
as, for example, one evening returning from work through
Hanley, he 'stepped into a dissenting chapel', when the minister
spoke from Numbers xxi : 4, 'And the soul of the people was
much discouraged because of the way', and of which discourse
Bourne wrote: 'I was much blest under his preaching . . . with
a flow of heavenly power.' Bourne cultivated 'a great zeal' for
attending preachings, being 'much edified' thereby. One
occasion, however, gave another emphasis to his thought and
experience. In July 1799 the Reverend Samuel Bradburn, an
outstanding Methodist preacher, preached on a weeknight at
Burslem. Bourne had heard him 'with admiration'; but he noted
that he seemed to disparage preaching 'as merely talking to
our fellow-creatures' and exalted praying 'as talking to
Almighty God'. This new emphasis lingered in Bourne's mind,
until in later years he tended to stress the importance of praying, and there is little doubt that here we have the spring of his
'companies of praying labourers', so important in his work for
open-air preaching and evangelism.

[32] Bourne MSS (Auto.), A Text, f. 40.   [33] ibid., f. 43.

CHAPTER THREE

EARLY LABOURS (1800–7)

A NEW SPIRITUAL opportunity now emerged for Bourne. Early in 1800 he purchased a quantity of oak timber, growing on a farm at Dales Green, between Harriseahead and Mow Cop,[1] some three miles west of Bemersley. The region was barren and unproductive; but Bourne's concern was about the scantiness of spiritual provision for the inhabitants, who were largely given over to ungodliness—bull-baiting, cock-fighting, plundering, drunkenness and profanity were widespread. Only one small chapel-of-ease, at Newchapel, was discernible for miles around. All this weighed heavily on his mind and heart.

Bourne's employment was exacting, for he was engaged in carpenter's work at mountain farms, and at the Stonetrough colliery a mile distant he had undertaken the timbering connected with the mine, so that there was no prospect of returning to Bemersley for some time. He found contact with a farrier and blacksmith, Thomas Maxfield, of Mow Cop, who had his smithy at Harriseahead, half a mile or so from Dales Green. The necessity for iron-work in addition to timbering required frequent visits to Maxfield, and these occasions afforded Bourne an opportunity of conversation on spiritual concerns, though he was hesitant about it. So he set down in writing for Maxfield the statement of his conversion to which we have already referred.[2] The opening sentence is significant:

It is with much diffidence that I attempt to give you some account of God's gracious dealings with me, as I am confident it will be in much weakness, but I trust that your cando[u]r will excuse me.

The document was to prove of immense importance. In the same village of Harriseahead there was also Daniel Shubotham, a relative of Hugh Bourne.[3] Daniel's father had left him an

[1] Mow Cop is a rough, craggy mountain running nearly north and south, ranging between Staffordshire and Cheshire, and situate in both counties. The name is a corruption of *moel* (Celtic for a bare chalk-hill) or perhaps A.-S. *mow*, a heap; 'cop' is A.-S. *caeppe*, a head or summit. cf. Moel Fammau in Denbighshire. See *Mow Cop and its Story*, W. J. Harper, Tunstall.

[2] *supra*, p. 18.   [3] Their fathers were first cousins.

independency in lands and houses, but he had squandered this
and had become reduced to a working collier. He was a fighter,
a poacher, and much given to profanity. One evening a
mountain-farmer invited him to a carousal, during which his
language became so outrageous that even the farmer remonstrated with him; he ceased at once. Although under conviction
of sin, a shoemaker of the village, in some fashion a preacher,
had prejudiced him against the Methodists. Now of all this
Bourne was unaware; indeed, these two had not had contact
since boyhood days, but as both were now working at the
Stonetrough colliery they met frequently. It seems that under
this sense of conviction Shubotham had turned to Maxfield;
dejected, he would sometimes cease his work and sit in the
smithy, brooding over his lost condition. On one of these occasions he spoke rather contemptuously of his cousin, Bourne,
criticizing his shyness, and saying that he seemed to have 'no
comfort of his life'. Maxfield pulled Shubotham up sharply with
words spoken in his moorland dialect: 'Aye lad! but he's a safe
mon.' That sentence became a shaft into his soul.

The written account given by Bourne to Maxfield had gone
beyond expectations; it had more than fulfilled its mission in
Maxfield's mind. Shubotham replied in an instant: 'I'll be a
safe mon, for I'll go and join him.' To Maxfield this effect was
startling indeed. Immediately Shubotham sought out his
cousin, their companionship became frequent, and with rustic
simplicity Bourne talked of the things of salvation. Yet in his
heart there was distress, for as yet Shubotham had not found
spiritual victory; this concern was especially deep on the afternoon of Wednesday, 24th December 1800, when he was con-
versing with Shubotham and another collier. The night was at
hand; Bourne had to go home, but he promised to see Shubotham
at his cottage on the following day. Here we must turn to
Bourne's own record.

Christmas Day, Thursday, December 25, 1800. Overnight I lay down
in sorrow, and I rose in sorrow this morning. The main cause of my
grief was my kinsman not being born again. My natural timidity
pressed upon me, so that it was a task indeed to go. But my mouth
had been opened before the Lord, and to have drawn backward
would have been awful: so off I set, taking with me a book written
by R. Barclay,[4] the Quaker: and I took the written account of my

---

[4] Probably *An Apology of True Christian Divinity* (1691), which had passed through
several editions before 1800.

own experience. It was a sorrowful journey: but I found Daniel
waiting for me, so my introduction was easy.

Having never prayed in public, and not judging myself capable of
it, I did not pray with the family.[5] But knowing him to be hindered
by an erroneous notion, I read him a piece out of Barclay, with
which he declared himself satisfied. So the way was open. Next
followed a little general conversation. I then rose up to go, requesting him to accompany me a little way. I was full of sorrow, but as
soon as we were in a suitable place, I set to preaching the Gospel to
him with all my might: and taking up John xiv: 21, where the words
of Jesus Christ are: 'I will love him, and will manifest myself to him',[6]
I told him that Jesus Christ must be manifested to him, or else he
would never be born again. . . . And being all the time in deep
sorrow . . . I dwelt very fully on the manifestation of Jesus Christ
unto him. At parting I put into his hands the full and large account
of my own conversion and experience . . . written with the zeal and
fire of a new convert.

I then took leave, but parted from him in sorrow, fearing that he
did not take sufficient notice; and I passed the day in sorrow. But
God's thoughts were not as my thoughts. And Daniel afterwards
told me that when I was talking to him that morning, every word
went through him. . . . It was the laying of a foundation. . . . The
'seed of God' word was sown in Daniel Shubotham's heart.[7]

Returning home, Shubotham immediately entered into severe
temptation, for his companions were awaiting his coming. The
challenge was immediate. With rugged determination he
declared: 'If you will not go with me to heaven, I will not go
with you to hell'; and seizing a Bible he began to read amidst
the confusion. Leaving the house his old companions declared
that he was mad, inciting thereby the fears of his own wife that
this was true. 'But he set his face as flint' against all opposition.

The effect of Shubotham's conversion produced an extraordinary stir amongst the colliers of the neighbourhood, 'from
Mow Cop to the vale of Kidsgrove'. More than forty years
afterwards, Bourne spoke of this as 'one of the extraordinary
events in my life'.

There being no Methodist preaching near, and also now being
aware of Shubotham's prejudices against the Methodists,
Bourne advised him to attend the Church of England service at
the village of Newchapel, a mile distant, but he declined. As
we shall see presently, the way opened.

We must notice here the conversion of Matthias Bayley,

---

[5] Daniel Shubotham was married and had two children.

[6] These words echo repeatedly through the years of Bourne's own spiritual quest.
and were therefore most applicable.

[7] Bourne MSS (Auto.), A Text, ff. 58–60

another collier, who lived at Dales Green; this had taken place a few weeks before, through hearing an open-air preacher belonging to the Burslem Circuit. So these three men became companions in the new faith, and they began to proclaim the Gospel:

Our chapels were the coal-pit banks, or any other place; and in our conversation way, we preached the Gospel to all, good or bad, rough or smooth. People were obliged to hear . . . and we soon had four other colliers in deep distress, deeply awakened.[8]

Bourne now applied to the Burslem Circuit for assistance, laying the situation before one of the travelling preachers, but without success. Yet he was undaunted. In connexion with the circuit there was planned preaching at the house of one, Joseph Pointon, on the Cheshire side of Mow Cop; Matthias Bayley had also joined Pointon's class. Bourne prevailed on Shubotham to visit Bayley, which he did regularly for some time, having doubts resolved thereby. One day, 'when he was just finishing a day's work', he 'obtained a glorious manifestation', and immediately communicated his experience to his neighbours, and then from house to house'. It was a bold venture, yet 'there was such a kindness in his forcible way of speaking, and the unction of the Holy One so powerfully attended his words, that he hardly ever gave offence . . . his words frequently reached people's hearts'.[9]

One of the occasions of Shubotham's visits to Matthias Bayley was important. They talked of praying: prompted by inexperience, 'having been a church singer', the latter turned to a *Book of Common Prayer*, but 'they found no suitable prayers'. So they attempted to pray unaided, and 'the Lord owned it and brought them into liberty'. This prompted the establishment of a regular prayer-meeting, which came to be held in the house of Jane Hall,[10] the only Methodist in Harriseahead. At this meeting it was determined that Hugh Bourne should pray publicly: 'This to me was trying . . . yet, by the blessing of God, it was as if heaven opened in my soul.' It was a significant

[8] Bourne MSS (Auto.), A Text, f. 70.
[9] ibid., f. 71.
[10] Some years afterwards Jane Hall suffered a severe mental breakdown and became violent, but was delivered through intense prayer in her home, on the part of William Clowes, Daniel Shubotham, and others. Clowes' *Jour.* (1844), pp. 77-9. 'After this she lived a number of years, was firm in religion and died happy in the Lord' (Bourne MSS (Auto.), C Text, f. 43*n*). Bourne also quotes another example of prevailing prayer in a case of lunacy (ibid., f. 41).

personal victory. The meeting became established, and its influence spread. 'The Lord had chosen ourselves ... there was soon an amazing change: hymns were sung at almost every house, and the country far and wide was surprisingly moralized.' [11]

It seems that on occasion some members of this meeting for prayer 'were zealous to go to greater lengths' than the disciplined order of the meeting, carefully planned by Bourne, would allow. One one occasion Shubotham declared that some Sunday there should be 'a whole day's praying on Mow'. This was a shadow of events to come, though some years had to pass before it happened.

The things referred to above took place in the spring of 1801.

II

The revival of religion in Harriseahead and the neighbourhood was carried on for some considerable time without the aid of preachers from the Burslem Circuit, appeals for support having proved unavailing. Although preachers were planned fortnightly to take service at Joseph Pointon's house, appointments were not always kept, and the ministrations were interrupted. Apart from Matthias Bayley, none of the new converts was a member of the Methodist Society, but Bourne was growingly anxious that they should be formed into a class, at Harriseahead, the meeting at Joseph Pointon's house being more than a mile distant, and on the Cheshire side of Mow Cop.

These men also pressed Bourne to undertake preaching on a Sunday when no preacher was planned, and the day was fixed —12th July 1801—for two o'clock. It was an important decision, which reluctantly Bourne accepted. His own words are illuminating.

... This was my first attempt, and I felt much trial of mind. I was much discouraged ... this from a fear lest my attempt should injure the cause of God. .... In climbing up the Staffordshire side of the mountain, I was in deep sorrow. I did not expect more than ten or a dozen of a congregation. But the Lord's thoughts were not as my thoughts: there had been mighty praying and His arm was made bare. ... The Lord had so moved the neighbourhood that the house was filled, and a host could not get in.[12] ... It was settled fine weather: I stood up at the end of the house, and the people lined the hill-side

[11] Bourne MSS (Auto.), f. 75.
[12] Some had come 'as zealous Methodists' from Biddulph Moor, four miles away, and in the Leek Circuit.

in the field, sitting on the dry, warm ground, as if they had been in a gallery. The view was delightful. Almost everything showed the work of the Lord.

I mounted the stand, gave out a hymn and prayed; gave out another and then read a text,[13] and began to preach. My feelings may be judged of when it is known that I held my left hand on my brow, so that I did not see the congregation during the whole time of the delivery of the sermon; yet the Lord gave me one seal to my ministry: one person started for heaven under the sermon. . . . Most of what I had thought of was quickly gone from my mind, and I was at a pause; but it came to my mind to speak as if addressing a single person. This threw me on a track to which I had been accustomed, and a field opened before me. I also gave an account of my conversion. . . . I felt unwell, and retired to the house, leaving my brother to conclude.[14]

But the meeting did not end thus: 'there opened out a great course of prayer', which so strengthened Bourne that he returned. 'New life was imparted to me . . . and Mow Cop was that day consecrated to the Most High. . . . The Lord began a new dispensation; He caused a camp-meeting to be held without a name.'[15] Thus the 'camp-meeting course' had really begun.

It is important to notice here the origins of Bourne's zeal for open-air preaching; though he himself shrunk from it he entreated the preachers of the Burslem Circuit to undertake it. The primary source was undoubtedly the example of John Wesley, who had himself made rules for its conduct, and had published them to the Conference on 28th June 1744.[16] In addition, through his reading, Bourne had been impressed by the open-air witness of the Quakers. So he writes:

. . . Through reading Mr. Wesley's writings, and other primitive records of Methodism, with the writings of the first Quakers, the desire of open-air worship was so implanted in me that nothing could shake it. I was in that respect quite primitive.[17]

There was an important outcome of the meeting held on the Cheshire side of Mow Cop. Just over a fortnight later, on

---

[13] Walford (p. 77) states that the text was Hebrews xi : 7.
[14] Bourne MSS (Auto.), A Text, ff. 86–7; B Text, ff. 11–12; C Text, ff. 47–8.
[15] ibid., f. 139.
[16] See *Mins. of Conf.* 1744, p. 10. Bourne quotes these (MSS (Auto.), A Text, f. 79). cf. ibid., f. 121. 'As Mr Wesley, John Nelson, and others of the first race were in the way of field-preaching and getting souls converted to God, I had taken these as sound proceedings of Methodists.' At another point, Bourne adds the examples of 'Charles Wesley, J. Haime, and others'.
[17] Bourne MSS (Auto.), A Text, f. 82.

Friday, 31st July, the colliers waited on Bourne to tell him that
they had agreed to have a chapel at Harriseahead, and that
Daniel Shubotham had given a portion of his garden as a site
for the building. Bourne was at once committed to this new
venture.

. . . This was an undertaking indeed; but believing it would forward
the cause of God, I promised to give the timber. As I had saved
some money it was in my power, and the Lord gave me a heart to do
it, although the timber would cost about thirty pounds.[18] In a few
days they waited on me again, and said they might dig the founda-
tions, but could do nothing further in it.[19] . . . I was soon involved
from head to foot. Materials had to be brought from a great distance, and the roads were not good, and in some parts very bad;
and there was no one to advance a single pound, and it was difficult
at times to get materials carried. The chapel was built of brick and
slated; it was large enough to accommodate about two hundred
people . . . but before I could get the roof covered, one of the gables
was blown down and the roof fell in. . . .
In praying I had an inward conviction that the Lord required it
at my hands to build the Harriseahead chapel, and I durst not
draw back. The trials of faith were heavy . . . but at length after
many difficulties it was completed.[20]

The infant cause at Harriseahead was not without its
troubles; in particular, two potters belonging to the Methodist
Society at Golden Hill, some two miles to the south, sought to
disaffect the new cause, as being contrary to normal Methodist
practice; they made frequent visits, and the issue became
serious. Bourne had to take his stand. 'I was under one of the
greatest trials I ever was under in my whole life.' Years afterwards he wrote: 'It was evident they aimed their shafts at me,
and they did what they could to stir up the people against me.'
Thus the Harriseahead revival was checked for a time, though
none fell away. 'By the blessing of God, the lesson they learned

[18] An entry in the Jour. (12th March 1803) suggests that a further sum was
given: 'I brought £14 for the furnishing of Harriseahead chapel.'
[19] Bourne notes that the degree of poverty in Harriseahead was severe. If it be
asked as to why he did not secure the help of the circuit authorities, the answer is
clearly in his own words. 'The cause of God was rising so powerfully as to make it
evident that a chapel would be needed; and the circuit authorities turned a deaf
ear to all I could say on behalf of the place' (Bourne MSS (Auto.), A Text, f. 95).
Note also the following, 'I had never been concerned in building a chapel, but they
knew that I was in some degree an architect, and had been a good deal concerned
in building, and they pressed strongly on me to make a beginning' (ibid., B Text,
f. 12).
[20] Probably the chapel was not completed until 1803, for in an entry dated 17th
May 1803, Bourne writes: 'The bricklayer being plastering the ceiling of the
chapel, today caused me after school-time, a great deal of trouble in cleaning.'

led them to abide by what the Lord in His Mercy had taught them ... so although they suffered deeply, their sufferings turned to good'.

In all this work at Harriseahead and the region round about Bourne was deeply troubled by the unwillingness of the Burslem authorities to realize its importance, and to share some of the responsibility arising out of it. His words are plain.

I long wished the circuit authorities to take the Harriseahead, Mow Cop, and Kidsgrove converts into society. And perhaps as they were weary of my applications they at length put a class paper into my hands and told me to take them into society myself. This was rather a knockdown blow; but in the fear of the Lord I undertook it; so I was forced into a kind of headship point blank, against my own inclinations, and the cross was heavy.[21]

So Bourne came to constitute a class at Harriseahead, under the leadership of Daniel Shubotham, at whose house it was held on Monday evenings, 'till the chapel was ready', Bourne himself assisting: the new converts at Mow Cop he joined to Joseph Pointon's class, which met on Sunday mornings. As for Kidsgrove, the colliers there had long been a concern of Bourne, for although there had formerly been a few Methodists in the village, it was, in 1801, 'a forsaken place'. He resolved, therefore, to journey there himself on Sunday mornings in order to lead a class for these men, to be held in the house of Joshua Bayley, brother to Matthias. Eventually he persuaded the latter to undertake the leadership.

Some time towards the end of 1801, or early in 1802, these three groups were united to the Burslem Circuit, bringing an increase of some eighty members.

It is worth observing that the attitude of the Burslem authorities to revivalism such as Bourne and his co-workers were carrying forward in Mow Cop and its vicinity was not an isolated one; allowing for local differences, it is to be contemporaneously met with in many parts of Methodism, where the conflict between 'modern' and 'primitive' Methodism had become a vital issue in the early years of the nineteenth century.[22]

At this point we must notice an important personal contact which greatly influenced Bourne. The junior travelling preacher in the Burslem Circuit, the Rev. John Grant, who had been stationed there in 1802, was the first of the staff to visit the new

---

[21] Bourne MSS (Auto.), A Text, f. 121.
[22] For an excellent discussion of this matter see Kendall, I.38–43.

Harriseahead chapel. He came expecting a congregation of
about thirty, but to his great surprise it numbered some two
hundred. Bourne found in him a true companionship. He
writes:

... He conversed well on almost every subject, scientific, religious, or
literary. I was favoured with his conversation several times: and it
was a blessing to me. He bought me Parkhurst's *Greek Lexicon*, and
Bell's *Greek and English Grammar*; and Parkhurst's *Hebrew Lexicon*, and
Bayley's *Entrance into the Hebrew Language*: and he gave me lessons in
Greek and Hebrew.[23] But through family affliction he was obliged
to leave the circuit, and this was a trial to me.[24]

This friendship was determinative for Bourne's future intel-
lectual development, as the following will show. Bourne's
labours for the spiritual revival in this region must have withdrawn him a great deal from his daily occupations, and, probably towards the end of 1802, he determined upon still further
sacrifice.

Having so many calls and so much on my hands, and having a
desire to be acquainted with the Hebrew and Greek languages, I
undertook to teach a school (a thing much needed) in the chapel. I
taught about a twelve-month: during which I gained an acquaintance with the Greek and Hebrew. . . . What time I could spare
from work and study was spent in prayer-meetings and exhortations; and in preachings I generally managed to get into the open-
air.[25]

In this decision there is illustration of the principle which
probably he had learnt from his earlier study of 'the first race
of the Quakers', namely, that of seeking to be led in all things
by the Spirit of God. There is evidence that pursuit of these
linguistic studies was on the background of prayer for diligence
and understanding; in this matter, as in all else, he had an eye
to the glory of God, through better equipment for his labours.

There is no surviving Journal for the year 1802; but from
Walford [26] we learn that not only did he teach in this weekday
school, but, about this time, he also established a Sunday-
school at Harriseahead, and this became the parent of similar
ventures in the neighbouring villages.

---

[23] An entry in the MS Jour., 1st November 1803, reads: 'This day I made large
progress in the French and Hebrew'—an indication of further linguistic study.
[24] Bourne MSS (Auto.), A Text, f. 127.
[25] ibid., f. 137.
[26] op. cit., p. 91.

During this year accounts of American meetings for open-air worship held during 1801 (though without being described as camp-meetings) began to appear in the *Methodist Magazine*.[27] These 'flaming accounts' so roused the colliers that they became eager for the fulfilment of Shubotham's suggestion made earlier in the year, for a whole day's gathering for prayer on Mow Cop: the enthusiasm of the latter, however, had lessened, due to lack of encouragement from the circuit authorities,[28] and this effectively postponed the venture. Nevertheless Bourne declared: 'The Methodist magazines opened upon us like the light of the morning. . . .' The matter now became more and more the subject of intercession, 'till about the year 1803 when . . . instead of interceding with the Lord to grant us a day's praying, our minds were so enlarged that we besought the Lord to open our way'.[29] To this, however, we shall return.

III

Early in the year 1803 Bourne seems to have undergone severe inward conflict. The first entry in his extant MS journal reads thus: '1803, Feby 12: This week I had greater tryals than I ever had since I set out.'[30] It would appear that at times he had been outspoken concerning the criticism of the revival, and it had been stated that the preachers of the circuit had had something of a charge against him in consequence. 'I thought it was hard that I should continually be a man of strife'; yet he believed it was the will of God that in these matters he 'should deal plainly with everyone'.

He was also greatly concerned about the completeness of his dedication to the work.

I have for some time had a great backwardness to self-denial, through which I find the enemy has got some advantage over me. I find self-denial easy to be talked on, but hard to be practised.[31]

[27] op. cit., p. 263. 'Religion has got to such a height here that people attend from a great distance. They encamp on the ground, and continue praising God for a whole week, day and night before they break up. . . . Twenty thousand meet at once, and continue encamped for twelve days.'

[28] The exception seems to have been the Rev. Thomas Allen, an ardent supporter, whom Bourne naturally commended.

[29] Bourne MSS (Auto.), B Text, f. 18.

[30] We may note also under the same date an entry which must have given Bourne deep satisfaction. 'On Wednesday night my brother William was brought in.' William Bourne (b. about 1773) was a man of great physical strength; after his conversion he joined the Quakers, emigrated to America some time before 1811, and became a travelling 'minister' amongst them.

[31] Bourne MSS (Jour.), 17th March 1803.

At this period he was carefully reading the *Journals* of John Wesley;[32] he seems to have felt the challenge of this great example, for on Friday, 1st April 1803, he sets down his own covenant with God.[33]

Today I reviewed and examined my conduct through the late temptations. I also read in Mr. Wesley's writings, and made the following resolutions: 1. To put away all trifling talk and follow after godly seriousness. 2. To put away all slothfulness and to be always (and if possible diligently) employed. 3. To put away all softness and indulgence, and endeavour to endure hardness. 4. To avoid sitting as much as possible as I have already been weakened by it. 5. To pay more attention to health and cleanliness, which I have of late foolishly neglected. 6. To endeavour every Wednesday and Friday to fast, as was the custom with the primitive church, and has been with some Methodists. 7. To take up if possible every cross, and never flinch at any self-denials or sufferings for Christ. . . . 8. To be given up to prayer and always endeavour to act with faith on the promise for strength to walk perfectly before Him. O Lord, help me and establish me!

This was set down just before his thirty-first birthday. During this year his labours in the neighbourhood greatly increased: he now had to divide his time systematically in order to cover the meetings on week evenings. He was apparently back at Bemersley again by this time, and he attended the Burslem and Tunstall chapels for Sunday meetings. Harriseahead, Norton,[34] Brown-edge, Whitfield, Ridgway, and other places were on his own private weeknight plan, and at each he laboured successfully, mainly through prayer and 'conversation-preaching', though on occasion he appears to have preached publicly. His comment on this is valuable.

The chief qualification for exercising in public I find to be a clean heart; a clean heart stands in stead of much study, and all study is weak without it. The stream of grace descends into a clean heart, flows out again to all round, with force and vigour.

At Harriseahead he continued as schoolmaster during most of 1803, diligently pursuing his own studies at the same time.[35]

[32] ibid. Bourne's estimate of Wesley is worth quoting here. 'Equally surprising, on whatever side we view this great man, whether we consider his unbounded zeal, his deep penetration, his steady perseverance, his moderation of spirit, his faithfulness in reproving, or his wisdom in managing. . . .'
[33] Bourne MSS (Jour.), loc. cit.
[34] Bourne had established a Sunday-school here some time before 1803.
[35] He records (8th November 1803) that he purchased the pamphlet *Improvements on Education*, just published by John Lancaster (1778–1838), teacher and educationist.

Although the year 1804[36] brought many occasions of search-
ing of heart for Bourne—indeed, such experiences marked his
spirit throughout his whole life—yet it was a period of great
spiritual uplifting.

At the Conference of that year the Rev. Edward Jackson was
appointed to the Burslem Circuit. Under his ministry a gracious
revival took place throughout the whole area. Of this his
biographer writes:

> It must be admitted that some irregularities attended the work
> ... but as drunkards became sober, and the idle diligent in business
> ... as the power of reigning sins was broken, the friends of religion
> acknowledged it to be the work of God.[37]

During this memorable year more than three hundred persons
were added to the Methodist churches of North Staffordshire,
and particularly in Burslem and Tunstall. Of outstanding
importance is the fact that this revival resulted in the conversion
of William Clowes, James Nixon, Thomas Woodnorth, and
William Morris, men who were afterwards to be in the van-
guard of one part of the movement which became 'Primitive
Methodism'.

Another centre of this impulse of spiritual awakening was
Congleton, where a blacksmith named Clark, at his own expense, brought a group of revivalists from Stockport, in Cheshire,
to attend the September love-feast of 1804. It was held in the
Methodist chapel, and a number of neighbouring Methodists
attended, including Hugh Bourne, who was deeply impressed
by the fervour and piety of these men.

> I thought them readier in the exercise of faith than we were, but
> they neither laid open doctrines, nor explained the mystery of faith.
> ... On our return we conversed freely and appeared to have an
> increase of faith.[38]

At a meeting at Harriseahead shortly afterwards, there was an
unusually great outpouring of the Spirit; 'the surrounding
country was shaken; the veil was taken from many hearts'.

On Christmas Day following, the Stockport revivalists came
again to Congleton, and once more Bourne was present.

> They spoke of having labouring love; and I thought that this was
> labouring love. ... I was much established by going among them.

---

[36] Unfortunately, only a fragment of MS Jour. for 1804 has survived.
[37] *PMQR*, 1906, p. 222 : see also *PMM*, 1900, p. 827.
[38] Bourne MSS (Auto.), C Text, f. 67.

. . . Since their first coming, it has quite altered the society at Harriseahead, and the Lord has worked powerfully there.[39]

The same Christmas week a love-feast took place at Harriseahead, and, 'when the time came, people flocked in from east, west, north, and south'. James Steele[40] of Tunstall took a leading part. Bourne was exultant:

Thou, Lord, hast filled me with Thy love; Thou hast made me glad with Thy salvation; my heart rejoices in the living God.[41]

We have already spoken of Bourne's frequent seasons of disquietude in regard to his own inward condition; it was the urge towards holiness, and the sense of failure to attain it, that so often perplexed him. This period illustrates this mark of mystical Christian experience in the case of Bourne. We quote one or two passages.

One Sunday night at a meeting near Stonetrough colliery he experienced loss of confidence:

A number of temptations came dashing at me on all sides. . . . Had I a clean heart now? . . . I applied immediately to Jesus Christ. I had a sharp struggle; but directly it came that I was clean through the word spoken . . . the noise of the temptation was gone.[42]

Again:

One Tuesday night I had a most absolute liberty, which continued till the Thursday; then a temptation came. . . . I had not then learned to go straight to Jesus Christ. It seemed to slacken, but in a few minutes it struck through me like a flaming dart. . . . I strove against it, and cried unto the Lord; it was taken away.[43]

Following a love-feast at Burslem, on Sunday, 5th January 1805, there was a season of exaltation once more.

I was rarely established. . . . I was full of love, peace, and joy, and had as much as the body would bear. I saw all things clearly.[44]

But a week later, having joined in some talk that was 'not expedient', the vision faded: 'I did not view Christ so plainly';

---

[39] Walford, p. 99.
[40] James Steele was one of the first members in the Methodist Society at Tunstall, and since 1785 'a steady, sensible man of great influence, a local preacher, a leader of two large classes, a superintendent of the Sunday School, and withal a person highly respected' (*An Account of Wesleyan Methodism in Tunstall*, A. Leese).
[41] Walford, p. 99.   [42] ibid., pp. 100–1.
[43] ibid., p. 101.   [44] ibid., p. 101.

a week of distress followed, but hearing a young praying lad, the vision returned:

> It came down on me. . . . I felt that it joined me to God . . . it shone brightly in my soul—then it began to burn, and I found it to be 'a spirit of burning'. This established me. . . . I now thought I could go to the ends of the earth to speak of Jesus Christ.[45]

This is indeed the language of Christian mysticism. It may be noted in passing that often during these seasons of difficulty, Daniel Shubotham, who, as we have seen, had been brought to Christ by Bourne, was the source of counsel and strength.

> Daniel told me that the unction of the Holy One was a burning love. He advised me continually to pray for the Lord to shew me my heart more and more, and Christ at the same time; to pray for light and wisdom.[46]

We venture to add yet another passage:

> Coming home, at the praying place in Mr Heath's field, I felt as if I was held by an irresistible power, and I sank down into nothing before it, and everything that I did was contrary to God. I felt it die away—I gave myself up to God. Immediately came 'the spirit of burning', and I was made 'a habitation of God through the Spirit'. I wondered at myself; I could scarcely believe what the Spirit witnessed.[47]

It was in this year, 1805, that a new spiritual bond was found in association with William Clowes, of Tunstall, who had so recently come into the new faith.[48] The younger of the two men, by some eight years, Clowes was deeply impressed by the quality of Bourne's spiritual experience: none rejoiced more than Bourne at the conversion of Clowes. As early as 10th March 1805 we find the following:

> I cautioned him against every temper that is contrary to love. . . . Before I received the Holy Ghost, 'the spirit of burning', I had a happiness which almost melted me: and I was at times as if my heart would draw out of the body to God. This agreed with his experience. After many instructions we parted. God bless him, for the sake of Jesus Christ![49]

---

[45] Walford, pp. 101–2.   [46] ibid., p. 103.   [47] ibid., p. 104.
[48] Clowes's conversion took place, in his twenty-fifth year, on the morning of 20th January 1805. See Clowes *Jour.* (1844), p. 21.
[49] The passages quoted are from Walford, pp. 105–10. There is no MS Jour. extant for the year 1805.

Again Bourne writes, on 23rd March:

I went to Burslem. William Clowes was there. We had a rare time. . . . He is now very solid. . . . I went to his house and stayed till after midnight; such a man for faith I scarcely ever saw; he gains any blessing almost immediately.[49]

On 30th March:

William Clowes grows at a vast rate. Being at play part of the day, he shut himself up in the chamber, with the Bible. He felt 'the spirit of burning' . . . the Lord gave it to him till it filled every part of his body, burning to his finger ends, and his eyesight seemed for a time to be taken away. . . . This man is such an example of living faith as I scarcely ever met with, and which I am not at present able to follow; but he is uncommonly strict; and if he happens to drink water without asking the Lord to make him truly thankful, it drives him to God for pardon.[49]

Nearly a month later, on 20th April, we find Bourne still deeper in rejoicing:

William Clowes has become a labourer, and the Lord owns his work. He is one raised up immediately by God—a man of uncommonly deep experience, of an unusual growth in grace, deep humility, steady zeal, and flaming love: such a man I scarcely ever met with. O God, this I desire, that Thou wouldest make me like him. I desire it from my heart. . . . It seems as if the Lord has raised him up to keep the revival steady. . . . I stayed advising, instructing, and talking with him till after midnight, when we prayed and parted by force.[49]

Such passages from the diary of Bourne leave us in no doubt as to the depth of this newly-found friendship, each influencing the other at the deepest level of spiritual experience.

We must note here another development belonging to the year 1805, namely the building of a chapel at Norton. Some four years earlier Bourne had manifested concern for the slender condition of the cause, and in his own mind had planned extended open-air preaching to counteract the influence of the Norton 'wakes', held each year in August, this being a special source of temptation to the young people of the neighbourhood. Although this did not come to full fruition until 1807, he seems to have preached at Norton, and in 1801 had formed a small class, for the leadership of which he took personal responsibility. In addition a Sunday-school was founded, similar to that at Harriseahead, where he taught. In 1803 Norton had been taken

[49] Walford, pp. 105–10.

on to Bourne's private weeknight plan for visitation and meeting. The society so developed that he could record in his
Journal for 20th March 1805:

This day at Mr David Leake's we concluded the size of a chapel
at Norton: at this meeting we subscribed £25 5s.

He appears also to have delighted in visiting the people of the
parish in order to collect donations. As illustration of this zeal
for the moral and spiritual welfare of youth we find that in 1807,
at his own expense, he prepared and printed a scripture
catechism for use in the schools at Norton and Harriseahead.[50]
The passionate care for the souls of children became one of
Bourne's greatest ministries; his Journal shows that on most
occasions when he preached he devoted part of the service to a
special discourse for children; also he held gatherings in the
open air to which he invited any children who might be available.

IV

We have no account of the detailed movements of Bourne
during the year 1806, as the portion of his Journal for that
period has not survived. But one or two hints are available.[51]
During 1804 the spiritual revival which had been manifest
in the Burslem Circuit had temporarily withdrawn the attention
of many from the idea of the proposed camp-meeting, but
afterwards this began to reassert itself, particularly in the mind
of Bourne. He was troubled because for most of a year there was
a dearth of conversions in Harriseahead and the region round
about, something which he set down to the policy pursued by
the travelling preacher, the Rev. William E. Miller, who had
been appointed by the Conference of 1805. Bourne esteemed him
as a man of revivalist spirit, but he was distressed by the fact
that in conversation he had turned Daniel Shubotham against
open-air worship:[52] so the question arose as to whether a new
camp-meeting impulse was not the necessary thing for resuscitating the work. So came a new stirring of desire, and it is certain

[50] *The Great Scripture Catechism, compiled for Norton and Harriseahead Schools and
intended for Sunday Schools in general*, 1807. This is printed in Walford (pp. 127–39),
and the 'Address' is dated: 'Bemersley, April 27th.'
[51] Bourne, *HPM* (1823), p. 8.
[52] This explains the difference between the estimates of Mr Miller by Bourne
and Clowes respectively, the latter holding him in highest esteem as a spiritual
counsellor. See Clowes *Jour.* (1844), p. 45; also art. 'The Mentor of William
Clowes', *PMQR*, 1906, pp. 215–26.

that the stimulus was partly strengthened by the numerous and vivid accounts of 'religious encampments' in America, which appeared in the *Methodist Magazine* for the years following 1802.[53]

There was another determinative factor, namely the visit of an American travelling preacher, Lorenzo Dow (1777–1824), to England, at the end of 1805.[54] In his travels Dow came to Macclesfield, in Cheshire, where Daniel Shubotham heard him preach, and was restored to the conviction of the value of open-air preaching, which he had lost. This was late in October, or early November, 1806.[55] One day in the following April, Bourne was informed that Dow would preach that same day at Harriseahead; he and his brother James attended. 'I heard him preach and speak of the American camp-meetings. This was the first sight I had of him.'[56] In the afternoon Bourne heard him again, at Burslem; Clowes was also present, and took tea with him, and afterwards listened to him again at Tunstall in the evening. The following morning Dow preached at Congleton, at five o'clock, and again at nine; Clowes was present at both services, and noted that at the second service Bourne and his brother James were there, 'and they purchased some tracts from the preacher, when he had concluded'.[57]

For some time past, as we have seen, Bourne had contemplated open-air preaching in order to counteract the 'wakes' at Norton-le-Moors, held late in August.

[53] See op.cit., 1803, pp. 131–2, 275, 249; 1804, pp. 233–4; 1805, p. 573; 1806, pp. 94–5. cf. *Thoughts on . . . Camp Meetings*, Lorenzo Dow, Liverpool, 1807. Also *NHM*, II.120–4; *The Secret of Mow Cop* (WHS Lecture, 1950), by Dr W. E. Farndale.

[54] See *Vicissitudes in the Wilderness: or The Journey of Life exemplified in the Journal of Peggy Dow*, 4th ed., Liverpool, 1818, p. 12. Dow arrived in England on 24th or 25th December 1805, and returned to America on 6th May 1807. ibid., p. 27.

[55] ibid., pp. 18–19.

[56] Bourne MSS (Auto.), B Text, f. 23. cf. Clowes *Jour.* (1844), pp. 66–7. Dow appears to have attended 'a religious encampment' in America for the first time on 15th September 1803, 'where there was about two thousand people, and upwards of thirty ministers or preachers of the Presbyterian, Baptist, and Methodist orders . . . I spoke in the night' (*The Travel . . . of Lorenzo Dow, written by himself*, 1806, p. 199). 'After visiting Tennessee and Kentucky, I saw the propriety and utility of the Camp Meetings which stimulated me to introduce them, first into the heart of Virginia; then into the State of New York; afterwards in Connecticut and Massachusetts' (*Thoughts . . . on Camp Meetings*, L. Dow, 1807, p. 45).

[57] Clowes *Jour.* (1844), p. 67. cf. Bourne MSS (Auto.), B Text, f. 30. 'I bought of him some American camp-meeting publications.' These tracts almost certainly included: *An Account of the Origin and Progress of Camp Meetings and the Method of conducting them*, Lorenzo Dow, 1806; *A Defence of the Camp Meetings* (North America), by Dr S. K. Jennings, A.M., 1806; *Queries, Observations and Remarks, or Thoughts on the Times and Camp Meetings, with a word to the Methodists*, L. Dow, 1807; *A Collection of Spiritual Songs used at Camp Meetings in the Great Revival in the United States of America*, Selected by Lorenzo Dow, Dublin, 1806.

This has given me much concern, and it came into my mind that if we could hold a camp-meeting for about three days, it would engage our young members and preserve them. . . . And it appeared to me that I and my brother, and Thomas Cotton, of Mow Cop, would be sufficient for the preaching, and I believed I could get a host of praying-labourers from Harriseahead and Mow Cop.[58]

So Bourne appealed to the class-meeting at Harriseahead for assistance: 'they were all in a zeal in an instant'—and immediately there followed the suggestion that there should be a similar meeting on Mow Cop. Regular preaching being planned, there was the problem of a day for the purpose; taking up the preachers' plan, Daniel Shubotham noticed that Thomas Cotton was planned at Harriseahead for Sunday, 31st May 1807. Of this moment Bourne writes:

In an instant we were all on our knees, and everyone praying with all their heart, mind and voice . . . till everyone had faith to believe that the Lord would stand by.[59]

Once determined upon (although notice of it was only given to neighbouring Christians, it being intended as a gathering in prayer, 'for their own edification'), 'the report flew through the country as if it had gone on the wings of angels'.

Bourne has left an account of the occasion,[60] from which the following picture of the scene is taken.

The morning proved rainy, and unfavourable . . . but about six o'clock the Lord sent the clouds off, and gave us a very pleasant day. The meeting was opened by two holy men from Knutsford,[61]

---

[58] Bourne MSS (Auto.), A Text, f. 163.   [59] ibid., f. 163
[60] *Observations on Camp Meetings, with an Account of a Camp Meeting held on Sunday, May the 31st, 1807, at Mow, near Harriseahead* (Newcastle-under-Lyme, 1807). Reprinted in Walford (pp. 119-25). The pamphlet seems to have had a wide circulation, for it is probably to this that Bourne refers (Auto., A Text, f. 179): 'In Staffordshire it got into circulation, and others printed it without my consent, and sold it apparently by thousands; and it shook the country. . . . Mr Riles put out a posting-bill against it, but wished me not to answer it; it remained unanswered.' cf. the account given by Clowes *Jour.* (1844), pp. 68-71.
[61] One of these was Peter Bradburn (Clowes *Jour.* (1844), p. 68); the other, an Irish lawyer who had been converted under the ministry of Lorenzo Dow and who related the troubles he had passed through in Ireland: 'in the late rebellion in that unhappy land, he had been deprived of thousands . . . he had since given up his profession as an attorney, because he found it too difficult to keep his religion in that profession: he exhorted all to pray for our gracious King, who was worthy because he gave us liberty of conscience' (*Observations on Camp Meetings*, p. 4). Bourne also mentions a third (ibid., p. 4), a world-wide traveller, probably as a soldier, having lost a limb in Africa, once having renounced Christianity, then having turned to deism, and finally to atheism, but now reclaimed under Dow's preaching. 'He showed the happiness of our land, and the gratitude we owed to God for being exempted from the seat of war' (ibid., p. 6).

Captain Anderson,[62] having previously erected a flag on the mountain to direct strangers, and these three, with some pious people from Macclesfield, carried on and sustained the meeting a considerable time, in a most vigorous and lively manner. They conducted it by preaching, prayer, exhortations, relating experiences, &c. The Lord owned their labours, grace descended, and the people of God were greatly quickened. The congregation rapidly increased and others began to join in holy exercises. . . . The wind was cold, but a large grove of fir-trees kept the wind off and made it very comfortable. So many hundreds now covered the ground, that another preaching stand was erected in a distant part of the field, under the cover of a stone-wall. Returning over the field, I met a company at a distance from the first stand, praying for a man in distress. I could not get near, but there found such a measure of the power of God . . . that it was beyond description. I should gladly have stopped there, but other matters called me away. I perceived that the Lord was beginning to work mightily. . . .

About noon the congregation was so much increasing that we were obliged to erect a third preaching stand . . . by the side of the fir-tree grove. I got upon this stand after the first preaching, and was extremely surprised at the amazing sight that appeared before me. . . . I had not before conceived that such a vast multitude were present; but to see thousands [63] hearing with attention solemn as death, presented a scene of the most sublime and awfully pleasing grandeur my eyes ever beheld.

The preachers seemed to be fired with an uncommon zeal . . . numbers were convinced and saints were uncommonly quickened, and the extraordinary steadiness and decorum . . . seemed to make a great impression.

Many preachers were now upon the ground, from Knutsford, Congleton, Wheelock, Burslem, Macclesfield, and other places. . . . Persuasion dwelt upon their tongues, while the multitude were trembling or rejoicing around.

The congregation increased so rapidly that a fourth preaching stand was called for. . . . To see thousands of people all in solemn attention . . . and four preachers dealing out their lives at every stroke—these things made an impression on my mind not soon to be forgotten; this extraordinary scene continued till about four o'clock, when the people began to retire; and before six, they were confined to one stand. About seven o'clock in the evening, a work

[62] Captain Edward Anderson had been a shepherd-lad at Kilham in Yorkshire; later he took to sea, endured many hardships, and finally settled in Hull, where he became a prayer-leader, anti-slavery advocate, and temperance reformer. He attempted a record of his experiences in a poem: *The Life of a Sailor: A Poem in Three Parts* (1807). Part of this he used at the camp-meeting (Clowes *Jour.* (1844), p. 70), and this may have prompted its publication the same year. He was the brother of the Rev. Henry Anderson (d. 1843), a Wesleyan travelling preacher; both are buried in Kilham churchyard. Captain Anderson was doubtless the main influence behind the camp-meeting held at Langtoft-in-the-Wolds, near Driffield, in Yorkshire, on 9th August, 1807. See *Remarks on the Life and Death of Captain Anderson*, W. Sanderson (*PMM*, 1848, p. 49). Also Kendall, I.66–7

[63] The numbers were estimated at between two and four thousand.

began among children. . . . At about half-past eight the meeting was finally closed. A meeting such as our eyes had never beheld; a meeting for which many will praise God in time and eternity. . . .

In this pamphlet, Bourne gave notice of a second camp-meeting to be held on Mow Cop, planned for 18th July, 'at 4 o'clock in the afternoon'; and also another at Norton-le-Moors, 'to begin on Saturday, August 22nd 1807, at four o'clock in the afternoon, to be held day and night'. He also pointed out that the experience of the first meeting had suggested the need for more elaborate arrangements; tents would henceforth be provided against inclemency of weather; coal, lanterns, and candles 'to light the camp day and night'; provision of food for those coming from a distance. In addition, there was the significant resolve 'to get the ground regularly licensed under the Toleration Act, that all interruption or mis-behaviour . . . may be prevented or punished as the law directs'.

v

In June 1807 Bourne made acquaintance with James Craw-foot [64] of Delamere Forest. This contact was to prove so important that we must examine it in detail. Born in 1758 at Stapleford, in the parish of Tarvin, near Chester, Crawfoot had become a local preacher on the Chester plan, and had removed to a remote part of the Forest about 1793, where he had established monthly meetings of a special character in his own house.[65] Those who gathered became known as 'Magic Method-ists', or 'Forest Methodists', because, under the influence of the meetings, they frequently fell into a 'trance' or 'vision'.

Bourne's approach came about in the following way. A farmer named Joseph Lowe, of the Moss House Farm, near Mow Cop, who had been converted under the Harriseahead revival in September 1804, had removed to Gresty Green, near Coppenhall, in Cheshire, some five miles north-east of Nant-wich, where he formed a Methodist Society. Occasionally he returned to Staffordshire, and early in 1807 he pressed Bourne, who greatly esteemed him, to visit the Methodist meeting at Delamere Forest, which he himself knew. 'The report was

[64] The name appears as 'Crowfoot' in the Chester membership roll for 1790 (*WHS Proceedings*, XXVI.77), and also throughout Bourne's MSS (Jour.); this is probably the correct spelling, but 'Crawfoot' being more familiar, we retain it.

[65] Herod, pp. 241–72; *PMQR*, 1902, pp. 578–92.

current that these people used magic, and were in league with Satan.' Lowe affirmed this to be false, and said to Bourne: 'I do not understand them; but you must look into them.' Bourne was naturally curious, but was equally shy of any approach. In June Lowe saw Bourne again and said: 'I have opened your way; but you will have to come round by Coppenhall.' This involved a considerable detour, but it was suggested that he should come to Gresty Green on the Friday, and that on the Saturday William Harding, who sometimes attended the Delamere meeting, would take him along, and that he should stay with Ralph Harding, a brother, who lived near. 'There I have provided board and lodging for you; so now your way is open.'

Bourne did not make the journey alone, however, for he was accompanied by Clowes,[66] who had also heard of these people when visiting in Cheshire. On 27th June they met near Coppenhall, and came to Crawfoot's house, which was in a lonely part of the Forest. Bourne records his impression of the meeting:

There were some people present, and a tall, aged man sat in a two-armed chair preaching, as I thought; but it seemed an idle way. Still I thought he spoke good things. But soon the people spoke of beginning. I was then aware the old man was redeeming the time. . . . He now read a few passages of scripture, and a brisk, sharp prayer-meeting commenced; and ere long I noticed a woman[67] struggling, as if in distress, and wondered why they did not pray for her. But two women placed her on a chair, and she appeared to have fainted away . . . and she was there for a length of time without any notice being taken of her. . . . The old man stopped the meeting, and put up a Mrs Prescot, a farmer's wife, from near Great Budworth, to exhort; and she spoke some time with apparent zeal. At length the woman on the chair clasped her hands, and praised the Lord, and went on speaking occasionally without stopping or opening her eyes. She spoke of ' a fine green meadow . . . of a fine river . . . of trumpets. . . .' Shortly after that she awoke up and came out of her visionary state. I then went up to the woman to enquire, but all in vain; only one of the women said: 'These things strengthen our faith.'[68]

The meeting began about seven o'clock and lasted until midnight. Bourne and Clowes departed about two o'clock in the morning. The next day Bourne heard Crawfoot preach; but his

[66] See Bourne MSS (Auto.), A Text, p. 169; Clowes *Jour.* (1844), p. 65; J. T. Wilkinson, *William Clowes 1780–1851*, pp. 26–7.
[67] The name of the woman was Nancy Foden.
[68] Bourne MSS (Auto.), A Text, f. 169; C Text, f. 111.

H.B.—4

impression was at first unfavourable.[69] 'I did not like him.' The next day he returned, with Clowes, to Staffordshire; but he was to make more visits to the home of Crawfoot. To this matter, therefore, we shall return.

VI

On the day of Bourne's return—Monday, 29th June—from his visit to Crawfoot he records the following in his Journal:

I came home to undergo trials beyond the common lot. . . . My flesh had no rest, but I was troubled on every side—without were fightings, within were fears.

He was concerned about the preparations for the forthcoming second meeting on Mow Cop. He found his brother, James, upon whom he had counted for help, busy in the hay-harvest: still more serious was the report that one, Mr Stevenson, of Cobridge, near Burslem, was proposing to indict the meeting under the Conventicle Act,[70] under which each preacher was liable to a penalty of £20, and each hearer to one of five shillings. So he writes:

I now concluded that the way was not providentially open, and thought to put posting-bills up to say that no meeting would be held; but, in mighty terror, the Lord gave me to know that I must stand by the camp-meetings.[71]

So he went forward with the project. Choosing a suitable site on Mow Cop, where it was common, he obtained a grant of occupation from a freeholder, and then 'drew up a brief' to present to the Bishop's Court at Lichfield, some thirty-seven miles away, the journey to which he made on foot. But he was to be disappointed, as the registrar refused his application for a licence, because there was no building on the site. So he had to retrace his steps, but before leaving he visited the cathedral, and later wrote an account of his experience.

I went into the minster. After the service began, it ran through my mind: 'Get thee out of this place, and beware of the woman that has the golden cup in her hand, and those that are with her; their ways

[69] With this contrast that of Clowes: 'I was greatly satisfied and benefitted. . . . The next day I heard the old man preach in the open-air, and afterwards had a private conversation with him, the result of which was a more determined resolution to seek a knowledge of the deeper things of God' (Clowes *Jour.* (1844), p. 66).
[70] The Act was not repealed until June 1812.
[71] Bourne MSS (Auto.), C Text, p. 113.

are death; sin no more, lest a worse thing come upon thee . . . .'
This startled me, as I had before taken delight in their singing of the
service. I saw much lightness and sin among the parsons. It seemed
like gross idolatry in them to spend their time in such a manner; but
then I thought the words of the service are good. It then struck me:
'These people draweth nigh unto me with their lips &c.' I prayed
God that if the impression to go out was from Him, it might increase;
if not, that it might go away: it increased till I was quite miserable.
I then thought to go out, and a voice came: 'Escape for thy life.'
They were singing the *Te Deum*. I took my hat as soon as they had
done, and went out, and the burden was removed. It looked as if
judg[e]ments hung over that place. I stopped all afternoon in Lichfield,
and such a travail of soul came upon me as I never before experienced—it was for the city. I mourned greatly. . . . I trembled for
the place and people. O my God! have mercy on them![72]

Returning, Bourne resolved upon the erection of a building on
the site he had chosen. By his own money he purchased timber
and with his own hands reared a structure capable of holding
a considerable number of people; also, he erected three tents,
after the American fashion. Under these conditions the licence
was granted, being sent through the post to him at a cost of
fourteen shillings; for the building he had expended £30. On
16th July he walked to Stafford, where he obtained a licence to
preach.[73] Still further preparation was necessary; so Bourne
went to Macclesfield to secure preachers. He discovered, however, that the travelling preachers there had posted large bills
in the town disclaiming all connexion with camp-meetings.
Undaunted, he enlisted the help of some, and then went also to
Knutsford for the same purpose.

[72] This has not survived in MS, but is recorded by Walford, p. 45. cf. the visit of
George Fox to Lichfield in 1651 (*Jour.* Everyman ed., pp. 39–40). Bourne may
have read this.
[73] This would be under the Toleration Act (1689), and on the same day James
Bourne obtained a similar licence. (The names appear in the *Quarter Sessions
Order Book for Translation*, Staffordshire County Record Office.)
The licence was granted in the following terms:
I do hereby certify, that at the General Quarter Sessions of the Peace of our
Lord the King, holden at Stafford, in and for the County of Stafford, upon
Thursday, the sixteenth day of July, in the year of our Lord, One Thousand and
Eight Hundred and Seven, Hugh Bourne personally appeared in open court
between the hours of nine and twelve in the forenoon of the same day, and did
then and there take and subscribe the oaths of allegiance and supremacy, the
declaration against Popery, and the declaration by law directed to be made and
subscribed by Protestant Dissenting Ministers and schoolmasters, pursuant to the
several statutes in that behalf made.
Witness my hand, the sixteenth day of July, in the year of our Lord One Thousand Eight Hundred and Seven.

ARTHUR HINCKLEY
*Clerk of the Peace for the
County of Stafford.*

Finally, but not unimportant, he purchased crockery [74] and provisions to meet the physical needs of those who might travel far to attend the meeting.

But further discouragement lay ahead. Daniel Shubotham, who had laboured heartily for the first camp-meeting, now wavered, having been influenced by those opposed to the movement, and was brought only by much persuasion to support this second meeting, to withdraw, however, before the gathering took place. Bourne records:

Many persecuted and opposed, especially the head preacher. . . . They put out papers, and sent them to the societies and circuits around.[75]

In reply, however, printed bills were posted in Burslem and Tunstall, stating time and place of the meeting, and these bore the signatures of Hugh Bourne, James Bourne, Daniel Shubotham, Matthias Bayley, and Thomas Cotton—afterwards to be known as 'The Camp-Meeting Fathers'.

The day proved fine and favourable, and 'about six o'clock on Sunday morning, 19th July, the voice of united worship sounded'. Large numbers assembled, including many from the Independent Methodists of Macclesfield; people from Stockport and from Knutsford; and some of the Quaker Methodists, from Warrington, in Lancashire, nearly forty miles distant. In the afternoon, Mr Stevenson, who was accompanied by a master-potter, both on horseback, presented his challenge, and the presence of Bourne was demanded. He was not to be found, for he was in a distant part of the hill praying earnestly for the work. Eventually he was discovered, and he calmly presented himself (dressed in working attire, for in the pressure of the preparations he had forgotten to change into his Sunday clothes) before the intruders. He handed over his preaching licence; that for the 'conventicle' he had inadvertently left at home, and it could not be shown. Threatening the assembly, the great man rode away in anger, but, observing the notice of licence which Bourne had fastened to a pole, he returned and began to argue the rightfulness of such a meeting, the licence notwithstanding. The tables were turned, however, for he himself was now under law because of his intrusion; so he changed

[74] 'Hugh Bourne called upon me and desired me to accompany him to purchase some pottery . . . accordingly I went, and the articles were bought and paid for by Hugh Bourne, at the works where I was employed' (Clowes *Jour.* (1844), p. 73).
[75] Walford, p. 148.

his demeanour and departed. Bourne counted this to be 'like light out of darkness'.

On the Monday the congregation was smaller, but on this day more than twenty conversions took place, the number on the Sunday being even greater. On the Tuesday still less were present, and in the evening the meeting closed. More than sixty souls had entered into the new life: in particular 'the tide of the New chapel wake' had been stemmed in the parish of Wolstanton. 'The flood of wickedness . . . never rose so high hereafter.'

It is rather a grim comment to have to record that Shubotham and others received the thanks of the travelling preachers and the quarterly meeting for not attending! Shubotham had come to the meeting on the Tuesday, however, to declare his opposition. Not long afterwards he left the Methodist society, and broke away from religious connexion altogether. This deeply saddened Bourne, who, however, continued to visit him in the hope of his spiritual recovery.

VII

Without rest, Bourne had now to undertake the preparation for the Norton meeting a month later, on 23rd August, and which was to be carried through upon a background of strong opposition that broke out against him.

But in this brief interval he made two important journeys. The first was to Macclesfield, 'to the house of a friend who was a member of the Independent Methodists', who were holding their first Conference; one of the main matters was to arrange for interchange of preachers. This was to prove important.

The other excursion was to the Quaker Methodists at Warrington and the neighbourhood. Bourne was 'much edified among them', and he preached several times; in particular at Rizley, amongst a society recently raised up by Lorenzo Dow.[76] 'I had much cause to bless God for this journey.'

[76] This society, whose members were spoken of as 'Dowites', eventually accepted the oversight of Bourne, being regarded as one of his societies. With a membership of about twenty it appeared on the first printed plan of 1812. This has led to the supposition that Rizley was one of the earliest churches of the Primitive Methodist Connexion. It would seem however, that the arrangement was made to mark and secure Bourne's periodic visits to the Quaker Methodists. (See *A Short History of Independent Methodists*, A. Mounfield, 1905, pp. 20–1.) Of this society, Bourne wrote in his Journal, 23rd April 1809: 'Here each one does that which is right in his own eyes. They stand, sit, kneel, pray, exhort, &c., as they are moved. I was very fond of their way.'

On his return, he preached at Runcorn, and then made his way to Delamere Forest, where he called upon the woman, Nancy Foden, whom he had seen 'in vision' at Crawfoot's house. In conversation with her—'a motherly woman who conversed well on religion'—Bourne spoke of his natural hesitancy in preaching. She affirmed that during her ecstasy she had seen his reluctance, and then she observed that his very reluctance was the sign of a call to preach, and that he must undertake it as the will of the Lord, whatever the cost. This conversation was determinative, and concerning it, years afterwards, Bourne wrote:

Truly this was a new lesson . . . it marked one of the most extraordinary events in my whole life, and I went home a different man.[77]

We must note the important development which had taken place during this time whilst Bourne was in Cheshire and Lancashire. In July, at the Conference in Liverpool, the ministers had considered the question of camp-meetings in America, and had expressed their opinion:

It is our judg[e]ment that, even supposing such meetings to be allowable in America, they are highly improper in England and likely to be productive of considerable mischief, and we disclaim all connexion with them.[78]

Reasons for this strong attitude have been suggested.[79] The ministers assembled may not have appreciated the difference between the meetings, as held in America and marked by emotional extremes, and those already held in England; in the light of the controversy of some ten years before, which led to the founding of the Methodist New Connexion, under Alexander Kilham and others, they may have feared new agitation; they may also have learned something of the eccentricities of Lorenzo Dow, and were thus prejudiced.

However, on returning from the Conference, the travelling preachers at Burslem declared themselves in opposition to camp-meetings, and required their office-bearers to do likewise. This at once created a tension in the circuit. The superintendent preacher, the Rev. John Riles, put all local preachers and leaders under edict in regard to attendance at such meetings,

---

[77] Bourne MSS (Auto.), C Text, f. 129.
[78] *Mins. of Conf.*, 1807.
[79] *The Secret of Mow Cop* (WHS Lecture, 1950), Dr W. E. Farndale, p. 33.

and urged them to persuade members similarly. It is not surprising, therefore, that some of Bourne's previous supporters became hesitant and withdrew. Even James Bourne wavered, but he was restored to his conviction, through a dream; William Clowes did not attend the Norton meeting, when the time came.[80]

Although there was opposition, it must not be supposed that there was any personal quarrel between Bourne and the circuit superintendent. Bourne writes:

I had a very sore travail for a great part of Burslem society: it appears as if the Lord had a controversy with them and that Mr R[iles] had done a sore thing. O my God, pardon him.[81]

In spite of discouragements, Bourne continued in this conviction regarding the Norton camp-meeting. In a meeting for prayer at the house of Joseph Pointon it was strongly impressed upon his mind that 'camp-meetings should not die but live', and he came to believe that he was called of God to stand by the new venture, and that if he deserted the cause it would be at the peril of his soul. So the preparations continued. He writes:

My sufferings were heavy, and my sorrows were great; but by labours and diligence, I got all things ready by Saturday evening, August 22, 1807. We had a course of praying, and the Lord was with us, and I so far copied after the Americans, as to sleep all night in one of the tents.[82]

On the following morning many were in the field before six o'clock: it was fine and the meeting opened with four preachers —one from Macclesfield, one from Knutsford, and Hugh and James Bourne—together with 'a good number of pious, praying labourers' from Harriseahead. Bourne was troubled in spirit by the arrival of a Tunstall local preacher and schoolmaster, who declared opposition to the meeting and then departed. Not long afterwards came the unexpected arrival of

[80] On 16th August 1807 a small camp-meeting was held at Brown Edge, mainly attended by hearers from Harriseahead, the preachers being Hugh Bourne and Thomas Cotton: 'Many came out to hear who scarcely ever heard the gospel in their lives.' One point in the entry in Bourne's Journal is noteworthy: 'At two o'clock we went into the chapel: W. Skinner preached. We then returned to the common and continued until six o'clock.' It shows that Bourne's practice was to avoid any interference with normal preaching appointments, an instance of his discretion.

[81] Walford, p. 160.

[82] Bourne MSS (Auto.), A Text, p. 213.

one, Dr Paul Johnson, M.D., from Dublin,[83] whose coming 'was like light out of darkness'; he had been informed of the occasion by the Irish preacher of Knutsford, who had attended the Mow Cop meeting, and who had written an account of it. 'Being much in the Quaker way',[84] Dr Johnson's powerful preaching impressed the company, and greatly encouraged Bourne. The meeting continued until eight in the evening. The following day, Monday, it commenced again at eight in the morning, proceeding throughout the day. It was necessary for Dr Johnson to return, and the meeting closed again at eight o'clock. On the Tuesday the service was held from noon until six, when the camp-meeting terminated.

Two things stand out as significant in regard to this Norton meeting. The arrival of Dr Johnson was regarded by the camp-meeting fathers as a token of Divine encouragement to continue; the purpose of the meeting, namely to counteract the influence of the 'wakes', had been fulfilled, not one member being drawn away.

Further, an incident arose out of the holding of the meeting which was to prove determinative for future development. A female preacher from Macclesfield, Mrs Dunnell, who had intended supporting the meeting, was asked to supply an appointment of the superintendent preacher at Tunstall, it would seem, in order to forestall her intention of being at Norton. This had an important outcome some few weeks later, when the same pulpit was closed to her. Of this Bourne writes:

Towards the close of this year, 1807, being at the house of Mr John Smith [85] at Tunstall, I found him and Mr James Steele in trial of mind. The female preacher being again at Tunstall, was shut out of the chapel under a plea of Conference. They said it was enough to make a secession and they had determined to fit up Mr Smith's

[83] Dr Johnson had attended Lorenzo Dow, who had been afflicted with small-pox during his visit to Ireland in 1800. 'He had me carried to his own house, though he was neither with the Quakers nor the Methodists' (*Travels . . . of Lorenzo Dow*, 1806, I.128).

[84] It would seem that by 1807 Dr Johnson's position regarding the Quakers had become more defined.

[85] John Smith was the brother of Joseph Smith. The latter, a man of somewhat eccentric habits, owned considerable property in Tunstall, and for some twenty years had preached widely in Cheshire and North Staffordshire, but on settling at Tunstall had ceased. In his dining-room the first Methodist services in Tunstall were held, and his family gave the site for the new chapel, of which John Wesley wrote, on 29th March 1790: 'At nine I preached in the new chapel at Tunstall, the most elegant I have seen since I left Bath' (*Jour.*, Std. ed., VIII.55). At his death, Joseph Smith bequeathed his property to his brother, John, named above. See art. 'Our First Preaching House and Pulpit', A. A. Birchenough, *PMM*, 1900, pp. 609 f.

kitchen for a place of worship. Their talk gave me alarm. I dreaded a secession. I spoke strongly to Mr James Steele, they having requested me to fall in with them; so they concluded that the kitchen should be for preaching only, and no society should be formed in it. I then fell in with them, and I obtained a licence from the Bishop's court, and it was settled for preachings to be on Friday evening.[86]

So before the end of 1807 regular preachings were held, and these continued without remission for the next five years or thereabouts. This new work sprang out of the opposition to the Norton meeting; later on Mr. Smith's home was to become an asylum for the camp-meeting fathers. This account makes plain the fact that Bourne had an abhorrence of any suggestion of departure from the Methodist fold.

VIII

One result of the camp-meetings had been a partial sweeping away of Bourne's timidity. 'I was like a new man, and was ready to preach the gospel wherever the Lord in His Divine providence opened the way'. It is not surprising, therefore, to find new calls pressing in upon him. Thus he was invited to undertake a preaching at a house at Lask Edge, near Leek, the result of which was the formation of a society, eventually to be taken over by the Leek Circuit, but which was alternately supplied by Bourne, who preached regularly, assisted by his brother, James, and by his friends, Thomas Cotton and William Maxfield.

Similarly at Kingsley, near Cheadle, in Staffordshire, some fifteen miles distant from Bemersley, the work was 'opened' early in 1808, though under considerable persecution.

At the end of February, a more distant call came from Market Drayton, in Shropshire, to which labour he returned in the following month, in the hope of resuscitating the weak cause by visitation and preaching. It was on his return journey, whilst passing through Wellington, that it was impressed upon his mind that, on account of the widespread irreligion, he should write a tract on *Rules for Holy Living*.[87] Some four thousand copies were printed a few weeks later and were widely distributed. We know from the *Journals* of William Clowes [88] that a Bible and

[86] Bourne MSS (Auto.), A Text, f. 227.
[87] It was printed at Newcastle-under-Lyme, May 1808. The text is reprinted in Walford, pp. 169–70. See *infra*.
[88] op. cit., pp. 60–2.

Tract-distributing society had come into being, as a result of which 'the country became greatly moved': regular preaching became established and societies were formed. To this work Bourne gave his willing support. 'The tract work is bringing great things to pass.'

Another venture also claimed his warm interest at this time, namely the 'Association for the Suppression of Sabbath-breaking', composed of persons resident in Tunstall and Burslem. Bourne was probably responsible for the selection of the printed literature,[89] as well as being an ardent defender. 'I find great thankfulness to God for calling me in some degree to stand up in defence of this Association.' The movement was unhappily frowned upon by the circuit authorities, its advocates being threatened with expulsion from the societies. 'The wicked, now encouraged by our spiritual guides, broke in upon us with redoubled fury . . . to stem the opposition was impossible . . . we were wounded in the house of our friends.' [90]

It is interesting to record that on one of his return journeys Bourne attended the class of Mrs Fletcher, of Madeley, and, on the following day, the service at Madeley Church. His impressions are worth recording:

She spoke much of faith, and seemed to be a woman of great faith herself, but the class was not such as I had expected: we have classes whose religion is deeper, whose faith is stronger, and who are much more given up to God. . . . Mrs Fletcher's language is not so well adapted to common people and they look upon her as a person quite out of the common way; they are rather dazzled with her than stirred up to imitation. . . . At Madeley Church, the scene of Mr Fletcher's labours,[91] for the first time I heard a gospel sermon in the Church.[92]

Whilst near to Wellington Bourne learned of the custom of holding revelries on the summit of the Wrekin, on the first

[89] The Association, which began late in 1807, printed an abstract of the law on sabbath-breaking: the proclamation of George III (*A Proclamation for the Encouragement of Piety and Virtue, and for the prevention and punishing of Vice, Profanation and Immorality*. London, June 3, 1781); a sermon by John Wesley on the same subject (Sermon LII); and an address by the Rev. David Simpson (incumbent of Christ Church, Macclesfield (1776–99), who was imbued with Methodist sympathies), entitled, *A Discourse on the Royal Proclamation for the Suppression of Vice: with a Letter to the Magistrates of the Borough of Macclesfield* (1787). Bourne writes (7th March, 1807): 'Coming through Hanley we agreed to have printed 500 of Mr. Wesley's sermon. . . . This is at this time needful because the Methodists are risen up against the Association.'
[90] Clowes *Jour.* (1844), pp. 47–52.
[91] The Rev. John Fletcher had died in 1785.
[92] Bourne MSS (Jour.), 3rd April, 1808.

Sunday in May each year. 'It immediately arose in my mind to get preachers, and hold a camp-meeting there.' So we find that on the appointed day, Sunday, 1st May 1808, forty miles distant from Bemersley, Bourne and a small band of preachers opened the meeting, which lasted for five hours. 'The Lord so bridled the revellers that we had not much trouble from them.'

Later in the month, new 'openings' were made at Ramsor and at Wootton-under-Weaver. On 15th May a small but useful camp-meeting took place at Buglawton, near Congleton, during which copies of *The Rules for Holy Living* were distributed.

This period proved a time of testing for Bourne. Intermittent return to his daily occupation was found necessary for his own material support: at this particular time he was engaged in felling oak trees, yet he was uneasy lest this spiritual ministration should be interrupted.

I have been more engaged in worldly business now than I have been for a long time. . . . My mind was full of wonderings. . . . But I had not comfort nor settled peace till I turned my mind to the ministry. . . . The light of grace appeared to be that I must go out in general and trust God for a living. This has been the greatest obstacle, but I felt willing to be in the hands of God. . . . I made no promise but simply gave myself into the hands of God to be moulded into His will.[93]

Sunday, 29th May, brought the day of the third camp-meeting on Mow Cop. 'It was neither too hot nor too cold, and the place under the mountain was exceedingly pleasant . . . all the day the company was solemn.' The meeting lasted from nine o'clock in the morning until seven in the evening. It was a day of remembrance and power, but there was some sadness: former friends, in particular Daniel Shubotham and William Maxfield, forsook the enterprise, and there was some opposition, the token of more serious challenge which lay ahead.

Two important happenings occurred during the following month. On Sunday, 12th June, Bourne attended the Conference of the Independent Methodists at Macclesfield, 'by appointment'.[94] A discussion arose concerning the ministry of women in the societies, and, on request, Bourne 'agreed to write an answer to the propositions'. The following day he had a conversation with Dr Paul Johnson (who had visited the

[93] Bourne MSS (Jour.), 17th–18th May 1808.
[94] Probably this means 'by invitation'.

Quaker Methodists around Warrington somewhat frequently) regarding the whole subject of Quakerism. Of this he writes: 'He honestly tried to convert me to Quakerism, but could not succeed.' This association and Bourne's decision were important for the future, and the nature of his decision is interesting when we remember how deeply he had already touched Quaker literature, admittedly with great profit.

A week later Bourne took a journey to Delamere Forest, where he heard Crawfoot preach; the next day he set off to Warrington, coming to the home of Peter Phillips,[95] a young and rising leader of the new Quaker Methodist movement which centred in that region. It was to be the beginning of a life-long friendship between the two men. Bourne had completed his tract arising from the Macclesfield Conference, and under the pressure of Phillips he agreed that it should be printed, after further revision.[96] It seems that Bourne became responsible for the entry of Hannah, the wife of Phillips, into the work of preaching,[97] a decision which was to prove of immense importance in the expansion of the Quaker Methodist movement.

[95] For an account of Peter Phillips (1778–1853) see *A Short History of Independent Methodism*, A. Mounfield, pp. 10–13; Kendall, I.198.

[96] This tract, under the title *Remarks on the Ministry of Women*, is reprinted in Walford, I.172–7.

[97] 'I put the question to H[annah] Phillips, whether she was called to the ministry. . . . I found that it was known to her, and I believe that for this, among other things, the Lord sent me to Warrington' (Bourne MSS (Jour.), 23rd June 1808).

CHAPTER FOUR

EXCLUSION (1808)

I

IN HIS MS Autobiography,[1] Bourne makes a significant entry regarding his return from Warrington.

On Thursday, June 23, 1808, I set off for home: and on my way between Holmes Chapel and Congleton, it suddenly came to my mind that I should be put out of the old Methodist society, and should be more useful out than in: but having never heard a hint of the kind, being also a chapel trustee, and having spent scores and scores of pounds in promoting the interest of the society, and hundreds of members having been raised out of the world: and feeling as if wedded to the society, I concluded it could not be, and put the thought from me, hoping it might not arise from a Divine impression: but it returned until I found it difficult to walk along the road. . . . On arriving at home, I met the rumour of being likely soon to be put out.

Bourne was quickly to discover that the impression he had received was only too true. Again we quote his own words:

On Monday, June 27, 1808, the circuit quarter-day meeting held at Burslem put me out of the old Methodist society, without my being summoned to a hearing, or being officially informed of the charge, or charges alleged against me.[2]

We must add his own comment on this decision:

This was not upright. I was a member of the quarterly meeting: and as a private member of society, I might, if due cause had appeared, have been put out without quarter day: but in addition to being a private member, I was a chapel trustee, which by rule entitled me to a hearing before expulsion: and in not being allowed this, I was wronged. I was informed that Mr Walker, the circuit steward, spoke for justice . . . but to his words the meeting did not pay attention.[3]

---

[1] op. cit., B Text, f. 61.
[2] ibid., f. 62.
[3] The exclusion also applied to James Bourne. 'My brother James told me that both him and me were put out of the society. The Lord's will be done. I am put out of the society-class which I first joined together, whom I have supported and watered' (Bourne MSS (Jour.), 28th July, 1808).

A few days afterwards, Bourne went over to Norton-le-Moors.

> Having been out from home for several weeks, I paid up the
> arrears of class-money, that all might be clear. . . . Not being sum-
> moned to a hearing . . . I have remained in the dark respecting the
> real charge or charges on which they secretly put me out of member-
> ship.[4]

To Bourne himself the sorrow was increased because he knew
that some who were preachers and leaders in the meeting had
shared his confidences and supported his evangelistic enterprise.

At least at the time it seemed that this strange decision was a
tragic mistake.

II

Bourne had now no alternative but to go forward quietly and
diligently with his labours, no longer under the 'repose' of the
circuit authority.

> I was necessitated to have no other head but Christ, and I felt
> like a solitary being. I did not, however, lose respect to my old
> friends, although they laboured to set people against me. . . . My
> wish was to labour for the conversion of souls. . . . The decree of the
> Lord was gone forth to bring forward open-air worship and the
> converting work afresh.[5]

Shortly after Bourne's expulsion, Thomas Cotton was similarly put out of society. The 'pioneers' were few, but 'the company kept united'. Within a fortnight the work was renewed at
Kingsley, Tean, and Wootton-under-Weaver, and at Ramsor
and Lexhead. An incident is recorded which reveals not only
Bourne's search for spiritual direction towards new opportunity, but also that mystical quality to which we have
already referred.

> About half a mile short of Kingsley, I was walking along the side
> of a field, and a shining light appeared on the opposite side. . . . It
> was a pillar of glory. I stood still, and it kept moving until it came
> across the field, and it rested upon me and filled my soul, and was as
> if it clothed my body . . . giving me light and holy instruction in
> regard to the ministry of the gospel. And while that heavenly glory
> was upon me, I waited on the Lord, to inquire where it was His will
> that my brother and I should go . . . and the direction was 'Wootton-
> under-Weaver'.[6]

---

[4] Bourne MSS (Auto), B Text, f. 63.   [5] ibid., f. 64.
[6] ibid., A Text, f. 255.

On 17th July another camp-meeting took place on Mow Cop: and its fruits were offered to the Methodist Society. Yet a new movement had been born.

The world was open before us; we could have had more if we could have done it. And the bond of our union was the grace of God . . . and our hands were so pure from proselytising that we were free to labour in other communities.[7]

Early in July Bourne returned to Warrington, again to be welcomed into the household of Peter Phillips; also he entered the home of Thomas Eaton,[8] where for long time to come he was to find the warmest hospitality. 'I may bless God that He ever caused me to set foot in that house.' Another contact was with Anna Richardson, who became an eminent and hospitable member of the Quaker Methodists. Of her Bourne writes: 'She was indeed to set out for heaven under my ministry. She was well-to-do in the world, and became a mother in Israel. . . . She soon became a preacheress, and laboured in the ministry many years',[9] until her death in 1848.

On his earlier visit to Warrington Bourne had found a copy of *The Life of Benjamin Abbott* (1732–96), an American Methodist evangelist, much devoted to field-preaching. He had brought it home with him, and had prepared an abridgement of it for reprinting. He now finished the work, and 'rather at the instance of the Warrington friends', he set off on foot to Leeds on 28th July, in order to discuss the material with one Mr John Sigston,[10] a schoolmaster, who was evidently known amongst the Warrington Methodists. The record of Bourne's journey is interesting:

I went through Knutsford, Altringham, Manchester, Middleton, Rochdale, Halifax, and Bradford. There are many villages and many Methodist chapels. When I first stepped into Yorkshire, I kneeled down and prayed. . . . I found a great nearness to Jesus.

[7] ibid., B Text, f. 66.
[8] Thomas Eaton came to reside at Stockton Heath as the local manager of the Bridgwater Canal. For his relation to the Quaker Methodists see A. Mounfield, *A Short History of the Independent Methodists* (1905), p. 18.
[9] Bourne MSS (Auto.), A Text, f. 223.
[10] John Sigston was a friend and biographer of the Rev. William Bramwell, who had sympathies with the revivalist movements in Leeds and Manchester; it had evidently been proposed that in the reprint of Abbott's *Life*, Bramwell's 'Letter to the Preachers' should be included, as also W. E. Miller's 'Letter to the Manchester Revivalists'. Later Sigston became a leading spirit in the troubles arising out of the Leeds organ case, which led, in 1828, to the formation of the Protestant Methodists.

Lancashire and Yorkshire are parted by large, barren mountains.
. . . Yorkshire is very hilly, abounds in stone, water, and coal: they
get up cloth. The building is chiefly stone, and they have stone doors
and window-cases, but chiefly sash-windows.[11]

He arrived at Leeds 'a little before noon' on the following day,
and found Sigston 'rather learned but not communicative', and
the interview did not prove fruitful. 'We did not add one line
to the book.' Four days later he returned.

I set off from Leeds taking the coach to Manchester, which cost
me 7/–, for my feet being sore and all things considered, I thought
it to be the cheapest way. I started with a Methodist coachman.
From Manchester I walked eighteen miles to Warrington, and then
to Stockton-heath.[12]

Here he found Dr Johnson, whom he had met at the Norton
camp-meeting, and who had arrived during Bourne's absence,
and with whom he had a long conversation. 'It was useful to
me to hear him comment upon the Scripture, and to see his
native honesty: a man so free from guile I hardly ever saw.'
The next day Bourne completed Abbott's *Life* and then went to
Delamere, and on to home.

The following weeks saw the increase of the work, and on
Sunday, 4th September, the first Ramsor camp-meeting was
held,[13] at which some forty souls found spiritual release. This
was followed, a month later, on 9th October, by the second
meeting, which was to have important consequences. This
meeting lasted from nine in the morning until five o'clock,
and of it Bourne writes:

I believe the Lord is about to give a powerful call to the people all
about this country. . . . I believe much seed sown at this meeting
will take root. O my God, water it![14]

Amidst all this new adventure Bourne was labouring in the
study of the Scriptures, as the following extract from his Journal
reveals:

[11] Bourne MSS (Jour.) 28th July 1808
[12] ibid., 2nd August 1808.
[13] Under the official attitude, William Clowes had not attended a camp-meeting
for fifteen months. He now renewed his loyalty to the enterprise, and set out with
Bourne to Ramsor. Whilst walking together along the canal-side 'between Endon
and Denford' [Dunwood], Clowes seems to have spoken critically, and Bourne
reacted strongly, even hastily. Clowes was silenced and they proceeded without
further words. Bourne MSS (Auto.), B Text, f. 68.
[14] Bourne MSS (Jour.), 9th October 1808.

I have been now for some time very much engaged in the Greek: this week I read much in the Greek Testament. I have been much assisted in the language through prayer. I believe the Lord requires it at my hands to learn Greek and Hebrew.

And a little later we find this:

October 29. This morning I got up about five o'clock to pray . . . and the Lord impressed the Greek language upon my mind . . . with great sweetness, particularly the Book of Revelation: it was as if I saw the language in its colour. I now saw what the gift of tongues was. . . . I have had hard work over studying it, but the Lord has made it joyful.

Of his diligence in pastoral service we may note that he furnished the newly-formed class at Bradley Green with a library; at his own home he began family prayers in the Bemersley kitchen, having hitherto desisted because of his father's violence; at the Cloud he wrote 'spiritual directions' for a young girl, Hannah Goodwin, of whom he said: 'She is minded to follow Ann Cutler's steps,[15] and I think she will succeed'; to one William Krinks he wrote urging him to consider the call to the ministry of preaching. We cannot but observe that at this time Bourne must have spent considerable sums of money in printing, for his own tracts,[16] as we have seen, were produced in thousands, and those written by others were purchased, all for distribution at camp-meetings and on his travels abroad.

This period of the Journal also affords us further glimpses of the mystical quality of his mind. We add the following:

November 3, 1808. I sat with Crawfoot and others . . . and I breathed my soul to God for the Holy Ghost to come upon that church. I turned my head and Crawfoot was looking at me: his face shone: I could not bear it, but was near to fainting away. I felt as if my inside was rising out of me, and going to God . . . the Lord made great discoveries to me.[17]

In conversation with Clowes:

[15] Ann Cutler was a saintly Methodist, at Macclesfield, who died on 29th December 1794 at the age of thirty-five. See *The Life and Death of Ann Cutler*, W. Bramwell. Bourne makes frequent references to her spiritual example, and distributed copies of her *Life*, e.g. to a soldier travelling to Ayrshire, whom he met when journeying to Warrington. 'By him I sent some of Ann Cutler's *Life* to Scotland. O God, follow it with Thy blessing.'

[16] Late in December, Bourne printed a new tract which he had written, entitled *Advice to Young Women.*

[17] Bourne MSS (Jour.), loc. cit.

We fell to talk; my heart was opened, and the Word seemed to soak into me like rain.[18]

At a meeting for prayer in Tunstall:

I felt extraordinary things at the thought of being a friend of Christ. . . . I had an uncommon time. It seemed as if Jesus Christ embraced me in His arms. After this He seemed to move to the church at Cloud, and He sat there as is represented in Isaiah's vision; and He seemed to put His arms around me, and say that I should reign with Him. . . . I felt unutterable things.[19]

It is not surprising that he wrote towards the end of 1808:

It is now very edifying to me to read letters of full sanctification. . . . I grow more and more spiritual every day. O Lord, fill me with Thy love and Thy glory, and guide my steps in all things, through Jesus Christ. Amen.[20]

The year closed with a journey to the Forest, accompanied by Clowes. 'We went to the watch-night and prayed the old year out.' It had been a year fraught with the deepest consequences; so much in the future was to depend upon his own loyalty and labour.

[18] Bourne MSS (Jour.), loc. cit.   [19] ibid., 20th December 1808.
[20] ibid., 27th December 1808.

CHAPTER FIVE

PASTORAL WORK (1809–10)

I

IN Bourne's MS Autobiography [1] we find the following:

Now standing clear of all other Methodist connexions, it may be asked how we proceeded.... Mr Wesley began with labourings; and it was the same with us. We endeavoured to follow the openings of Divine Providence.... The Lord appointed us to labour at large in promoting open-air worship and the converting work. And our hands were so clean and our motives so pure, that we could labour among the Wesleyans with all freedom.... We were as free among the Independent Methodists at Macclesfield, and the Quaker Methodists at Warrington.... Although for a time it appeared to be the Lord's will that we should labour considerably in benefitting other communities, still our settled places kept increasing; already, on our side we had Gratton, Lask Edge, Gillow Heath, Congleton Edge and Brown Edge. In the other direction there were Tean, Wootton, Ramsor, Caldon Lowe: and other places kept opening. ... At first we had no direction from heaven to immediately form new classes, as our call from the Lord appeared to be to labour for the benefit of other communities as well as our own. This was evidently the Lord's will, and we were blest in the doing of it. God was glorified, communities were strengthened and souls were saved.

This represents the spirit and purpose of this early period following Bourne's exclusion.

So we find Bourne fulfilling pastoral service wherever opportunity was afforded. Typical of this are the following extracts from his Journal:

1809. Monday, January 16th. Clowes and I visited from house to house at Wootton and talked and prayed with the families.

Sunday, February 5th. I went with Clowes and Nixon to Lawton-wich. We visited from house to house and were at the preaching in the afternoon.

Sunday, March 12th. I visited Miss Anne Mear of Norton Green. Above a year ago I visited her a few times and she was light and averse to religion. Sorrow struck in my heart, and then the Lord spoke in me ... I had now more hope of her than before. I lent her *Ann Cutler.* [2]

[1] A Text, ff. 273–7. [2] *supra*, p. 65, n. 15.

In addition we find service through pastoral letter, an example of which has survived [3] written to one of his 'spiritual daughters', possibly Betty Howell of Stableford Mill:

> I feel thankful to God for the great work He has wrought in you, and I am fully satisfied that our Lord Jesus Christ intends you to be extensively useful. . . . The spirit of your Father that is in you will speak, and will open the Scriptures as needs be: and if the people do not immediately hearken, yet you will receive a blessing in your own soul. . . . Our conversation was made a great blessing to me; and this also was a further testimony that the Lord had called you to bring many to Christ. . . . Therefore I wish you goodspeed in the Name of the Lord.
>
> HUGH BOURNE.

Quietly during the year 1809 'The Lord granted us an increase in our ministry'. William Maxfield, Thomas Knight, Thomas White, William Allcock, and William Turner began to preach, so that by August of that year the number had grown to eight. Bourne writes:

> The weight upon me was great. The making and writing out plans was a deal of work. And as I had opened my mouth before the Lord not to allow my worldly business to distract me in the ministry, I was by degrees obliged mainly to relinquish my temporal business and devote my time to the ministry.[4]

We should note at this time the deepening understanding between Bourne and Clowes, and the consequent increase of their labours together in the new cause. This is indicated by many passages in Bourne's Journals.

> We were praying at Mr Berrisford's and Clowes touched me with his hand, and power came from him and it was a great blessing. I rejoice that he has the gift of laying on of hands.[5]
>
> Having stayed all night with Clowes, we had a grand time in reading the Scriptures and at prayer this morning.[6]
>
> I went to see Clowes; better in body and driving on as usual; he said, 'I have always Christ and He always satisfies me.' [7]

There is evidence also that Bourne's own spiritual experiences were at a deeper level. Thus we read:

> *Mar. 20. 1809.* Coming through Kingsley I was set upon by a few abandoned people. I spoke a little to them. I saw the need of the

---

[3] Walford, I.203–4. [4] Bourne MSS (Auto.), A Text, f. 276.
[5] Bourne MSS (Jour.), 22nd January 1809. [6] ibid., 13th February 1809.
[7] ibid., 28th August 1809.

gift of discerning spirits. . . . I looked unto the Lord till such a spirit of love came upon me that it appeared impossible for me to feel any resentment to anyone, except I first cast away my faith. If a man were to rob or murder me I believe I should only feel tenderness, pity, and love.

At times he felt 'a great flow of light and love'. He could write: 'Another fold of power spread over my soul'; again, 'I had that sacred awe that dares not move, and all the silent heaven of love.' Again, 'My heart was like a glowing coal and I felt the power move from me to all the ends of the earth'. Yet again, 'As I came home I felt the seventh seal open in me, and I was more in God than ever. . . . I found quite a deadness to the world.' As part of his spiritual discipline he resolved upon stated periods of fasting in which he found purification and renewal. 'I believe it is my duty to fast on Wednesdays and Fridays, and to leave the event to God.'[8]

A deep impression concerning the solemnity of his life and labours was made upon him by a visit to Bucknall Chapel in July 1809, where many of his former schoolfellows were interred:

I felt very awful while examining their tombs. I almost felt as if I should not long be an inhabitant of this world.[9] O Lord, Thy will be done. I then went to Fordhays where I was born, and where I lived sixteen years. I went over the field in which I was convinced of sin.

Although Bourne had relinquished his occupation in order that he might fulfil the work of the ministry, it was necessary at times for him to engage in other labours for the sake of his own maintenance. So we find him taking time for timbering and carpentry, building and gardening, haymaking and harvesting; sometimes, however, setting off upon a long journey on foot for visitation and preaching after the day's work was over, lest a spiritual opportunity should be lost. Often he became extremely tired.

I worked at Milton and was kept in peace over rearing [i.e. of a barn-roof]. I felt much strained with heaving and could scarcely keep awake at family prayers; afterwards I fell asleep at the bedside.[10]

[8] cf. Jour., 22nd March 1809. 'I solemnly engaged with Thomas Knight and my sister-in-law Sarah, and Hannah Mountford our servant, to fast and pray a month for the Lord to revive His work, that is to fast on Wednesdays and Fridays. O Lord, assist us, through Jesus Christ. Amen.'

[9] Perhaps it was the sense of foreboding that prompted him to make a will at Tunstall on 19th October 1809. The document so far as we know is not extant.

[10] Bourne MSS (Jour.), 13th September 1809.

We find interesting glimpses of him during these toils.

> *Friday, July 14.* Haymaking and studying Greek. *Saturday, July 15.*
> Haymaking: today I made great progress in Greek.[11]

And later, in the harvest field:

> I worked very hard in the corn. I was strong in faith. In the after-
> noon I was setting up corn after three scythes, and by working
> quickly I often got a little time to kneel behind a *kivver* [i.e. a shock
> of corn] which was well for me. I felt nothing in me more desired
> anything but God.[12]

It should also be remembered that Bourne's occupations in this
way were intermittent, and it is astonishing that through his
life he performed so great an amount of labour upon a mini-
mum of sustenance. From a letter written many years later
we learn of this.

> I know he used to walk forty or fifty miles a day, and was under
> circumstances of self-denial little practised and even known by
> most. He used to put into his pocket two or three hard-boiled eggs,
> and a little dry bread in the morning, and during his journey he
> would sit down by a well of water and take his humble fare, and
> then travel on in pursuit of the great object of saving souls.[13]

During 1809 Bourne's labours expanded into what he called
the 'Cheshire round', a home mission field extending from the
Forest of Delamere to Warrington and Rizley in Lancashire,
and Stockton Heath and Runcorn in Cheshire on the one side;
and on the other to Tarvin and Stapleford, near Chester, and
to the neighbourhood of Altry, in Flintshire. His visits to the
Quaker Methodists at Warrington and the neighbourhood were
regular and prolonged—he made some five visits during the
year, and he was regarded as their spiritual counsellor, yet he
himself received a spiritual blessing in return:

> I had a severe controversy with Peter Phillips, he having adopted
> some of W[illiam] Law's opinions. Spoke at Stockton Heath and
> had a good time: Ellen Eaton is full of simple faith. I fasted and
> spent the forenoon in this lovely pious family. I talked further with
> P. Phillips and showed that some of his opinions had no founda-
> tion.[14]

---

[11] Bourne MSS (Jour.), 13th September 1809, loc. cit.
[12] ibid., 22nd September 1809.
[13] T. Steele to J. Walford, 22nd December 1853 (Walford, pp. 210–11).
[14] Bourne MSS (Jour.), 3rd–4th October 1809.

Similarly, Bourne made frequent visits to the Independent Methodists at Macclesfield: the cause was low, and, along with Clowes, he became the means of revival. During one of these visits the problem of funds for the maintenance of preachers was discussed, and Bourne was hesitant, though Clowes supported the idea. 'I spoke against funds . . . but I mean to examine this point.' The matter was not unimportant in the light of future developments.

Further important expansion took place eastwards around Ramsor, to which region Bourne made even more frequent journeys, opening new places, though as yet in the main doing work auxiliary to visiting societies. During his visit on 25th June he met one, Elizabeth Evans, the wife of Samuel Evans of Derby, who preached at Wootton on that day. She was to become the prototype of Dinah Morris in George Eliot's novel *Adam Bede*, and Bourne's description of her is worth recording:

She began about two o'clock; her voice was low and hoarse at first from having preached so much the week past, but she got well into the power. She appears to be very clear in Scriptural doctrine and very ready in Scripture, and speaks full in the Spirit, and from the little I saw of her she appears to be as fully devoted to God as any woman I ever met with.[15]

During July three camp-meetings were held at Runcorn, Biddulph, and Mow Cop. The movement of open-air preaching was expanding. Late in October Bourne journeyed southwards to Market Drayton, in Shropshire, where he laboured with much success. We have a glimpse into Bourne's sensitiveness in his note of conversations with John Whitaker, who sought to persuade him of the rightness of accepting proffered hospitality, and to whom Bourne made admission: 'I believe I have not done the best way in these points.' A later conversation was about Bourne's preaching, the style of which had evidently been in vernacular speech:

John Whitaker talked to me about using the best language as I had it in my power, and he pressed it much. I told him I would pray about it. . . . Appearing to be illiterate when I am not illiterate seemed to be quite wrong. O Lord, I beseech Thee, direct my soul, touch my lips. O Lord, if Thy will be that I should use fine language . . . touch my lips with a live coal from the altar. O may the love of Jesus flow from my lips in accents mild as the evening dew, and in

---

[15] Bourne MSS (Jour.), 25th June 1809. See Kendall, I.142–4. Betsy Evans was the aunt of George Eliot by marriage.

beauty as the falling of the fleecy snow. O let the honey distil from my lips.[16]

Two important things must be recorded for the year 1809. Early in his labours Bourne recognized the ministry of song in relation to the spread of the Gospel. Existing hymn-books were expensive for many of those who were brought in; moreover, a more simple form of expression seemed required. To meet this Bourne made a selection of hymns and songs, printing them at his own expense and selling them at a low price. The title-page of this first hymn-book was as follows:

> *A General Collection of Hymns and Spiritual Songs for Camp Meetings and Revivals*, selected by Hugh Bourne. Newcastle: printed at the office of C. Chester 1809.[17]

This collection, which was largely an adaptation of a similar collection published by Lorenzo Dow in 1807, went through many editions and became widely used.

The second important event arose out of the association with James Crawfoot of Delamere Forest, to whom frequent visits were paid by Bourne and Clowes in their journeyings into Cheshire. Bourne's first impressions of Crawfoot were tinged with dislike, but he recognized spiritual values in him. He writes:

> He was illiterate, but very conversant with the Bible. His views of the mystery of faith were clear, and in the knowledge of present salvation he excelled. Sometimes his conversation was deep and clear, and both edifying and improving. His knowledge of the converting work was extensive. I received much information from him relative to bringing souls into liberty in conversation. I went to his house with reluctance; but found myself so much a gainer that I was glad to call on him from time to time, always taking care to remunerate him.[18]

On Friday, 17th November 1809, on his return from Warrington Bourne called at the house of Crawfoot, and found the latter in serious domestic difficulty. It was so slack a time of work that, as a farmer's labourer, he could not get employment, and he and his family were in hunger. Moved with pity

---

[16] Bourne MSS (Jour.), 4th November 1809.

[17] The first notice of this in Bourne's MSS (Jour.) is under date 18th February 1809. 'I stayed at R—— and had with me some camp-meetings and revival hymn-books which I have got printed in a cheap form.'

[18] Bourne MSS (Auto.), A Text, f. 289; B Text, f. 75; C Text, ff. 150–1.

and as a deed of charity, Bourne determined to help him through the winter, and so proposed to give him ten shillings a week till Lady Day (25th March) 1810, by which time the farmer's spring work would commence and employment become possible. In return for this, during the winter Crawfoot was to 'labour in the Gospel' at places in the neighbourhood indicated by Bourne and in particular to make one journey into Staffordshire. So in the Journal for that year we find the entry:

I agreed with Mr James Crawfoot to give him ten shillings a week till Lady Day, to labour in the vineyard. This I believe God required at my hand.

Crawfoot remained beyond the date specified, and the expense, amounting to some £40, was shared by Bourne and his brother James, until it was undertaken by the newly-formed Connexion as a whole.

Many passages in the Journal bear witness to the early success of Crawfoot's labours, at first on the Cheshire and Lancashire side, and early in 1810 in the region of Tunstall and on to Ramsor. Bourne speaks in terms of astonishment at Crawfoot's spiritual insight, and his power in prayer and preaching.

Tuesday, August 14th. I stayed with Crawfoot . . . and had a most extraordinary opening in faith through his instruction. *Wednesday.* I set off with him to Dudden: by the way he opened the Scripture very much.

So for the time being we must leave Crawfoot engaged in his pastoral labour.

II

After labouring in Cheshire and Lancashire for several weeks Bourne returned to Bemersley to discover that in his absence his brother James and William Allcock had engaged Mrs Mary Dunnell,[19] a woman preacher, to assist in the work for the Mission Stations in North Staffordshire. With characteristic caution

[19] Mary Dunnell had been a local preacher in the Methodist Society at Tunstall, and as early as 1807 had manifested her interest in camp-meetings, in consequence of which (so it was believed) the Superintendent preacher had asked her to take his appointment on Sunday, 23rd August 1809, the day of the Norton camp-meeting, in order to prevent her attendance. In January 1810 this pulpit was closed to her (probably due to the Conference ruling regarding female preachers). This incensed Mr Smith, in whose house meetings had been held since 1807, and he invited her to take service there, the outcome of which was an invitation to the Bourne household at Bemersley. She then became an itinerant preacher in the camp-meeting community.

Bourne was rather hesitant in approval, but her power as a preacher soon convinced him. This was an important decision. Early in February 1810 he set off again to Market Drayton. As he passed by Broughton Church he put copies of his *Rules for Holy Living* through the broken panes in the window. 'I believe God will direct them' is the comment in his Journal.

It was at this time that, stimulated by the news of the great revivals there under the Camp Meeting Movement, Bourne came to have thoughts of leaving England for America, but he waited in order to be obedient to the Divine Will. It was whilst on his way from Market Drayton to Moreton Wood that he received deep intimation that he must remain in the homeland.

I had an impression by the Spirit, showing me why I was to stay in England, and not go to America. I was very happy, and much staid upon God.[20]

In the light of after events the decision was a right one.

We have a glimpse at the kind of pastoral work pursued by Bourne in his journeyings in the following entry from his Journal:

I called at a poor cottage near Stanton Heath, and the woman told me that she had been very ill for above four years, and went to doctors but was no better. She then prayed and pleaded with the Lord . . . till she was instantaneously healed. I was happy whilst she related it. She called in her father-in-law and the family: they lived in the other end of one of the poorest homes I ever beheld. I talked to the poor old man and the Lord broke his heart. We kneeled down and prayed and the old man was made happy. For this, perhaps, I was sent to the place.[21]

Another aspect of his labours is seen in the following:

I rose early and had much time in private. Went to Drayton and put up the candlesticks and repaired other things in the Chapel. I went under a greater travail for sinners at and about Drayton.[22]

Bourne returned to Staffordshire at the beginning of March, calling upon Clowes at Tunstall.

We engaged in talk about deep things. . . . If any persons must go into very deep things, death must pass upon the body, but this must be done by the Holy Ghost: they then enter into true revelations,

[20] Bourne MSS (Jour.), 14th February 1810.
[21] ibid., 17th February 1810.
[22] ibid., 16th February 1810.

and then take the body again. Clowes has fasted now four days. He is a man of great resolution.[23]

Bourne also learnt that there was some opposition being raised against Crawfoot's labours. 'The preachers are warring against him, but at present they cannot prevail.'

He also discovered the further success attending the labours of Mary Dunnell in North Staffordshire, and heard her preach 'a most extraordinary sermon'. One of her appointments at Standley, four miles from Bemersley, was to prove significant. As far back as 1802 William Bourne, a cousin of Hugh, lived there, and his daughter had been one of Bourne's converts. 'She grew well in grace.' After a time she had married a forgeman, Joseph Slater, who had declined in his Methodist loyalty, and Mary had done likewise. By 1810 they had come to live at Standley, and now sought to return to the fold, but there was no place of meeting. Slater's employer agreed to open his house if Mary Dunnell could come for preaching: so the Standley appointment was made.[24]

On Wednesday, 14th March, Hugh Bourne went to Standley to make preparation for the evening; James Bourne and Mary Dunnell followed on horseback, but as the road was difficult they were late in arriving. Bourne opened the meeting. Of this occasion he writes:

M. Dunnell preached ... we had a good time. This place has been tried and given up several times, but now the work is begun. O Lord, continue it. I stopped all night and Mary Slater was set at liberty.[25]

The following day others were also brought into salvation. 'We prayed the light down.' Then a new class was formed, Joseph Slater, now restored, being appointed leader.[26] Some two months later Bourne wrote: 'There is a great work going forward.' But a crisis was imminent. John Brindley of Norton 'thrust himself forward' to join it to the Circuit, and after an interview with the Superintendent preacher, the Rev. Jonathan Edmondson, the latter agreed and placed it upon the plan, but upon his own terms, namely that he should have 'the sole rule ... and thrust us out though we had been the sole instruments

[23] ibid., 5th March 1810.
[24] Bourne MSS (Auto.), A Text, f. 253; C Text, f. 153.
[25] Bourne MSS (Jour.), 14th March 1810.
[26] The names of the members of this class are recorded in *PMM*, 1845–88.

of raising the work.'[27] This brought apprehensiveness, because some seven years earlier there had been a large class at Standley under the hand of the then preacher and it had proved unsatisfactory. At the Quarterly Meeting John Brindley proposed that the class might be under joint direction for the first quarter, but Mr Edmondson replied that it must be under his sole control or else he would have nothing to do with it. Brindley said sharply: 'Then you must lay your hands off it.' That settled the matter. The die had been cast.

We must note Bourne's reflections upon the decision:

I cannot but look back and admire the wonderful hand of God. It was not my intention to have had anything to do with raising separate societies, but to have raised up as many people into the service of the Lord as I was able to do, and then to have encouraged them to join other societies. This view I had from a vehement attachment to the old Methodists, and a peculiar aversion to having any ruling part. But Mr. Edmondson's conduct has quite put a different turn upon things. Here necessity is laid upon us, and we are obliged to go on in the work without them.[28]

The importance of the Standley class with reference to the origin of the Connexion has often been exaggerated, probably due to the fact that its date, March 1810, was printed, but without authority, on the Class Tickets from 1829 onwards as being the first class. The real significance, however, is that the refusal of the parent body to incorporate that class strengthened the official policy against the fathers of the camp-meeting movement, and inevitably precipitated independent development.[29]

Bourne makes still further comment on this issue.

Up to this time we had laboured among the Wesleyans . . . but now they made a law to keep their members from attending our Camp Meetings; so they drew a clear line of distinction between the Wesleyan and Primitive Connexions; but there was cleanness of hands on both sides. They did not take one member from us, and we did not take one from them. There were various places at which we had laboured once a fortnight, and they had done the same: but these we left without taking away a member, and made our leaving as easy as it could well be. At first we had no direction from heaven immediately to form new classes, as our call from the Lord

---

[27] Bourne MSS (Jour.), 22nd May 1810.

[28] ibid, 23rd May 1810. It should be noted that at this point in the MSS a page has evidently been torn out by some (probably later) hand; a remaining fragment of the missing page indicates that it was written upon both sides. Doubtless it contained further details of the episode.

[29] cf. J. T. Wilkinson, *William Clowes 1780–1851*, pp. 94–8.

appeared to be to labour for the benefit of other communities as
well as our own. . . . But from providential circumstances as well as
Divine impression, it now appeared to be the will of God that we as
a Camp Meeting community should form classes and take upon us
the care of Churches in the fear of God . . . and as the Lord opened
our way we went forward in it, and by the blessing of God there had
been some preparation, for I, my brother and others, had laboured
much in conversation from house to house in opening the Scriptures
and the mystery of faith. . . . It was owned of the Lord. The classes
raised at Kidsgrove and Harriseahead in 1801 were originals: and
the leading of those classes was in accordance with the principles of
Primitive Methodism: and our Standley society proceeded in the
same way.[30]

III

In March 1810 the extent of the work under the camp-meeting
fathers stood as follows:[31] In the Cheshire and Lancashire
Mission there were five places—Macclesfield, Warrington,
Stockton Heath, Rizley, and Runcorn—the three preachers
being H. Bourne, James Crawfoot, and Thomas White, of
Runcorn. The Rizley class of some twenty members had been
raised up by Lorenzo Dow, and that at Runcorn of five members by Thomas White, and as early as 1808 these had come to
regard Hugh Bourne as their overseer, and he had come to
count them as his own people. In the Staffordshire Mission
there were six places—Ramsor, Wootton, Tean, Caldon Lowe,
Lask Edge, and Standley—and nine preachers were listed:
H. Bourne and James Bourne of Bemersley, Thomas Cotton of
Mow Cop, Thomas Knight and William Maxfield of Harriseahead, Francis Draycott of Ramsor, William Allcock of
Bemersley, William Turner of Brown Edge, and Mary Dunnell
of Bemersley. The new converts at Ramsor and Wootton in
1808 had been joined to the Methodist Society, the Bournes
still continuing to supply preachers fortnightly; it was natural
that these people should consider themselves as belonging to
the camp-meeting community, and when the care of Standley
fell upon the Bournes in 1810 their association was strengthened
still further.

Three days after the Standley Meeting on 14th March
Bourne thrust eastward in excursion to Ramsor and on to
Derby, returning at the end of the month. On the last day he
accompanied James Crawfoot (who had been re-engaged

[30] Bourne MSS (Auto.), A Text, ff. 302, 305; cf. B Text, f. 79; C Text, f. 135.
[31] Walford, I.270.

beyond Lady Day under the pressure of James Bourne) on his
return to Delamere, a journey which would mean some twenty
miles' walk before Bourne reached Tunstall again.

> I went with old James a little beyond Sandbach: he opened many
> things. I came back to Tunstall and talked with Clowes.[32]

In April he set off for Warrington, where he stayed for just over
a fortnight, mainly in the home of Peter and Hannah Phillips,
and visited neighbouring places. 'I had much discussion about
a present salvation.' Whilst at Warrington he met one, Mary
Ward, and a letter to her is extant,[33] which we quote in illustration of Bourne's pastoral care. It was written on 21st April 1810.

DEAR SISTER,

I am thankful to you for the great blessing whereof the Lord hath
made you a partaker. I am perfectly satisfied that the Lord has
accepted you in the situation you are in. I saw you come into the
transfiguration: I saw the glory shine in your face when you fully
believed: but when you reasoned about your situation in life your
faith sank and the glory departed.

But it may probably be that you may bring more glory to God
and more benefit to mankind in that line of life than in any other. . . .
You must look unto the power that worketh secretly. You have the
Fountain in you, and if you breathe your soul the power will move
on the people you are in company with. This is all by faith. . . .
Christ is in you and you are the instrument, and by thus being the
willing instrument you bring much glory to God and benefit to your
fellow-creatures, for your faith sets the arm of heaven at work. . . .
Herein is the excellency of the work of faith—it will have its effect
upon the people either in silence or when you are doing your
worldly business. Thus you may work for God at all times and in all
places, and nothing can hinder you: and if there be an opening you
may also talk about religion and offer a present salvation without
money or price.

But there is one point that you should be well acquainted with.
. . . As the power of God flows from you upon others to enlighten,
convince, convert, heal, so the powers of hell from others will strike
upon you to hurt, wound, and slay. Therefore when this is the case
be not alarmed, nor think you have lost ground, for this is only bearing the burdens of others, and by faith you will conquer and they
will be much benefitted.

Yours in the Lord,
HUGH BOURNE.

STOCKTON HEATH. *April* 21. 1810.

On his return journey Bourne came near to Runcorn.

---

[32] Bourne MSS (Jour.), 31st March 1810.   [33] Walford, pp. 263–5.

Sunday, April 29. We crossed over to Hale Wood; we held meeting at 2 o'clock. I had hard labouring. I stood up nearly two hours. The sun was hot. We had a good time, but it was with hard labour.

Thence he came to Delamere Forest. 'I found old James Crawfoot at home doing the spring work.' Bourne stayed to help him, and during these days had further evidence of the experience of vision which characterized some of these 'magic' Methodists, though, as the Journal shows, this visionary power was to be found elsewhere, and the phrase 'went into vision' often occurs.[34] Usually the persons concerned were pious women.[35] The most frequent form was an indication of the precedence of those who were the leaders of the new movement, and whose transfigured form the visionary appeared to behold. Each figure bore a trumpet and a cup, the symbols of their office as proclaimers of the Divine truth and offerers of the Divine salvation. They were seen usually as if on an invisible ladder, and great significance was attached to the position occupied in the vision, as interpreting their real status in the sight of heaven and their value to the little society of the faithful on earth. If a trumpet lay upon the ground or the cup was not firmly held, then its owner was spiritually at a discount. Lorenzo Dow is always the leading figure and next is usually James Crawfoot. Clowes is always above Bourne and James Bourne below him.[36] At least we may affirm that an examination of these visionary experiences indicates the general estimate of those who touched the spiritual ministrations of these men.

It is noteworthy that never on any occasion did Bourne experience such 'vision' himself, though for a time it seems that he accepted both the genuineness and usefulness of these manifestations. Only once does he record a desire for its possession.[37]

[34] Kendall rightly points out (I.153) that the word 'vision' is better than 'trance' as a description of these spiritual experiences, for the person was able to relate the revelation which had been experienced, however insensible during the experience itself.

[35] e.g. Nancy Foden; but sometimes others, e.g. John Smith, 12 years old.

[36] As an example we may take the following: *Sunday, May 6, 1810.* We went to New Church. I spoke from 'Pray without ceasing': it was a powerful time. Nancy Foden went into vision. It appeared to us that the man who stood above James Crawfoot, dropping honey from his finger in the vision, was Lorenzo Dow. Of course, old James is the second trumpeter: Mary Dunnell the fourth, Clowes the fifth, myself the seventh, Thomas Knight the ninth, and my brother James a few below him. Mary Dunnell has had the cup as well as the trumpet, but had rather left it. Clowes, Hugh Bourne, Thomas Knight, and James had each a cup as well as a trumpet. For this I was thankful to God. About twenty of the trumpeters had breastplates. These shone exceeding bright (Bourne MSS (Jour.)).

[37] Bourne MSS (Jour.), 20th July 1810. 'I felt a desire to look and feel more after the visionary power.'

The Journal indicates that as time passed these experiences tended to extravagance. They reached their highest point in 1810–11, and after July 1811 they disappear. This mystical extravagance, which might have proved disastrous, was probably averted by the spiritual insight of Bourne himself.

Another interesting fact of Bourne's experience at this time is his acceptance of the widespread belief in the existence and power of witches, as the following entry in the Journal shows:

I visited Clowes. He has been terribly troubled with the woman we saw at Ramsor. I believe she will prove to be a witch. These are the head labourers under Satan, like as the fathers are the head-labourers under Jesus Christ. So we are fully engaged in the battle. These, I believe, cannot hurt Christ's little ones till they have first combated the fathers. It appears they have been engaged against James Crawfoot ever since he had a terrible time of praying with and for a woman who was in witchcraft. For the witches throughout the world all meet and have connection with the power of the Devil. . . . The Lord is strong, and we shall soon have to cope with the chief powers of hell. I am certain the Lord will give us the victory.[38]

On Sunday, 3rd June 1810, a camp-meeting was held at Ramsor, beginning at eight o'clock in the morning, and continuing until nearly six in the evening. 'It was a very powerful time.' Crawfoot (who had not previously attended a camp-meeting) spoke, as also did Hugh Bourne and Mary Dunnell. William Clowes was present also and spoke. This camp-meeting had important consequences.

Shortly afterwards Bourne made another excursion into Shropshire.[39] Whilst away he had deep spiritual concern. On a journey to Market Drayton he turned aside to pray. 'I felt that I had the whole race of mankind in my heart.'[40] It was 'under impression' that he returned home on 18th June.

I took leave of several. I then set off for Staffordshire. I came to Tunstall. I stopped with Clowes all night. The preachers at Burslem are raising up war against him.[41]

The following day they 'talked a deal about the ministry, and about travailling in birth for the whole world', the very con-

---

[38] Saturday, 9th June, 1810.
[39] We have, however, another glimpse into the manual labour of Bourne by the following revealing entry: *Friday, June 1*. I had a very hard day's work of felling oak trees.
[40] Bourne MSS (Jour.), 16th June 1810.
[41] ibid., loc. cit.

cern which had been in the heart of Bourne but a few days before. It was the burden of new spiritual responsibilities. For Clowes it was a time of crisis.[42] It was from the preachers' plan of the June quarter 1810 that Clowes's name was omitted, to be followed by the withholding of his ticket of membership in the following September. Clowes writes in his *Journal*:

I was told that my name was left off the plan because I attended Camp Meetings contrary to Methodist discipline and that I could not be a preacher or leader amongst them unless I promised not to attend such meetings. . . . But to promise not to attend, that I could not conscientiously do, for God has greatly blessed me in these meetings . . . and my motive was simply to glorify God and bring sinners to the knowledge of the truth as it is in Jesus. I was then told that I was no longer with them; that the matter was settled. I therefore immediately delivered up my class papers . . . and became unchurched.[43]

Doubtless Clowes's attendance at the Ramsor meeting on 3rd June was the immediate ground for the exclusion of his name from the plan for the June quarter. We do know that before setting out he had conferred with Hugh Bourne,[44] whose judgement in the light of the official ruling was against his coming, but it would seem that Crawfoot decided the issue by urging that it was 'better to obey God rather than man'. So Clowes laboured at the Ramsor meeting, with the result we have named.

Another consequence of this Ramsor meeting came from the successful preaching of Mary Dunnell, not only there but in the region around. Of this Bourne writes:

The Camp Meeting not only went on well, but was a means in the hand of the Lord of opening our way into a further part of Derbyshire. The female preacher had an invitation and arrangements were accordingly made, and she went into Derbyshire, and I shortly followed. She had great success . . . some ripe fruit was gathered.[45]

It was the expansion of the work into Derbyshire that enabled Bourne to write: 'On a fair muster in July 1810 we were more than one hundred strong with our ten preachers.[46] By September it had reached nearly 140.[47]

---

[42] See J. T. Wilkinson, *William Clowes 1780–1851*, Ch. II, for a more detailed account.
[43] op. cit., pp. 84–5.   [44] Bourne MSS (Auto.), A Text, f. 307.
[45] ibid.   [46] ibid., f. 305.
[47] ibid., f. 313, C Text, f. 164, where Bourne gives some details: Boylestone (22), Rodsley (10), Hollington (10), Wootton and neighbourhood (50), Standley (10), Bemersley (9), Rizley and Runcorn (25).

From Derbyshire Bourne returned to the area around
Ramsor on the last day of June, remaining for some eight days
in the home of the Buxtons at Wootton Park Farm. During
this period the wakes took place at Ramsor and the bear-bait-
ing particularly distressed him. 'I felt the spirit of the wake
dash upon me like a flood.' But he seized the opportunity and,
labouring amongst the people who had gathered, he brought
some into the way of salvation. 'I felt very thankful to God.'
He reached home early on Sunday, 8th July. Ramsor and its
neighbourhood, including Wootton-under-Weaver, Lexhead,
Kingsley, and Farley, was a very fruitful field of missionary
labour, at first as auxiliary to the Methodist cause, and then,
following the Standley episode, conducted on independent
lines. In this region were the homes of several families, generous
in hospitality and rich in spiritual power, opening their houses
for preaching and prayer. There is constant reference in the
Journal to the Heatons of Farley, the Sergeants of Kingsley, the
Buxtons, the Critchelows, the Draycotts, the Salts of Wootton,
and the Brothers Horobin of Lexhead. As far back as May 1808,
on Bourne's first visit to Ramsor, Francis Horobin had pointed
out half a dozen spiritually destitute villages, and promised
help, which was afterwards fully given. Concerning James
Horobin Bourne wrote:

This man and his wife have been and are abundantly kind to me
and the cause of God. May God reward them.[48]

A week later was the important occasion of another camp-
meeting on Mow Cop, 'a day that will be long remembered',
which had the result of impressing still more deeply on the
mind of Bourne that this was indeed the work of God.

I believe the Lord has now fully established the Camp Meetings.
O Lord, attend them with Thy power and may Thy glory be manifested, and the Kingdom of God and of Christ be brought forward
and precious souls saved. O Lord, support those who labour at the
Camp Meetings from evil and unreasonable men.[49]

He spent much time in visiting neighbouring hamlets, but he
was also engaged in heavy manual labour:

We reared the building today, the roof of Bemersley house. . . . I
worked grievous hard at home . . . it was very late when I gave over
work.[50]

[48] Bourne MSS (Jour.), 24th November 1810.   [49] ibid., 15th July 1810.
[50] ibid., 17th July 1810.

Towards the end of July a new sphere of opportunity opened. One named David Buxton,[51] a native of Stanton, had moved from Ramsor to Wyrley Bank in South Staffordshire; on a visit to his native hamlet he left a pressing invitation to Bourne to go southwards. So on 27th July Bourne walked thirty-four miles —'it was a long walk and it rained a great part of the way'— and he reached Buxton's home about five o'clock. The next two days were given to visitation and preaching. During this excursion Bourne met John Benton. Though illiterate, he had begun to exercise a preaching ministry amongst the colliers of the Cannock area. 'He is a lively, earnest man and highly called.' 'He is short of grammar but the Lord is with him. I opened many things to him and we had a good time together.' For many years afterwards he was to prove a successful pioneer missionary in Derbyshire, Nottingham, and Leicestershire.[52] Bourne returned home early in August; by this visit he had begun that work which was ultimately to prove the centre of a large Darlaston Circuit. It was the spear-head of a new advance.

The rest of August was given to Delamere and to Warrington and the region round about, fulfilling preaching and pastoral service and being encouraged by the ministrations of those households, the Eatons at Stockton Heath and the Phillipses at Warrington, he so greatly valued. During this stay Bourne was concerned to lead the Rizley society into a knowledge of the Scriptures in which many were deficient. He writes:

Today I bought a Bible: cost 13/6d for Jno Webb of Rizley. Thomas Eaton gave me the money. I also ordered Peter Phillips to purchase half a dozen of Testaments to go to Rizley and told him to buy half a dozen more if wanted. I trust they will take to the Scripture.[53]

It was whilst at Warrington early in September that through one John Shegog, a call came to Bourne to visit London.

This kept me waken a good while. It was tender to part with my friends. . . . I left it to the Lord and it seemed as if the Lord directed me to go to London. O Lord, Thy will be done.[54]

On Thursday, 20th September, he set off, accompanied by James Crawfoot, and that evening they came to near Stafford;

---

[51] Not to be confused with David Buxton of Wootton Park Farm.
[52] Kendall, I.354–6.
[53] Bourne MSS (Jour.), 11th September 1810.
[54] ibid., 3rd September 1810.

the next day on to Wyrley Bank and Cannock. On the 24th at noon they went to Birmingham and at six o'clock took coach for London, journeying through Henley, Stratford-on-Avon, and Oxford. They reached their destination the following evening between four and five o'clock. Preaching both inside and out of doors, together with visitation, fully occupied the days, and there was little opportunity for sightseeing, but there is this entry for 1st October 1810:

We saw many places in London and Westminster, the King's Palace, Westminster Abbey, and St Paul's Church. We were at the top of St Paul's, and had views of the City. It is wonderful, but, O Lord, what shall be done for the multitudes of the inhabitants. O Lord, have pity on them. We also saw the Lord Mayor's procession.[55]

Two other interesting episodes are recorded. They listened, though without edification, to the preacher associated with Joanna Southcott,[56] the religious fanatic, of whom Bourne writes: 'Her writing frequently contradicts Scripture; it appears to me that she is really in witchcraft; her people are strangely deluded.' Bourne also writes: 'I saw Lancaster's free school: this is wonderful and noble.'[57]

Leaving London by coach for Newcastle-under-Lyme at six o'clock on Monday, 8th October, they arrived about five o'clock in the morning of the Wednesday, and set off on foot to Bemersley.

[55] Bourne MSS (Jour.), 1st October 1810.
[56] Joanna Southcott (1750–1814), a Devonian and originally a Methodist, about 1792 became persuaded that she possessed supernatural gifts; she wrote prophecies in rhyme and announced herself as the woman spoken of in Rev. xii. Coming to London she began to 'seal' the elect; her followers are said to have numbered 10,000. See art. *ERE* XI.756.
[57] Joseph Lancaster (1778–1838), English educationist, for some time connected with the Society of Friends, and who was one of the inventors of the monitorial system of instruction, had a thousand scholars in his school in Borough Road, London, teaching them reading, writing, and arithmetic at very low cost.

CHAPTER SIX

PROBLEMS AND PERPLEXITIES (1810–19)

I

THE REMAINDER of the year 1810 was used by Bourne in evangelistic and pastoral labours in Staffordshire, Cheshire and Lancashire, and Derbyshire, giving general superintendency to the work. Much time and labour were involved in securing appointments of preachers, and it became Bourne's custom to write out a separate plan for each preaching-place, leaving them at the meeting-houses, and also furnishing each preacher with a note specifying his appointments.

It was shortly after Bourne's departure for London that the Burslem Circuit withheld Clowes's ticket of membership. This brought a critical situation. Bourne writes:

I went to Tunstall. Clowes goes on well, but the travelling preachers seem determined to destroy the work of God. O Lord, do Thou still guide and direct Clowes that he may perfectly do Thy will. And, O Lord Jesus, direct the people and enable them to abide by the light.[1]

For Clowes the position was indeed a delicate one. The two classes at Kidsgrove and Tunstall (numbering almost forty members), of which Clowes was leader, insisted on remaining with him; not long afterwards others from the Methodist societies joined them. Clowes speaks of the feelings of 'indignation, astonishment, and sympathy' which arose from this decision.[2]

During these last months of 1810 one thing is outstanding: namely the closer association of Bourne and Clowes in the new situation which had arisen. It is rather strange that although a licence for the kitchen of Mr Smith, of Tunstall, as a preaching-place, had been procured by Bourne as early as 1807, and appointments had been arranged by him, neither he nor Clowes had ever preached there. The utterances of Clowes appear to have been too vigorous for Mr Smith,[3] and it is said

---

[1] Bourne MSS (Jour.), 23rd October 1810.　　[2] Clowes *Jour.* (1844), p. 85.
[3] ibid., p. 57.

that Bourne had stated that he would not preach there if his friend were excluded! However, the expulsion of Clowes so roused Mr Smith that he now pressed both Bourne and Clowes to preach in his home. Bourne writes:

I preached at Tunstall for the first time . . . when I began to speak I was strait awhile, but I got liberty afterwards.[4]

We now find that Bourne and Clowes are spending more time together, the former visiting Tunstall and the latter Bemersley more frequently. Each is touching societies under the care of the other, and we may note that (on Christmas Day, 1810) a special meeting was held at Stockport [5] to which came Hugh and James Bourne and William Allcock from Bemersley, James Crawfoot from the Forest, William Clowes from Tunstall, William Turner from Brown Edge, and E. McEvoy from Ramsor. They met in the large room of an old cotton factory. 'It was a powerful time and some were set at liberty.' It is not without significance that Bourne preached from the words: 'Let thy priests be clothed with righteousness' (Ps. cxxxii: 9). These men were on the threshold of a new venture, and it is almost certain that the occasion provided an opportunity for considera-tion of what the future might hold in regard to the work of God.

The opening weeks of 1811 were marked by uneasiness and tension,[6] and this found expression in outspoken words by James Nixon, at a love-feast in Burslem chapel on Sunday even-ing, 13th January. 'It was so applied that it has caused no small stir among the old society . . . the war runs very heavy.' The following Friday Nixon was also put out of the society; shortly afterwards he joined the company of Clowes and his friends. It was he, along with Thomas Woodnorth, the brother-in-law of Clowes, who proposed that the latter should consent to become a full-time preacher, each being prepared to give five shillings weekly for his maintenance. Believing this to be the divine call, Clowes accepted. This decision marked a new beginning. 'The new movement . . . brought me into great exercise of soul, and what would follow I could not tell.'[7]

[4] Bourne MSS (Jour.), 16th November 1810.
[5] ibid., loc. cit.
[6] This is shown by the following entries in the Journal: *January 7.* At Kingsley and Newton the class is purposed to leave the old connection (*sic*). *January 10.* We called at Kidsgrove and found the travelling preachers are carrying on a war, but the people are firm. *January 12.* The travelling preachers are carrying on a heavy war against the Lord.
[7] Clowes *Jour.* (1844), pp. 84–5.

II

Bourne spent most of February in labouring at places in Derbyshire, where some persecution had caused increased difficulties. In March he came to the Ramsor area, and then on to the region of Warrington, where there was need of encouragement, particularly in the Rizley society, which had also suffered persecution.

In April there was new tension in the Burslem Circuit, which resulted in the exclusion of James Steele from the Tunstall society.[8] He had been a member for some twenty-four years and had held office. The charge against him was that he had joined in a love-feast—on Good Friday, 12th April—at the home of his cousin, Joseph Smith, of Tunstall, who had given hospitality to the new movement under Clowes. The fact is that he was not so present. On the morning of the Sunday following his exclusion, when he attended school as usual, an official of the chapel ordered him out; quietly he obeyed and, amidst confusion, the assembled school followed him. During the week, a master-potter, Mr Boden, offered a large room in the warehouse for the teaching of the scholars; it was to be later used for preaching,[9] the first of such services being held on 28th April 1811.

The two classes of which James Steele had been leader insisted upon coming to him for spiritual instruction, despite his plea that he was no longer a member of Society.

This occurrence directly affected Hugh Bourne, for this Tunstall group turned to him for counsel and assistance. He therefore now found himself called to bestow thought and labour upon the Tunstall cause in addition to his already expanding responsibilities in those regions already opened out. The success of the services in the temporary meeting-place was so great that a new building was found to be necessary. Bourne writes in his Journal: '*Friday, 10 May:* We were at Tunstall and had much conversation about a chapel. . . . I was much harassed.' Three days later, on the 13th: 'I was at Tunstall two days; we fixed upon a piece of land to build a chapel on.' On 6th June: 'We broke ground for a new chapel at Tunstall'; on

---

[8] Bourne has this entry in the Jour. for 21st April: 'In Burslem Circuit they have put James Steel[e] out of the society, and this has unhinged all their classes at Tunstall.'

[9] See Kendall, I.108–9; J. T. Wilkinson, *William Clowes 1780–1851*, p. 34*n*.

11th June: 'We signed the writings and secured the land.'[10]
Six days later another commitment was undertaken:

At night after much difficulty we set out a chapel at Boyleston[e]
to be 16 feet wide and eight yards long [11] clear within. O Lord, bless
and prosper the undertaking.

During 1811 another important decision was made. For
some time the Ramsor people had urged the propriety, and
indeed necessity, of having quarterly tickets of membership, a
suggestion which appeared to gain still wider approval. The
offer of Francis Horobin to defray the cost of printing the
tickets decided the whole matter, the Tunstall friends being in
entire agreement. So we find this entry:

Thursday, May 30, 1811. I ordered tickets to be printed for the first
time.

The ticket bore the date 'May 1811', and the initials 'H.B.',
together with the text, Acts xxviii : 22 : 'But we desire to hear of
thee what thou thinkest: for as concerning this sect, we know
that everywhere it is spoken against.' This was deliberately
chosen on account of the peculiar situation of the new movement.[12] Bourne made his own comment:

It may seem strange that quarterly tickets were not sooner introduced. But it should be considered that the Connexion was begun in
the order of Divine Providence, and not in the wisdom of man, nor
by the desire of man. . . . Being begun in the order of Divine Providence it was held together by a zeal for the Lord of Hosts. This
formed its bond of union.[13]

[10] The chapel was opened by James Crawfoot on 10th October 1811 (Bourne
MSS (Jour.), loc. cit.). A print of it is in Kendall, I.109. (Note, however, that Kendall,
having misread the date of the entry in Bourne's Jour., is mistaken in stating that
the chapel was opened on 13th July.) 'The building measured sixteen yards long
by eight wide, and was galleried half-way . . . it was furnished in a plain manner;
the walls were not coated and it had no ceiling. . . . In the erection of it the house
form was chosen in preference to the chapel form, so that if not wanted, it would
form four houses, according to the plan on which houses are usually built at
Tunstall . . . because it could not be known whether or not the connexion would be
of any long continuance' (Bourne *HPM*, pp. 30–7, 1823).
   Bourne not only undertook considerable manual labour in the building of the
chapel, but when others, probably fearing the weight of legal responsibility,
declined to sign a deed of conveyance, he and his brother, James Bourne, shouldered
the responsibility. The chapel was vested in them and remained their private
property until 1834, when it was transferred to the Connexion. Ten years later a
superior building was erected near by, and the original was turned into cottages.
[11] Bourne MSS (Jour.), 17th June 1811.
[12] For facsimile of the first ticket see Kendall, I.112.
[13] Bourne *HPM* (1823), p. 39.

The introduction of tickets tended to the consolidation of the interests of both groups, now rapidly increasing in numbers. The camp-meeting community was enlarging its borders in Derbyshire—at Turnditch, Mercaston, Hulland, and Weston-under-wood—and new societies were also springing up around Ramsor, and at the Cloud and Biddulph Moor; the Tunstall men were also making advance in Cheshire and in places around the Potteries.

A further important circumstance at this time was the problem of the financial maintenance of Clowes as a full-time preacher: James Nixon and Thomas Woodnorth were working potters and fluctuations of trade made it difficult for them to continue their contributions. Moreover, the work had so extended that it could no longer be sustained by a few individual subscribers [14] for the support of the ministry. There had been hesitancy about asking for contributions from members of the classes, in part influenced by the doctrine of an unpaid ministry held by the Independent and Quaker Methodists at Macclesfield and Warrington. But decision in this matter could not long be withheld. So we find in the Journal the following important entry, dated Friday, 26th July 1811.

At night I was sent for to Tunstall. . . . We then had a society meeting, very agreeable. The preachers were examined:

Qu. 1. Whether they would be satisfied with any appointment without choosing; and that every one might as far as possible be appointed where they were most likely to be useful. To this they all fully agreed.

Qu. 2. Concerning John Boden, whether he should be admitted as a preacher, if he desired it, and it was unanimously thought that he should.

Qu. 3. Whether it was thought right for James Crawfoot and William Clowes to be given up to the work; which was agreed to.

Qu. 4. What was the best method of conducting the money matters. The number of society under our immediate inspection were stated at 200.[15] It was proposed that the circumstances be mentioned to the people, and what they voluntarily gave to be collected by proper persons and to be paid into the hands of a Steward; and what fell short to be made out by private subscription.

Qu. 5. Who shall be appointed Steward? This was put upon James Steele.

[14] In addition to his existing responsibilities Bourne took over the chapel at Brown Edge (Bourne MSS (Jour.), 17th July 1811).

[15] Walford (pp. 325–6n.) suggests the number was much greater, as the members on the Derbyshire mission, together with a large class under Joseph Bourne, had tended to form a somewhat independent group under Mary Dunnell, but were afterwards numbered in the new Connexion.

This first general meeting made for cohesion in the rapidly unifying groups.

Another indication of co-operation between the Camp-Meeting Methodists and the Clowesites[16] was the making of a written plan commencing on 2nd June and extending to 15th September 1811. It shows eight places and fifteen preachers.[17] A second written plan, covering the period from 22nd September to 15th December, gives seventeen preachers and seventeen places.[18]

A careful examination of these plans is revealing, in particular regarding the results of the labours of Bourne and his helpers, a work which had been carried on for some ten years, since 1801. Only two of Bourne's places—Standley and Ramsor—appear; there is little indication of the immense zeal which he had manifested. The explanation is that by far the greater proportion of the harvest of those labours had been gathered by others, clearly supporting Bourne's frequent assertions that he had never intended the creation of a new denomination. The societies to which he had given so much toil—Harriseahead, Norton, Kidsgrove, Tean, and Kingsley—had been taken over into the Methodist Circuit; the expenditure in time and energy given to the societies belonging to the Quaker Methodists in Lancashire and the Independent Methodists of Macclesfield; the society at Rizley which had originated from the preaching of Lorenzo Dow, and to which Bourne had given so much oversight—of all these labours there is no record in these written plans of the new and developing movement.[19] There is clear evidence from Bourne's Journal that his labours were auxiliary to other churches, in a large measure being that of supplying preachers on alternate weeks and giving constant and voluntary pastoral oversight. This was the case until the middle of 1810,

[16] The first recorded mention of this name is by Clowes himself in the Clowes MSS, A Text, f. 10.

[17] For facsimile, see Kendall, I. p. 559. The places are Tunstall, Bagnal, Badley Edge, Stan[d]ley, Brown Edge, Ramsor, Lax Edge, Gratten. The preachers are: J. Crawfoot, J. Steele, J. Bourne, H. Bourne, R. Bayley, W. Allcock, T. Woodnorth, E. McEvoy, W. Turner, J. Nixon, H. Mattison, T. Allcock, T. Hulme, J. Marsh. cf. Kendall, I.113, 559.

[18] For facsimile, see Kendall, p. 114. The plan is probably in the handwriting of Clowes, who writes 'Matthias' instead of 'Mattison'. The name is correct, however, in the list given in Clowes *Jour.* (1844), p. 97.

[19] It should be noted, however, that Rizley does appear on the first printed plan in 1812, with a monthly appointment. It should also be noted that Bourne MSS (Jour.), 27th September 1811, indicates the extent of the combined work. 'There are about 30 places we have to attend to.' In his Journal for 2nd October he lists these: three were '16 miles beyond Oxford besides London'; three others 'at Cannock side'.

when, as we have seen, the refusal of the Burslem Circuit to take over the Standley class entirely changed the situation.

Bourne spent the latter part of 1811 visiting the societies, preaching and establishing order, giving encouragement under persecution, opening new places, and at times working with his own hands so that he might not be chargeable in any way to the churches. The work was arduous; occasionally a remark in his Journal reveals deep tiredness of body: 'I was so fatigued that I could scarcely get home'—and there is indication that 'the care of the churches' weighed heavily upon his mind.

I have found a great alteration in my memory in the course of a few months. . . . It has been that I could recollect what I had said to persons about spiritual things to any one for a long time after: but this is now in a great measure taken away.[20]

In particular, there was his concern for the Derbyshire mission under the labours of Mary Dunnell, who had for some time caused him uneasiness, for in addition to some impropriety of conduct, she had used the influence of her strong though somewhat unstable personality[21] to gather the societies under her own leadership, and 'lording it over God's heritage' had urged separation from the general movement. Bourne writes: 'I came to Rodsley . . . there is much trial and complaint among the people on account of being separated from us.' So he determined to examine the situation carefully: he found 'it was like going into the midst of fire'. He was informed that Mary Dunnell had made an ill-advised marriage. All this was to Bourne 'a great and uncommon sorrow', on account of his 'dear children' in the faith. But 'the snare was now broken', and the work was resumed. Bourne was conscious of his own integrity and of the righteousness of the cause he had espoused.

III

Towards the end of 1811, in consequence of the coming of new itinerant preachers into the Burslem Circuit, there is evidence that an approach was made, inviting a return to the old society. This invitation was carefully considered, but reply was postponed until the opinion of the societies could be ascertained

[20] Bourne MSS (Jour.), 13th October 1811.
[21] The frequency and manner of her experiences 'in vision' recorded in Bourne's Journal is evidence of this.

by Clowes and Bourne. The decision not to return was definite.[22]

It is at this point that we meet the following entry in Bourne's Journal:

Thursday, February 13, 1812. We called a meeting and made plans for the next quarter, and made some other regulations. In particular we took the name of the society of the Primitive Methodists.[23]

Bourne is entirely silent as to any reason for the adoption of this title for the new community, neither was he responsible for the selection of it.[24] In a passing reference Walford suggests that the designation was connected with the practice of open-air preaching:[25] not until many years afterwards, however, does it seem that the precise origin became generally known. The source of the name seems to have been as follows. On 6th April 1790 Wesley addressed final words of advice to a company of his preachers at Chester:

Fellow labourers, wherever there is an open door enter in and preach the gospel: if it be to two or three, under a hedge or a tree, preach the gospel; go out quickly into the streets and lanes of the city, and bring in the poor and the maimed and the halt and the blind.[26]

Then, lifting up his frail hands, and with tears in his eyes, he exclaimed: 'And yet there is room; and yet there is room'—and then added: ' . . . *and this is the way the primitive methodists did.*'[27]

That night James Crawfoot was one of his hearers. Twenty-two years later at the Tunstall meeting, when taking part in the discussion regarding a name for the new community, he arose and, stating what he had heard Wesley say at Chester, remarked that he thought this was the particular emphasis of the new enterprise: so the designation was immediately adopted.

At this meeting it was found that the number of preaching-

---

[22] cf. Clowes *Jour.* (1844), p. 99: 'Not any were willing to such a course. . . . The resolution was unanimously carried that we should remain as we were. A letter was then sent to our old friends . . . stating that as soon as ever we saw that to incorporate ourselves with them would promote the glory of the Most High and enlarge the Redeemer's Kingdom . . . we would immediately do so.'

[23] See Kendall, I. p. 132.

[24] Several years afterwards Bourne told John Petty that owing to fatigue he had been overcome with drowsiness, during which time the meeting agreed upon the name in question (Petty, p. 39). Petty does not seem to have known in 1860 how it originated.

[25] op. cit., I.350.

[26] Herod, p. 250. *WHS Proceedings*, XXVI.78–9, art. by F. F. Bretherton on 'Wesley's last visit to Chester'.

[27] Antliff (p. 177) is the first to give an account of the origin of the name, and he includes the italicized sentence [italics ours]. He adds: 'We received it some years ago from a credible authority, though only verbally.'

places had now reached thirty-four, and that there were twenty-three preachers; this made it necessary for printed plans to be issued in place of the written plans previously supplied.[28] Another regulation was the appointment of quarterly meetings to be held in March, June, September, and December each year.

Following this entry in Bourne's Journal, there is a strange sentence. It reads: 'I left off keeping a journal for nearly a year. . . .' Bourne assigns no reason why he relaxed from recording the daily occurrences which had so long been his custom—and which afterwards, we may note, he continued unbroken to the end of his life. We are left to conjecture. Certainly he was a tired man, both physically and spiritually, and perhaps some relaxation of his labours was found immediately to be necessary, but if so, it is strange that he makes no reference to it. Perhaps, however, there is some hint of the reason in the additional clause which completes this solitary entry named above:' . . . during which time James Crawfoot declined from the faith and fell into sin.' Was this period marked by such saddening experiences in relation to his old friend and helper that he preferred to make no record? One thing is certain, namely, that during this year things did happen which made a deep wound in Bourne's spirit—something which may well account for his first entry when he recommenced his Journal, almost a year later, on Sunday, 7th February 1813.

I went under much temptation and trouble of mind to preach at the Cloud. It seemed to me that I was quite unfit for the ministry or anything belonging to it.

On the following Thursday, 11th February, we find this:

James Crawfoot having declined taking his appointments, we had a meeting to consult about the matter, when it was resolved 1. that James Crawfoot has acted improperly in withdrawing from the work in the manner he has done. 2. That he therefore be suspended till the quarter-day; but if he be hereby grieved he is at liberty to call another meeting to reconsider the matter.

If Bourne had kept his Journal during the period referred to above, we should doubtless have had more light upon this unhappy situation, passing reference to which occurs after the recommencement of the Journal, and of which the following may be taken as an example:

[28] A copy of the first printed plan—commencing 22nd March 1812—is printed in Walford, I.349; Petty, p. 41; Kendall, I.135.

Thursday, Feb. 25. I find that J. Crawfoot has gone on worse than ever, and has made cruel work, so things are now come to a point. I suppose the Lord will remove him from us. O Lord, Thy will be done. The preachers are more than ever tried with him.

Walford, however, affords some explanation of the situation, and this probably from conversation with Bourne himself.[29] He fully appreciates the value of Crawfoot's earlier ministry—as indeed we see also in the admiration of Bourne himself, both by word and action—yet he suggests that the position granted to him in leadership in the infant community had fostered in him a spiritual pride which gave him exalted notions as to his authority. In illustration of this he points out that in 1811 Crawfoot had introduced a demand for special dress amongst the preachers of the community, half-Quaker in style,[30] which was to many far from acceptable. Further, it seems that Crawfoot often spoke disparagingly of the travelling preachers of the Methodist societies, thus kindling prejudice against them—an attitude which was anathema to Bourne. Of this Walford writes: 'The habit of reflecting upon others was one of his besetting weaknesses.' Further, Walford indicates more personal matters: that Crawfoot had accused Bourne of being an enemy to travelling preachers as such, and that he was seeking to carry on the work by local preachers alone, with himself in charge, and that, in consequence, Crawfoot had planned secretly to depose Bourne and others from the community.[31] Most serious, however, was neglect of preaching appointments, so that the work suffered.

Whatever may be the truth in these explanations, and although we may make some allowance for sternness in Bourne's attitude, as well as perhaps some exaggeration in his account of the matter, the fact remains that Crawfoot refused to face the charges laid against him, by absenting himself from the meeting called to discuss the issues in his presence, and he therefore placed himself outside the Connexion.[32]

[29] Walford, I.357–62.

[30] Bourne himself has sometimes been held responsible for this feature, but such a view is mistaken, for he asserted that the 'hat-whim' had injured the work by attaching importance to what he felt were secondary matters.

[31] It is also stated that Crawfoot had acted foolishly in regard to a second marriage.

[32] Crawfoot continued to live for some time at Delamere, then moved to Dudden, where he commenced a small business; he preached when opportunity afforded. He died on 26th January 1839 in his eighty-first year, and was buried at Tarvin, Cheshire (Herod, pp. 268–9).

This was on 15th April 1813. He had laboured within it a little less than four years.

This break gravely affected the prosperity of the rising societies for the time being, and the whole matter distressed Bourne beyond measure. As late as 22nd August 1813, Bourne makes this confession: 'I have never been in full liberty to rest for above a year, chiefly through old J. C.'s wickedness.'

In taking our leave of Crawfoot in these unfortunate circumstances, the contribution he made to the infant community should in no way be discounted. His earlier labours, particularly in personal persuasion of others to the faith, were invaluable: his instruction, especially of Bourne and Clowes, concerning the nature of inward spiritual conflicts, deepened their own mystical experiences, though the visionary aspect of his own mysticism constituted a danger to the rising community, the seriousness of which was fortunately averted by the spiritual insight and common sense of Bourne himself. Crawfoot's contribution was real, but it must not be exaggerated.

IV

Returning again to the journals of Bourne, we find that the year 1813 was marked by labours as abundant as hitherto—bringing souls into spiritual liberty by private conversation and by public discourse; assisting those in need,[33] reclaiming those who had fallen away, warning the unruly, clearing up grievances and 'janglings' in the societies, arranging for chapel-building [34] and encouraging preachers [35]—in short, daily hard at work without remission upon the solemn commitment which he had undertaken.

One or two matters deserve particular notice.

During the early months the work of God spread widely into Derbyshire, and in order to aid the expansion, a 'tract society' was formed under Bourne's counsel and supervision. He writes:

[33] e.g. Mary Hawksley, persecuted by her parents on account of her faith, cast out of home and earning but a scanty living by lace-making: 'I promised to give her some assistance for a quarter of a year.'

[34] '*June 23.* We executed the deed of Rocester Chapel: so that it is now vested in the hands of trustees.' This seems to be the first chapel in the Connexion under a board of trustees: a facsimile of the deed, and the signatures of the nine trustees, appears in Kendal, I.173. Also before the end of 1813 Bourne had built a chapel at Talk o' th' Hill, at his own expense.

[35] '*Sept. 15.* I saw Daniel Leather, and lent him a Hebrew Grammar and Lexicon and put him in the way of learning Hebrew.'

Thursday, April 22. We talked about a tract society and I explained it at large. O Lord, bless and prosper every endeavour.

Friday, April 23. I came to Ashbourne, and providentially met with an account of a Church of England Tract Society. I ordered 9 different sorts and 25 of each . . . to be ready on 3rd of May.

So, when in the following month the tracts were obtained, a code of rules was drawn up and society established. The tracts were kept at Hulland, and those engaged in the work were sent out in companies of two, each visiting a particular area fortnightly on Sundays. They visited from house to house, lending a tract to those willing to receive it, and calling a fortnight later to lend another. Exhortation and prayer were made when possible. One rule was that they should neither eat nor drink with those whom they visited, lest offence should be taken. These labourers were themselves greatly enriched by the work, and several became preachers.[36]

We should also note the constant evidence in the journals of the strain under which Bourne himself was labouring. Thus, of a visit to Englesea Brook he writes:

March 29. I was exceedingly exhausted and fatigued near to falling down. . . . I travelled near 20 miles today and about sixteen of it in great haste.

A few days later he was compelled to see a physician, who 'bled me: the blood was black and thick, and it was with difficulty that he took it from me'.

It is in this year that we first find mention of the foottrouble which in after years was to bring disaster. On 15th April he records that he had walked thirty miles home to Bemersley, and adds:

I got a severe inflammation in my left foot today, by excess of travelling . . . the inflammation began at the root of my toes and extended to about the middle of the foot . . . my foot was so painful that I could not sleep.

Yet, two days later, he is journeying again, though with great difficulty, in order to supply an appointment vacant through the illness of William Allcock, at Hulland in Derbyshire:

April 17, 1813. I set out trusting in the name of the Lord. I took a mare nearly a mile but she was so lame that I then resigned her, and

---

[36] cf. Clowes *Jour.* (1844), pp. 60-1, concerning a similar society, working under the direction of Clowes and Nixon on the Cheshire border, as a result of which 'the country became greatly moved'.

set off on foot with much difficulty. I called at Latheredge and there got my foot dressed, and then set off again. I called at Swinscoe, and took tea and then rode in a cart rather above three miles to Ashbourne. I was now exceedingly lame. . . . However, by the tender mercy of God, I came safe though in great pain. I here met with the most extraordinary attention and kindness. They applied dock leaves to my foot, and by this means the heat and pain was assuaged. This was the most severe journey I ever remember to have travelled.

Bourne had walked nearly thirty miles.

We now turn to a significant entry, dated 22nd March 1813:

Today was the quarter day . . . and we passed several useful regulations. One was that no single preacher have more salary than £15 a year. . . . Another regulation was that all chapels and other burdens shall be borne by the society at large; that is, the expenses to be made one general concern. Also a committee was appointed to draw up a code of rules or regulations for the whole body and to submit them to the quarter days. . . .

This committee, which consisted of James Steele, E. McEvoy, and Hugh Bourne, found the task a difficult one, and was 'soon of opinion that the undertaking was too weighty and too great'. So the matter fell into abeyance for some six months, until the October meeting, when

. . . the people very pressing to have the rules completed . . . an order was made that sketches of rules should be immediately drawn up: and that, during the quarter, they should be read in every society by the preachers: and that all the objections and improvements suggested by the various societies should be brought in writing to the next quarter day. . . . [37]

It fell to Bourne to prepare this draft, which he did on the two days following.[38] The document was considered throughout the societies: 'during the quarter, prayer and supplication was made to God, almost without ceasing on this behalf.' At the meeting on 3rd January 1814 an order was made that the rules should be printed immediately. 'They were considered as the work of the whole Connexion: there being scarce a member but gave his opinion on them before they were completed.' [39]

This document not only formed the framework of polity for the new denomination, but also laid down that democratic principle in Church government, which was to be an outstanding

---

[37] Bourne *HPM* (1823), p. 46.   [38] Bourne MSS (Jour.), 5th–6th October 1813.
[39] Bourne *HPM* (1823), pp. 46–7.

feature for generations ahead. In this Bourne made an invaluable contribution.[40]

Another important decision was taken at the meeting at Tunstall on 3rd January 1814,[41] when the office of superintendent travelling preacher was instituted. 'This was done solely to cut off neglects.' [42] It was natural that Bourne should be appointed to this responsible position, though he opposed the appointment on two grounds: one, that he was unequal to the undertaking, and two, that a burden would be laid upon him from which his brethren would be exempt. How assiduously he fulfilled this office, not only during this early period when the Connexion consisted of but one circuit only, but afterwards when many who were leaders looked to him for guidance, the pages of his Journal show.

This year 1814 also marks a new development in Bourne's activities for the Gospel, for he began the formation of Sunday schools wherever the opportunity was afforded. This work was a deep concern laid upon him throughout the rest of his life. We find the record in his Journal of what seems to have been the first Sunday school established in the Connexion at Boylestone, in Derbyshire.[43]

Sunday, February 27, 1814. At 9 we opened the school with singing and prayer, and then came 41 children, and the school was conducted in a good manner the whole time.

He names eight teachers and speaks of others in preparation. This was rapidly followed by the establishment of schools at Abbots Bromley, Rocester, Hulland, and elsewhere. This new venture made a great demand upon both his time and substance: 'I bought some Sunday-school books'; 'I wrote directions for the Sunday schools'; 'I smoothed and cut some slates for the Sunday school.' In some places he spent time begging money from house to house for the new venture, and at others he had to meet opposition from the parish incumbent. It was an arduous undertaking, but great results accrued.

[40] These Rules were afterwards printed in *PMM*, 1822. We may note one concluding sentence : 'All the society is to be considered as one family, every burden is to be borne by the whole.' The term 'society' here refers to the Connexion as a whole.

[41] *PMM*, 1822, pp. 75–6. The early pages for the year 1814 are missing from the MS Jour.

[42] Bourne explains this, ibid., p. 76: 'The travelling preachers were greatly attached to labouring in word and doctrines: to teaching publicly and from house to house; but were reluctant to the cares of society discipline and management. On this account, when any matter of the societies wanted adjusting . . . they frequently referred it from one to another till the societies had to complain of neglect.'

[43] For an account of this, see *PMM*, 1824, pp. 90–4.

V

We must now consider at some length a situation which, in 1814 and for some time afterwards, caused Bourne the deepest anxiety.

As we have seen, in its early beginnings the Connexion was marked by missionary labours through which it greatly flourished despite opposition. After a time, however, when societies had been raised up, these missionary exertions began to decline, and the chief symptom was the diminution of camp-meetings. To Bourne this was in the nature of a catastrophe. In the early part of the year 1814, probably at the March Quarterly Meeting, a resolution [44] was carried in the conviction that the number of stations was now sufficient to give full employment to the whole staff of labourers. It was deemed wiser to retain and improve the stations already occupied than to open others, which could not receive proper attention. This seemed reasonable and prudent, though the decision was not unanimous. Thus Bourne writes:

> There was a diversity of opinion on the subject; some thought the societies already formed would flourish the more; others were of opinion that the missionary labours ought to have been pursued with diligence.[45]

Bourne expressed his own fears, and even if we allow that it was his temperament sometimes to magnify a situation of crisis, his estimate proved substantially true:

> After some time, it was found that the societies, instead of prospering more, prospered less. . . . It seemed as if the blessing of God was, in some degree, withdrawn from the societies, and there appeared so general a weakening that some thought the Connexion would absolutely break up. The suspension of the missionary labour produced a season of deep anxiety and painful experience.[46]

Those who disagreed with the resolution appear to have submitted patiently, however, with one notable exception, apart from Bourne. We find the following entry in the Journal respecting the next quarterly meeting:

> *July 4, 1814.* We had Qr day and settled things pretty well and were upon clear ground, *but there was some discussion with Jno Benton.*[47]

---

[44] Bourne afterwards designated this resolution as the 'Tunstall non-mission law', the leaders of that region having promoted it.

[45] Bourne, *HPM* (1823), p. 47.   [46] ibid.   [47] Italics ours.

The fact was that John Benton had chosen to ignore the resolution,[48] and, probably in the interim, at the invitation of one, William Ride, had missioned Belper, which lay beyond the regions in Derbyshire already touched. Almost certainly this was the reason for the 'discussion' just referred to. Without doubt Bourne was secretly glad that Benton had disregarded the decision, and that later it fell to his own lot to take over Belper, and incorporate it into the Tunstall Circuit. He writes on 9th September 1814:

I took up Belper, and put things in order, and the work soon began to move in other places, and the people in Derbyshire disregarded the Tunstall law against missionarying. And being superintendent I had additional labours in taking up new places, *but it was glorious labour*.[49]

Apart from this important exception it would seem that the policy of consolidation rather than expansion prevailed throughout the following year,[50] although Bourne suggests that during this time 'much prayer and supplication was made to Almighty God' for the renewal of missionary endeavour. We may certainly assume that it was a long period of spiritual distress for Bourne himself, whose convictions had long been that the decline of camp-meetings was due to the emphasis on preaching, to the neglect of 'the companies of praying labourers'. It was early in 1816 that this was reaffirmed when Peter Phillips, of Warrington, put into Bourne's hands the journal of a Methodist missionary, the Rev. Joshua Marsden,[51] in which there was a description of American camp-meetings, near New York, which he had attended, and in which this emphasis was present.

[48] For a full account of John Benton, see Herod, pp. 272–305; Kendall, I. 190–1. Benton's early missionary zeal is illustrated by his offer of £3 per quarter towards a missionary's maintenance; his refusal to be planned in the ordinary way, so that he might continue pioneering work; his printing at Leicester, at his own expense, of a thousand copies of Bourne's edition of *Hymns and Spiritual Songs . . .* for use in the Derbyshire mission (for facsimile of the title-page of a later edition (1818) printed at Leicester, see Kendall, I.190). Bourne spoke of the societies arising from his earlier labours as 'Benton's circuit'.

[49] Italics ours. It was at Belper that the name 'Ranter' originated with reference to the early Primitive Methodists. On occasion when a powerful meeting had closed, the praying company, in returning home, were accustomed to sing in the streets, and the name was given by a householder, Richard Turner, who was standing at the door listening (Kendall, I.185–6).

[50] MSS Journals between 15th September 1814 and July 1816 are not extant, and were apparently not in Walford's possession when he wrote the *Memoirs*, 1856. Clowes *Jour.* (1844) sheds no light on this period.

[51] Joshua Marsden (1777–1837) was a missionary who visited the United States in 1802, and later served in Nova Scotia and Bermuda. He returned to England in 1814 (see *Mins. of Conf.*, 1838, p. 269).

The Lord blessed my soul with understanding that this was what we wanted, only suiting it to the state of things in England. So I sketched out a plan for conducting camp-meetings, with praying services in companies, or circles; and sent copies to different places, hoping the system would take somewhere. And to my great satisfaction, old Mr Ride, of Weston-under-wood, got a copy; and the Lord so moved on his mind that he made preparation to hold Mercaston camp-meeting on that system.[52]

This important camp-meeting was held on Sunday, 9th June. Bourne was the appointed preacher and he was joined by John Benton. 'I was glad in my heart when I saw him come.' There was some opposition: a heavy shower drove the assembly into a barn, 'but we set on foot two praying companies . . . and the praying was powerful'. When the weather became better, they went out again: one who had opposed set up 'a praying-circle', and in this company was John Ride. 'They raised him into a preacher, and he was a preacher ever after.' [53] . . . Bourne writes exultantly:

The converting work broke out . . . this was glorious. . . . The Lord showed Himself the God of the camp-meetings, and the meeting kept rising in power till its close. . . . It was like a new founding of the Connexion.

This Mercaston camp-meeting proved of crucial significance: it created a resurgence of evangelistic zeal, the outcome of which we are shortly to outline. Clearly its origin was in the inner conviction of Bourne and his willingness to follow the dictates of his own conscience, guided by the Divine Spirit.

The new impulse made itself felt almost immediately in Derbyshire, and there was strong disposition against 'being under Tunstall'. 'It soon appeared there must either be a new circuit, or a new Connexion.' The outcome was that the Derbyshire places—with the exception of Belper, which remained—were made into a separate circuit, the second, therefore, to be founded in the Connexion. As early as 28th September we find this entry in the Journal: 'R. Winfield was at our house, and we made rough draft of Derby plan.' Bourne also says:

[52] Walford, I.407.
[53] John Ride (1821–1862), of Weston-under-wood, became a distinguished pioneer, particularly in Berkshire. He was arrested for street-preaching in Liverpool, and later suffered imprisonment in Winchester. In 1850 he went to the Australian mission. His early beginnings are noted by Bourne: 'John Ride, I think, will be a preacher' (Bourne MSS (Jour.), 18th April 1813); 'I had much conversation with John Ride about the work of the ministry (ibid., 7th May 1813). Clowes wrote of him: 'In him I have much joy' (*Jour.* (1844), p. 117).

The work of God went on rapidly . . . and additional preachers being wanted I engaged Sarah Kirkland,[54] of Mercaston, agreeing to pay her two guineas a quarter out of my own pocket. She laboured in the Derby Circuit with such success that the quarter day insisted on the right to pay her salary to employ her wholly in that circuit, . . . afraid if I paid her salary that I should take her to labour in the other circuit.[55]

The new missionary impulse extended eastwards; towards the end of 1815, when on a visit to Mercaston, Winfield made the suggestion of 'opening Nottingham'. It was on Christmas Day that Sarah Kirkland, accompanied by Winfield and his daughter, preached in a room in the 'Narrow Marsh', and shortly afterwards in the room of a disused factory in the 'Broad Marsh'. 'This room was made the birthplace of many souls.'[56] When Bourne came to the town, on 11th August 1816, he could write: 'I spoke to a great multitude from Ephesians 6. . . . It was a glorious time. . . . There has been a surprising work at this place.'[57] Bourne also records that on Whit-Sunday, 2nd June, 'we had a great camp-meeting on the race ground'; it was stated that some twelve thousand persons were present.

From what has been said it will now be clear that the policy of advance so dear to the heart of Bourne had established itself——there is no indication that those who had so persistently advocated a policy of consolidation attempted to resist it—and it was now gaining that momentum which was to result in great extensions in the near future. Derby and Nottingham form the strategic points for this new advance.

VI

Turning once more to Bourne's Journal it is interesting to find that much of the remaining months of 1816 seems to have been devoted to literary labours. We find indication of an intensive

[54] Sarah Kirkland (1794–1880) was the first female travelling preacher in the Connexion. She had received the faith during Bourne's visit to her home at Mercaston in 1811, and in September 1814, as a result of Bourne's discernment of her gifts, had begun to preach, eventually becoming a travelling preacher in February 1816. She had visited the Derbyshire outposts in 1815, at the invitation of Robert Winfield. (See Herod, pp. 305–6; *PMM* 1881, pp. 199–203; Kendall, I.176–7, 194–5, 201–4, 226–34.)

[55] Walford, I.413.

[56] Letter from Sarah Kirkland to John Barfoot (*PMM*, 1881, p. 227).

[57] Bourne MSS (Jour.), loc. cit. It should be noted that there is a somewhat different account of the first entry into Nottingham, given by Bourne (Walford, I.414), where he names Richard Weston, of Lexhead, as having 'a main hand in opening the town', but unfortunately he gives no date (Kendall, I.206–7).

study of the Scriptures [58] and the reason for this may be found perhaps in an entry for 18th August 1816:

This morning I began to write a commentary upon the Scriptures adapted to the capacities of children. O Lord be my wisdom. I intend to call it: 'The Children's Friend, or a Companion for Families and Sunday Schools', being a commentary with questions on the Holy Scriptures, adapted to the capacities and intended to assist the lovers of the rising generation.

The work was never completed, however—Walford speaks of a few chapters of Genesis in MS as in his possession—and it would seem that other duties came to override Bourne's intention; or perhaps in his simple eagerness he had not counted the cost of such an undertaking! It was this same zeal for the children which accounts for a further entry: 'I composed several Sunday-school hymns.'

Bourne continued to labour with his usual earnestness at all points of his extensive field; now at Derby and its neighbouring places; now at Tunstall and North Staffordshire; now at Warrington and in the Cheshire and Lancashire villages.

In January 1817, whilst in South Staffordshire, Bourne was taken suddenly ill with fever, and 'a violent gathering under the sole of my left foot', but with boiled turnips applied to the trouble and 'by the blessing of God', he made unusual recovery from what appeared to be a dangerous condition.

Much of the Journal for this year is a simple record of preaching appointments, visitation of members, making plans, and distributing them—he records that on one occasion he carried some seven hundred, together with a package of books, for many miles on his journey—discussion with preachers on the work of God and its improvement, assisting Sunday schools, and having constant concern for the spiritual welfare of the societies, and, withal, reading as he travelled on his way.[59] Once again we have insight into the extremity of his labours.

I went to Nottingham and had luggage for another person. It was excessive hot and I had to travel nearly 27 miles. It seemed to injure my inside.[60]

[58] cf. Jour., *25 January 1817*: I have lately made progress in the Hebrew; *24 July 1817*: I came home and read in the Greek Testament; *20 August 1817*: This week I have committed to memory the first seven chapters of St Paul's Epistle to the Hebrews.
[59] e.g., at Wyrley he borrowed a recently published edition of the *Pilgrim's Progress* done in verse by Burder (1804). He writes: 'The poetry is tolerable, but the work is far inferior to Bunyan's *Pilgrim* in prose.'
[60] Bourne MSS (Jour.), 21st June 1817.

We are not surprised at the entry the following day:

I went six miles to Radcliffe to preach; it was excessive hot. I preached there at 9, but felt the effects of yesterday's journey. I then hurried two miles to preach at Shelford at 11, but this was too much for me. I was suddenly taken ill and was obliged to come down as I was fainting away. This is the first time that I ever failed in preaching. I desired them to sing and I sat down and recovered very fast. I then stood up and spoke again, but ere long my strength again failed. I went to bed.

Yet in the evening he preached to the congregation and 'had a glorious time'. Such was his indomitable will.

Early in July he was back at Bemersley, to remain, however, only a few days before setting out again to Derbyshire. It was a departure that cost him much. 'My mother has been low this week,' he wrote, though she was not in bodily affliction, Bourne knew that when he left home he might see her no more. So it was, for whilst he was on his labours in Derbyshire, she died, on 7th August.[61]

I was out labouring in the ministry . . . and they did not think it necessary to send for me. When I first knew of her death, I was filled with sorrow, but this was mixed with joy when my brother James gave me an account of her death.[62]

A few days afterwards, journeying to Coppenhall, the horse upon which Bourne was riding, stumbled and fell, hurting Bourne on his left side, though not seriously.

VII

The year 1818 saw several important developments in the organization of the Connexion; for these Bourne was primarily responsible, and they became additional to his daily care of the churches. For Friday, 23rd January, we read: 'Morning I planned a small magazine. O Lord, Thy will be done.' The following days were given to preparation of material for this new venture. In the month of April, the first number, printed at Burslem, was issued, Bourne personally undertaking the financial responsibility.[63] The following quotation from the 'Introductory Address' indicates Bourne's purpose:

[61] *supra*, p. 15.
[62] On 3rd October there is this simple entry: 'Drew up an acct of my mother.'
[63] See Appendix IV, p. 189.

Grace, mercy and peace be multiplied unto you from God our Father and the Lord Jesus Christ. The Lord has evidently raised us up, among other societies, to assist in promoting piety and holiness. And therefore all the wisdom and all the talents with which God has entrusted the body should be employed in promoting His glory, and the good of our fellow creatures. . . .

A new chance of usefulness is opening; it appears now to be the call of God that our body should enter upon a magazine. . . . It may at present be considered simply as an improvement in the mode of publishing plans. . . . It will be suited to the present state of the body. . . . It will circulate a large portion of religious intelligence with much useful information of various kinds. It will form a record for happy deaths and striking conversions. It will promote and improve camp-meetings. It will be helpful and encouraging to the missionaries, and there is a fair prospect of it being a blessing to every member of the society . . . it will enable them, more fully to pray with the Spirit and with the understanding also. . . . It will form a repository of things new and old.

The most interesting feature of the magazine is the printed plan of the Tunstall and Derby Circuits which it contains. In the former we note sixty places and fifty-seven preachers; in the latter there are sixty-eight places with fifty preachers. Remembering that Bourne was the recognized superintendent of the Connexion, and therefore had oversight of both circuits, this gives some indication of his tremendous responsibilities. The plan shows no weeknight appointments, these being left to local arrangement.

The publication of the magazine was recommenced as a monthly issue in January 1819; the earlier numbers did not meet the cost, and Bourne undertook the loss.

As yet there was no connexional Book Room, though such a project had been considered, doubtless under Bourne's own suggestion, for there is a significant entry dated 7th January 1818: 'At Tunstall we took some steps to establish a book-room.' [64]

In illustration of the administrative problems with which Bourne had to deal we may take the following extracts from his Journal:

---

[64] The home of the Bournes, and the buildings which formed the printing and book-room, stood by the roadside some distance from the hamlet of Bemersley. The printing establishment adjoined the house, and the book-room a separate building a little farther distant from the road. A journeyman printer and an apprentice, together with John Bourne, the son of James, under James and Hugh Bourne, were the staff employed (Art. 'Reminiscence of a Residence at Bemersley' *PMM*, 1900, p. 751).

Saturday, Jan. 17, 1818. I came to Nottingham and was at the arch-deacon's registry. Licences had been refused at this place. I remonstrated with the Registrar, and he seemed almost persuaded to do his duty. I came then to Derby, very foot-sore.

Monday, September 21, 1818. Quarter day at Nottingham; the work is going on well, but the temporal concerns are very bad . . . things are much confused.

Behind this lay the story of a travelling preacher who had 'the concerns too much in his hands', and had expended the society money so unwisely that the Tunstall Circuit had to relieve the embarrassments, at considerable cost to itself. 'At this quarter day a committee was formed to arrange the temporal concerns and to put the affairs of the circuit into a more regular way.' This administrative decision, for which Bourne was responsible, was important in that it marked the beginning of circuit committees.

The Journal shows how often Bourne had absorbed time and strength in dealing with the affairs of societies to which preachers who declared that their sole energy must be given 'to saving souls' were frequently oblivious.

The following letter,[65] addressed to Thomas Jackson, of Belper, who shortly afterwards became a travelling preacher, illustrates Bourne's concern for the oversight of the preachers:

DEAR FRIEND,
        Grace, mercy and peace be multiplied unto you from God our Father, and the Lord Jesus Christ. I feel truly thankful to God that He has, in some degree, given you abilities for usefulness in the ministry of the Word. But when I consider the various trials, temptations, and difficulties which attend the course of the successful minister, I am impressed with anxious feelings on your account. You have a powerful, crafty enemy opposing you in every instance and every place. He will endeavour by every means to make his advantage, and to hinder your usefulness in every way. You will therefore find it needful to live in the spirit of prayer, of faith and watchfulness. It will also be useful to you to consult with those who have been useful in the cause, and who have had large experience in the ministry. These, by painful experience, have gained a knowledge of many things which you as yet are scarcely acquainted with. Let your mind also be always open to information and instruction in these things. . . .

I trust you will excuse me taking the liberty to say that there is one thing which I think you have not sufficiently considered. . . . You

[65] Bourne MSS (Jour.), 5th February: 'Saw Thos. Jackson, and had much useful and necessary conversation with him.' The letter is given in Antliff, pp. 208–10, is undated, but belongs to this period. (See also Kendall, I.182.)

will from time to time be introduced into various families, and much of your success in public will depend on your conduct in these families. Here, then, you will have to walk with the utmost care and circumspection. When you enter a house wait inwardly on the Lord for wisdom and direction, that the Lord may make your coming in useful, and that you may be preserved from speaking words out of place. Be very careful in making the first salutations or compliments. If the words 'honour all men' be properly in your mind, you will be enabled to show a respect for everyone in the house. . . . Beware of hasty freedoms: endeavour to speak with care, gentleness, and prudence. At the same time, wait on the Lord, that your mind may be kept solemn, and that no lightness or anything contrary to Christian gravity may appear in your behaviour. A preacher should always pay proper respect to the children and servants. Their souls are precious. He should shake hands with these, as if he neglect this, he will be thought to be unacquainted with the nature of Christianity, and in particular with the duties of the ministry. A preacher should certainly wait upon the Lord while in a family, that the unction of the Holy One may attend his words; without this he is liable to blunders and improprieties. The temptations of Satan are quick, powerful, and constant. Therefore, 'let your speech be always with grace, seasoned with salt'. And let it be 'that which is good to the use of edifying, that it may minister grace to the hearers'.

Your obedient servant in Jesus Christ,
HUGH BOURNE.

Early in July, Bourne received a letter from Thomas Eaton, of Stockton Heath, telling him that Lorenzo Dow had arrived from America. Bourne immediately set off and the following day heard Dow preach. He comments: 'During the day I had some talk with him, but not satisfactory.' Bourne stayed two further days: 'I was dissatisfied with him but after came to a better understanding with him.' There is no hint as to the reason for this dissatisfaction: we are inclined, however, to think that it may have been on some point of doctrine.[66] Later, he heard Dow at Tunstall, and still later, in September, at Nottingham, where he found Dorothy Ripley,[67] the Quaker evangelist, accompanying Dow. Of their labours Bourne writes: 'It was truly a time of liberty.' A few days later, when visiting Leicester for the first time, Bourne listened to Dow at the camp-meeting, with much blessing.

[66] Walford, II.33, suggests a personal reason: that Dorothy Ripley was travelling alone with Dow, something to which Bourne would not have agreed. This hardly seems a satisfactory reason, as there is no mention of her being at Warrington, and if so, Bourne would have made mention of it. Further, reference to her being with Dow at Nottingham later calls for no comment of dissatisfaction from Bourne.

[67] Dorothy Ripley was the daughter of James Ripley, of Ripley, Yorkshire; she embraced the Quaker faith, went over to America, and became a female evangelist.

VIII

During the remaining months of 1818 Bourne continued to
preach and visit the various societies in the neighbourhood of
Leicester and Loughborough.[68] In March, the Nottingham
quarterly meeting had formed a new circuit, with Loughborough at its head. The superintendency of the three Circuits
—Tunstall, Nottingham, and Loughborough—placed a great
responsibility on Bourne, who during much of this time
suffered from a painful affliction of the eyes. He had much
travelling, having to attend the three quarterly meetings,
'almost uniformly at my own expense'. 'I travelled chiefly on
foot: my feet were often sore, but this I endeavoured to bear
patiently.'[69] Thus, after attending the meeting at Nottingham on
21st–22nd December, we find him moving across to the
Tunstall meeting, 'where much important business was trans-
acted'; then, 'after making the plan and putting it to the press',
he returned to Nottingham on 6th January 1819, where an unexpected and critical situation demanded his attention[70]: two
days later he came to Loughborough, and on to Leicester,
where he put the plans and the MS of the first number of the
new monthly magazine to the printer. Six days afterwards 'at
a friend's house at Coleorton'—on Sunday, 17th January—he
collapsed under the strain. 'Overmuch fatigue and labour had
brought on an extraordinary weakness.'

There is no doubt whatever that this breakdown was due,
not only to the weight of Bourne's physical labours, but to the
inward anxieties which pressed heavily upon him. As we have
already seen, he had been deeply concerned about the decline

[68] It is interesting to note that much advance was made in this area by the holding of open-air meetings after dark, aided by the light of lanterns held aloft upon
sticks (*PMM*, 1819, pp. 15–16).

[69] It should be remembered that the distance from Nottingham to Tunstall is
fifty-four miles; from Loughborough to Tunstall about fifty-five, and from
Nottingham to Loughborough sixteen.

[70] Before the end of 1817 Hull had become an outpost of the Nottingham Circuit,
and at the December meeting of 1818 an urgent request that a travelling preacher
should be sent to Hull was received. Robert Winfield was appointed, but he afterwards declined to go, in consequence of which a delegate was dispatched to Tunstall (Bourne having left the Nottingham meeting), 'to request that William Clowes
might be stationed at Hull'. So Clowes entered Hull the following January (see
Jour. (1844), pp. 146–61; Kendall, I.361–2). The debate at the meeting on 9th
January was difficult, and shortly afterwards, under a sense of grievance, Winfield
separated from the Connexion, proceeded to Leicester where, under his influence, a
division took place in the society, and a new sect was formed—the 'Winfieldites'—
which came to number some thousands. Eventually Winfield joined the Methodist
New Connexion (Herod, pp. 310–11).

of the camp-meetings; he believed this was entirely due to the supplanting of praying-labourers by 'the long and wearisome sermons of the preachers'. This decline had haunted his mind almost daily for some two years or more. Something of a climax came at a meeting at Alton, on 5th January 1819, when

...the camp-meeting ruin in the Tunstall Circuit was laid open. This wounded me to the soul. And on getting into Leicestershire I was aware of the discord sown and the mischief made by R[obert] W[infield]. . . . The united weight reached both soul and body. I broke out into a fit of weeping. . . . Nothing appeared in view but death. I was pierced to the soul with the prospect of leaving the camp-meetings all in ruin, by the handiwork of my most intimate friends. . . . I had had no sleep for some time, nor could I get any: I could hardly bear my own weight, and I weakened every day: I made my will,[71] and set all in order.[72]

The foregoing extract gives some indication of the severity of Bourne's breakdown. After some days his brother James fetched him home to Bemersley for rest and recovery. His condition continued for several weeks, but he attended the quarterly meeting at Leicester in the following March. 'The journey brought a relapse, and at Leicester I was dreadfully ill; but after a time I got back home again.'[73]

A valuable element in Bourne's recovery seems to have been his friendship with James Steele, to whom he unburdened his 'concern' about the Tunstall situation and the future of the camp-meetings, and who offered sympathy and encouragement. 'He said he should hear me preach again.'

At the Tunstall meeting on 29th March, the findings of the Alton meeting [74] 'stating that the camp-meetings were beginning to be overthrown' were presented, and it was ordered that instructions for the conduct of camp-meetings should be printed on the back of the Tunstall plan. 'The camp-meetings underwent a regulation for the first time; this I trust will be of service.' It was a new beginning.

This regulation restored the praying services to the camp-meetings; and directed that the pious praying labourers should form in

---

[71] See Appendix III, p. 187. The will is dated 26th January 1819.

[72] Walford, II.48.

[73] The MS Journal from January to September is missing, but some glimpses of the period are available in Walford, II.48. Bourne's illness may account for no journal during this time.

[74] The findings of the Alton meeting are set out in Bourne, HPM (1823), pp. 56–7, and Walford, II.48–50.

companies, in order to carry them on in the most commodious and successful manner. This regulation cut the root of the mischief, and opened the way to restore both the camp-meetings and the Circuit. The society at Tunstall and the travelling preachers (chiefly young men) entered spiritedly into the work: and there was a very general concurrence throughout the Circuit. The Lord returned in mercy, restored the converting power and made the camp-meetings a means of diffusing unusual vigour and energy into all the other meetings. The preachers rose into vigour and usefulness: the praying labourers were as if let out of prison: more labourers were soon raised up: and the Circuit began to revive in almost every part.[75]

On Sunday, 23rd May, a camp-meeting was held at Wrine Hill, about nine miles from Tunstall, many people from there attending. This precipitated a system for conducting camp-meetings, with additional guidance as to the conduct of meetings generally [76] which was drawn up by Bourne, the details of which were afterwards circulated throughout the Tunstall Circuit and beyond.

At this March meeting Bourne withdrew from the superintendency of the Nottingham and Loughborough Circuits, and remained in charge of the Tunstall Circuit only. It is probable that he did not preach again until June, having been entirely out of action for almost six months. The whole experience had proved 'a fiery ordeal'.

The progress of the Tunstall Circuit was evident by the quarterly meeting in June—'it had begun to revive in almost every part'—and in the following September 'as it was grown strong the quarter day directed a collection to be made throughout the circuit to open the way for spreading the gospel and to relieve the circuit from the heavy debt incurred during the former two years [77]; the Lord so prospered this measure that the circuit rose out of its embarrassment and was greatly strengthened'.

Although Bourne had relinquished the oversight of the Nottingham and Loughborough Circuits, this did not mean a severance of contact with them, or of interest in their work. On the occasion of a visit to Nottingham after his illness, he

[75] Bourne, *HPM*, p. 58. cf. Walford, II.52. 'The circuit rose like the sun in its strength.' During the twelve months from this quarterly meeting to March 1820, the number in society in the Tunstall Circuit increased by 1,013.

[76] These rules are set out in Bourne, *HPM*, pp. 59–60.

[77] In March the amount had reached £30, and Bourne had written: 'I saw no human prospect of its being paid.'

observed the success of the new system of conducting business by an appointed committee.[78]

The Nottingham Circuit by this time had become very extensive, spreading into Derbyshire, Yorkshire, and Lincolnshire. The making of plans was difficult, and therefore at the March meeting of 1819 it was decided to divide the circuit into 'branches', each with its own steward, committee, and quarterly meeting, all of which was under the control of the general meeting at Nottingham. This was a natural step towards the formation of new circuits [79]; moreover, it enabled the travelling preachers to be planned more conveniently, the 'branches' being taken in turn, quarter by quarter.

At the June meeting, 1819, it was felt that in order to further the unity of the Connexion and to promote a regular exchange of travelling preachers, an 'Annual Meeting' of the whole Connexion would be advisable. The other circuits being in agreement, it was decided to hold a preparatory meeting at Nottingham in the following August, to be composed of delegates from the four circuits.[80] The meeting took place on Tuesday, 10th August, and continued until the Saturday evening following. There is no doubt that Bourne was the guiding spirit throughout the deliberations, and also that he was responsible for the final shape of the document, together with the address to the societies. In actual fact the meeting was much more than 'preparatory': it was a legislative assembly, and that to an extraordinary extent.[81] It laid down the foundation of the polity of the new denomination. This is implied in the first of the forty-three questions and answers, of which the document is composed. 'The object of this meeting is to organize the system for the general management of the Connexion of the people called Primitive Methodists.' 'Annual Meetings', to be composed of three delegates from each circuit, one only of which should be a travelling preacher,[82] were decided upon.

[78] 'Hitherto we had conferred by conversation, but now the company was too numerous. . . . My brethren had introduced the moving, seconding, and voting. This was new to me, but its excellence was manifest' (Walford, II.55).

[79] At this meeting the Hull 'branch' was made into a separate circuit.

[80] The delegations were as follows: Tunstall (2); Nottingham (6); Loughborough (4); Hull (3). Only two of the fifteen delegates were travelling preachers. See *Minutes of a Meeting held at Nottingham . . . by the Delegates of a Society of People called Primitive Methodists*, 1819. cf. Kendall, I.378–9.

[81] Petty, p. 78, where the names of the delegates are given. It is unfortunate that the MS Journals for this period are missing.

[82] Probably this proportion was suggested by James Rudd, of Nottingham, not by Bourne, though it became acceptable to him (Kendall, I.379, and Petty, pp. 78–9).

The document proceeds to establish regulations for examination and admission of travelling preachers, for their allowances,[83] their dress,[84] their stationing and discipline. All travelling preachers were required to keep written journals, so that 'the General Committee be informed of the spread of the work of God amongst us'; no preacher was allowed 'to carry on business on his own account or for his own profit'. Regulations were set down for administration of circuits and office-bearers; for admission of members,[85] and for their discipline. The final question is an interesting one. 'Shall a person be appointed to attend to the general concerns of the Connexion?' The answer was in the affirmative, and although an attempt has been made to discount this [86] in the light of the later presbyteral development, which was certainly the feature of the expanding Connexion, the implication seems to be that *at that stage* some such general oversight as had been exercised by Bourne from 1814 to 1818 was still necessary, and that none better than Bourne could undertake it.

At this Preparatory Meeting it was decided that the 'First Annual Meeting' [87] of the Connexion should be held at Hull, on the first Tuesday in May 1820, 'to begin at two o'clock in the afternoon'.

[83] £4 per quarter .or single preachers; £9 10s. for married, plus 1s. per week for each child under eight years. Female travelling preachers to receive £2 per quarter.

[84] 'A plain one: the men to wear single-breasted coats, single-breasted waist-coats, and their hair in natural form: and not to be allowed to wear pantaloon trousers, nor white hats: and that our female preachers be patterns of plainness in their dress.'

[85] 'Any person who earnestly desires to flee from the wrath to come may be admitted to our classes: but such earnest desire must be manifested at least three months before they are received into full membership.'

[86] Kendall, I.379.

[87] The term 'Annual Meeting' as a description of the first connexional assembly possibly reflects early Quaker influence, and Bourne may have been responsible for it in the light of his early contacts with the Quaker movement. The term 'Conference' was not used until 1825.

CHAPTER SEVEN

'IN LABOURS MORE ABUNDANT' (1819–21)

IT is now possible for us to turn again to the Journals of Bourne, which recommence on 26th September 1819. A few extracts will enable us to see how, alongside these responsibilities of leadership, he continued his daily ministrations to the societies.

Wednesday, October 6. Visiting from house to house the greater part of the day. Night, spoke at Tunstall. 1 Thessalonians, 'The Lord Himself shall descend &c'. Circuit Committee met and ordered several things.

Thursday 7. Wrote several letters and other matters; then fetched the plans and was busied about them till the evening. Spoke at Norton. Zechariah iii: 6-7: a time of liberty and prayer after was lively.

Friday 8. Settling Rocester accts. Noon set out for Cheshire, called at Talk o' th' Hill and ordered about the Sunday-school sermons. Came to Coppenhall: . . . came to Leighton. Friends all well.

Saturday 9. Writing out the instructions for the travelling preachers with other writings: examined the class-papers: twenty-one in society: going on well.

Sunday 10. Preached in the forenoon abroad, at Tiverton: then met and spoke to the class. 1 John i: 7: afternoon: spoke abroad at Spurstow to a large multitude: met society. The Lord much present. Spoke 1 Thessalonians iv: 6. Night at Eaton in a barn: a great company and a good time. Ezekiel xlvii: 1-5: met class in a house. Lord Jesus, let Thy blessing be upon us. I had today a great deal of business. . . .

Tuesday 12. Wrote a part of the history of the first rise of the society called 'Primitive Methodists'.[1] Came to Tiverton, then to Spurstow; left there the plans and an account book. Burland Green: spoke 'Scapegoat': a large company.

Wednesday 13. Spent the forenoon in writing and conversation . . . came to Burwardsley: saw T. Brownsword: I spoke John iii: 3. We were out of doors by candle-light. Four lanterns were tied to sticks and held aloft in different parts of the congregation.

Thursday 14. . . . A great part of the day I was employed with T. Brownsword, in making plan for praying companies. Night spoke at Burton Hall: Job: had much sorrow of heart.

---

[1] Bourne states (*HPM* (1823), p. 63) that at the Nottingham Preparatory meeting enquiry had arisen regarding the origin of the Connexion, and this was the cause of his determination to write an historical account.

Friday 15. Came to Weaverham about 14–15 miles: spoke abroad by the light of lanterns tied to sticks: met and spoke to the society.

Saturday 16. Came 22 miles to Macclesfield: saw and conversed with some of the friends. . . . Spoke in the market in the name of the Lord. To God be all the glory. . . .

Bourne reached home the following Wednesday, the 20th, but three days later he set out again.

Saturday October 23. Writing diligently in the forenoon and between 11 and 12 o'clock set off for Northwich: came there in due time, 21 or 22 miles.

Sunday 24. Was at morning prayer meeting at Northwich. Came to Great Budworth: preaching at 9: spoke. Ezekiel xlvii : 1-5, seven in class: the class has not met well . . . at 2 spoke at Northwich. I Thessalonians iv : 15-18: good liberty: met society and gave them some instructions and spoke to the whole: a great multitude. Took down some names to attend in praying-companies . . . and made plans for them. Night, spoke: stopped the society and instructed them about a leaders' meeting or committee of management. There are about 20 in class and more want to join.

Here again we see a good day's work and a fair specimen of Bourne's ordinary and constant labours. The greater part of this period was devoted to Cheshire, and in passing we may note an example of dream-experience which the Journal records. He was at Hampton Heath when the following occurred:

I appeared to be at home at Bemersley and it was night. I looked out and the moon shone bright, but I was surprised to see around it very large lettering. . . . The letters were very beautiful but did not stand in any regular order. Soon after this I had gone over a narrow part of Bemersley Green, opposite to my father's house, and was in one of my father's fields. I looked up to the moon; it shone bright and near it were a number of people: one was upon his knees . . . all in the attitude of adoration. . . . I never saw such a picture but I did not see the object of their adoration. . . . I never saw such a picture of happiness. After some time the whole disappeared. I then came out upon Bemersley Green and looking up, I again saw the moon in brightness, and a person appeared who far surpassed all I had seen before. I called my brother, James Bourne, who was working in a field near, to look at him. It then came into my mind that this was the Head Master and the moon denoted His church.[2]

In December we find Bourne planning a scheme for the building of a preaching-room—at a cost of £300—to meet a proposal of the friends at Macclesfield.

[2] Bourne MSS (Jour.), 12th November 1819.

In his Journal he sets forth a detailed statement:

	£	s.	d.
Interest on £300 per year	.	15	0	0
Ground Rent . . .	7	0	0
Total Rent per annum .	22	0	0

	£	s.	d.
The same room let to 5 silk-twisters at £3 each .	15	0	0
Sunday School to pay . .	3	10	0
Preaching to pay . . .	3	10	0
	22	0	0

and he adds: 'This it is thought might be accomplished: but it must be 26 yards long inside or else it would not do for the silk-twisters.'

Such is a glimpse into the difficulties of early chapel-building in these pioneering days. We find also that at the same time Bourne is planning nearly a dozen new 'openings' around Macclesfield as a centre.

The weather conditions in the closing weeks of 1819 and the early days of January 1820 were difficult for travel, yet we find Bourne pursuing his work in North Staffordshire and along the borders of Derbyshire. Here is an entry for Friday, 21st January:

Weatherbound: the wind was very high and the snow fell apace. At two o'clock I set out and with much wading got to Tunstall to the meeting of the circuit committee and arrived soon after seven: the journey was about sixteen miles.

Reaching Bemersley the following Monday, he drew up regulations for annual removals of travelling preachers and communicated these to the other circuits. The following day he was again at Tunstall, to deal with trouble concerning the chapel there, and at this circuit committee he read the historical account of the rise of the Connexion, upon which he had been busy for some time. The next day he set off for Cheshire. At Barnton, near Northwich, he had to deal with a problem in the society. 'An evil report had been raised of one of the members, and there had been much wrangling and confusion: I spoke, and afterwards explained the nature of discipline. . . . The Lord was present, and I trust the society will be more settled.' This occurrence led to a clear statement of class discipline for the future: [3]

It is the duty of a Methodist to believe evil of no one until it is fully proved: and even then, to put the best construction on all things. . . . It is his duty to pray with all his might for the persons complained of: and having done this, he may get an opportunity to speak to him, in the fear of the Lord. But if he can get no opportunity, or if he has spoken to him and can get no satisfaction, he may then speak to the leader, or to a travelling preacher, and to no one else, but preserve silence on the subject and keep his tongue as it were with a bridle. To this careful silence should be added fervent, effectual prayer: the man of God will then stand clear. It then becomes the leader's or preacher's duty to investigate the matter: and in them a degree of parental affection is expected to dwell.

Once again, therefore, we have illustration of Bourne's sagacity, as the shepherd of the flock under his charge.

Early in February Bourne reached Delamere Forest, where he had 'much discourse about the chapel', and wrote on discipline for the Forest people, 'and thought to print something on the subject'.[4]

Here is yet another example of Bourne's pastoral oversight.

Much of this month laid a serious burden on the shoulders of Bourne, owing to the widespread illness of the preachers— probably due to the severity of winter conditions: 'all the travelling preachers in Cheshire are unwell'.

Early in March he turned eastwards to Staffordshire, where he laboured throughout the month. On 6th April he moved on to Derbyshire, where he worked for three weeks. The cause at Belper caused him some concern, as the sum of £50 loaned upon the chapel was urgently called for: the amount had to be found, and Bourne shouldered the responsibility.

After two or three days in Nottingham, Bourne moved northwards through Lincolnshire, in view of the approaching 'Annual Meeting'.

Thursday, 27. Came in the steam-packet to Gainsborough.
Friday, 28. Came in the steam-packet to Hull: saw Sarah Harrison: led a class.

---

[3] Walford, II.74; *PMM*, I, 1821, p. 237.
[4] This document, which was printed in *PMM*, 1820, p.193, and afterwards as a separate pamphlet, was probably a revision or expansion of a similar statement which Bourne had drawn up after visiting Nottingham in the spring of 1819 (Walford, II.55). It was entitled *A Treatise on Discipline chiefly as it respects Meetings for Business*, and was prefaced by 'An Address to the Society of the Primitive Methodists'.

Saturday, 29. Was much with Wm. Clowes: at night was at a band-meeting.

Sunday, 30. Spoke at half-past ten in the great chapel [5] Ephesians vi: 18-20: at three, spoke again: 'Scapegoat': night I Thessalonians iv: 15: great liberty: one converted at prayer-meeting in the vestry before the three o'clock preaching.

This was Bourne's first visit to Hull: the 'Annual Meeting' was to commence on Tuesday, 2nd May, and the following entry in his Journal is characteristic of the man, particularly regarding his insistence upon punctuality.

At two o'clock in the afternoon I was in the chapel. No one else was present: so with the Lord's assistance, He being present, I opened the meeting with singing and prayer: I made some regulations, and adjourned the meeting; and concluded with singing and prayer, no one beside the Lord being present.

Shortly afterwards the delegates arrived by steam-packet, the delay being doubtless fully explainable! Bourne continues:

At night, Brother Skevington [6] preached, and a prayer-meeting commenced; several were converted.

The next day began with preaching at 5 a.m. 'Then the delegates met and began to settle preliminaries.' The President appointed was George Handford. [7] Difficulties arose, however, in the matter of delegation. Bourne writes:

William Clowes was presented as a travelling preacher, but upon examination it was found that he had not been regularly elected. He was therefore set aside, and the circuit committee was convened to elect one, and they elected W. Clowes. [8]

Further difficulties arose concerning arrangements for married travelling preachers, but of other details we are left uninformed, as the entries in the Journal are formal: 'business went on as usual'. Two things are noted, however:

[5] This was in Mill Street: it had been dedicated on 10th September 1819, and was destined to be the centre of the work for the next thirty years. A print appears in Kendall, I.373.

[6] Joseph Skevington, of Loughborough, who had been a member of the Preparatory Meeting.

[7] Of Sileby, Leicestershire. Bourne had been a guest at Handford's house in the spring of 1819: 'I conversed much with him about discipline.' Shortly afterwards Bourne prepared the first draft of his *Treatise* . . . (Kendall, I. 296).

[8] This procedure was probably due to Bourne's insistence upon exactness in observance of the rule. No list of delegates is extant. Bourne MSS (Jour.), 3rd May 1820.

Sunday 7. Camp-meetings at Hull, Holderness and Barrow in Lincolnshire. That at Hull immensely large: I was appointed to conduct it. In the afternoon two preaching stands and twelve praying-companies: there was some converting and a great awakening.[9]

Tuesday 9. . . . Evening, love-feast. I and T. Woodnorth led it: a vast company, and the work broke out largely: finally concluded between one and two: about forty converted.

The following day, Wednesday, 10th May, the 'Annual Meeting' closed. Bourne afterwards recorded some details as to the state of the Connexion:

Eight circuits [10]: forty-eight travelling preachers, and two hundred and seventy-seven local preachers: number of members, seven thousand eight hundred and forty-two.[11]

No 'general muster' of the whole Connexion had been taken since July 1811, at which time the number in Society had been estimated at 200.

An examination of the 'General Minutes' [12] of the Annual Meeting reveals certain important decisions. First of all the regulations drawn up at the Nottingham Preparatory Meeting of 1819 were adopted with few changes, and incorporated. In addition, a regulation was made for continuing a monthly magazine at threepence;[13] Bourne was appointed editor, and the delegates present were to be the committee for the year, in their respective circuits, 'to collect and transmit to the editor the intelligence of the circuits'. A further question concerned 'another collection of hymns', to be selected from Mr Wesley's'. A book steward was appointed—to be Edward Taylor, if the magazines were printed in Hull, James Bourne, if in the Tun-

---

[9] A fuller account is given in *PMM*, 1820, pp. 220–5. 'Evening preachings were carried on in one street or another on most nights.' We extract the following description of the scene of the Hull camp-meeting: 'The situation was between the town and the river; and it commanded various views of the surrounding country. On one side were docks, in which were numerous ships, elevating their tall masts, together with other vessels of burden which plough the mighty deep. . . . Another view displayed an expanse of waters, with here and there a vessel riding at anchor. Above us was the open firmament of heaven. The works of Providence and grace appeared upon a scale of magnitude. The great congregation was arranged in six companies, wrestling with heaven, and pouring out their supplication to the Most High: and a great solemnity rested upon the whole.'

[10] These were: Tunstall, Nottingham, Loughborough, Hull, Scotter, Sheffield, Derby, and Darlaston.

[11] Bourne, *HPM* (1823), p. 34.

[12] These are printed in *PMM*, 1820, pp. 206–20.

[13] A magazine had been begun in the year previously, but only eight numbers were issued. This volume was ordered to be completed, and then the issues were to be in regular monthly succession.

stall Circuit. The next Annual Meeting was appointed to be held at Tunstall, on the first Wednesday in May 1821.

A survey of all available information regarding this first assembly leaves no doubt that Bourne was the leading figure throughout the proceedings.

The day after the meeting Bourne came to Doncaster—'I was ill with a severe pain in my eyes'—and the following day, through Rotherham to Sheffield, where he stayed some four days, preaching as many times. He moved on to Chesterfield, Mansfield, and Belper, and reached home on 21st May, having been away from Bemersley almost three months.

CHAPTER EIGHT

A TIME OF CRISIS (1821–8)

I

BOURNE WAS now to be much engaged in editorial duties, but this does not seem to have lessened his pastoral labours. Repeatedly in his Journals we find such entries as: 'writing'; 'preparing for the magazine'. His mornings seem to have been absorbed by these editorial labours. Yet 'the care of the churches' was still laid upon him, chiefly in Staffordshire and across into Derbyshire. We find that between the end of May and early August, in 1820, there were no less than ten camp-meetings, for much of the organization of which he was responsible. During September, leaving Bemersley, he came to Macclesfield and journeyed northwards, on foot, to Sheffield, then to Rotherham and Doncaster, and at Thorne took steam-packet for Hull, where he preached and also attended the quarterly meeting which lasted three days: then he crossed over into Lincolnshire and came by way of Scotter to Nottingham. From there he went to Loughborough and on to Derby, and finally back to Bemersley. During the twenty-one days he had travelled some two hundred and forty miles, having done more than two hundred of these on foot, and having preached at least fifteen times.

The next four weeks were given over to an excursion into Staffordshire and Cheshire, not seldom 'visiting from house to house' in the places to which he came. We find this:

Sunday. October 15. Came to Macclesfield and visited Catherine Worrall,[1] a very pious young woman and a member of the society. She lay on a bed of death. I prayed with her and it was an extraordinary time. I visited her again in the evening, and on the Monday morning, and twice in the evening, and was present when she departed about half-past 7, spoke in the afternoon and evening in the room . . . Night, spoke to a large congregation at 8 o'clock. . . . I mentioned the circumstances and it was a solemn time.

---

[1] A memoir of this remarkable woman, and part of her journal, is printed in *PMM*, 1821, pp. 61–7.

On the 27th Bourne came to Congleton and 'wrote a brief for a licence'; thence he proceeded to Macclesfield and Stockport, and on to Manchester the following day for a special occasion. 'They opened the new room in Chancery Lane.' He remained ten days, and preached no less than nine times, in addition to daily visitation of the sick, writing, and 'endeavouring to arrange a matter that was difficult', satisfied, however, to record that 'there is a prospect of it being done away'.

We now come to a considerable period where direct information concerning Bourne's labours is scanty. There is a sudden break in his MS Journal,[2] and we are therefore unable to follow the course of events in detail. It is possible, however, from what sources are available, to gain some impression of Bourne's influence and activities during these years.

The second Annual Meeting commenced on 2nd May 1821, in the chapel at Tunstall, and lasted eight days. There were fifteen circuits and 16,394 members recorded, the increase for the year being 8,552.[3]

By strange coincidence, Bourne was not a member of this assembly, at least at its beginning, and for a reason similar to that in the case of Clowes at Hull, a year earlier, namely that he had not been officially elected by any circuit. Having been appointed editor, Bourne had taken it for granted that election by a circuit was not necessary.[4] The delegates from the Hull Circuit appear to have opposed his inclusion, on the rigid principle of circuit nomination.

So Bourne withdrew and 'returned to a friend's house in Tunstall',[5] and the assembly was left to shape its course without him. The situation was strangely anomalous, especially as the Tunstall chapel was itself the private property of Bourne and his brother. It seems that the recollection of this stirred him deeply, and shortly after the commencement Bourne decided to return to the session, where more than forty members were

[2] The MS Journal ceases with an entry dated 18th February 1821, and there is no further extant MS material until 9th November 1842—a period of more than twenty-one years. From the *Memoirs* (1856–7) it is evident that no MSS covering this period were in Walford's possession, as Bourne's literary executor, and we may reasonably conclude that they are irretrievably lost. We must not assume, however, that Bourne kept no Journal during these years, because printed extracts appear in the connexional magazines between 1828 and 1841. It has to be admitted, however, that the absence of any printed excerpts between 20th November 1820 and 3rd October 1828 is not easy to understand.

[3] Bourne, *HPM* (1823), p. 66; *Gen. Mins.*, 1821, p. 2.

[4] The Editor was made an *ex-officio* member of the Annual Meeting in 1823.

[5] Probably the house of James Steele.

present. Entering the chapel he soon disapproved of the proceedings, and especially of the presence of one member whom
he described as 'a speeching radical',[6] and so he declared: 'He
must not sit in this place.' Others present seem to have supported the offender, for Bourne states: 'They opened out against
me, against the King and against the government.' Bourne
made his reply, emphasizing the fact that under the recent Acts
of 1812 [7] greater liberty of conscience and worship had been
secured, and, in particular, this had made the holding of camp-
meetings possible without infringement of the law; therefore to
speak against the Government was unworthy and might result
in suspension of the new liberty, which would seriously injure
the progress of the work. The debate was prolonged. Bourne
says of himself: 'I got into strong and even peremptory
language.' Suddenly the argument was ended by a resolution
that the offender should withdraw from the assembly. Bourne
adds: 'Such was the effect that during the meeting no one lifted
a finger against the government and it was a blessing to the
Connexion.' Although Bourne's action was severe, his motive
cannot be questioned: he was concerned lest the religious purpose should be compromised by association with political
issues.

The matter being settled, Bourne withdrew again to the
house of his friend, soon, however, to be called into the assembly when the appointments of travelling preachers presented
an insoluble difficulty. James Steele seems to have been responsible for this approach made to Bourne, who had already worked
out a scheme for dealing with the matter in the light of the
connexional experiences during the years. So Bourne returned
and put before the assembly the proposal for the formation of
'districts',[8] each to station its own travelling preachers, and
each to have its own 'district meeting' composed of three delegates from each circuit in the region; the Annual Meeting

[6] The term refers to one who had some measure of extreme political opinion,
probably one of Luddite sympathies, and was therefore against ruling government
authority. There is no indication as to the person concerned.
[7] *An Act to repeal Certain Acts . . . relating to Religious Worship and Assemblies and
Persons teaching or preaching therein* (29th July 1812, 52 Geo. III. c. 155). By this
Statute the Conventicle and Five Mile Acts of Charles II were repealed and interference with religious meetings was made a punishable offence.
[8] The five districts were as follows: Tunstall (Tunstall, Darlaston, Macclesfield,
and Manchester Circuits); Nottingham (Nottingham, Loughborough, and Derby
Circuits); Hull (Hull, Brotherton, Pocklington, and Hutton Rudby Circuits);
Scotter (Scotter, Grimsby, and Lincoln Circuits); Sheffield (Sheffield and Barnsley
Circuits).

should henceforth be composed of these delegates from each
district, only one of whom should be a travelling preacher.
This was an important constitutional development, for which,
as we have seen, Bourne was responsible.

Despite the unhappy personal situation, Bourne counted the
meeting successful.[9]

Much preparation had been made for the reception of the delegates: and the kindness shown them by the neighbourhood [10]
exceeded all expectations. The Lord opened their way abundantly.
. . . Their labours in the various meetings for worship were
attended with an extraordinary unction, and many powerful conversions took place. . . . The labours were in all respects interesting
and important.

One further item we may notice. At this Annual Meeting the
rule concerning the dress of travelling preachers was made a
statute-law, which meant that they were restricted to one
particular cut of coat, and to the wearing of breeches and
stockings instead of trousers, the latter being strictly forbidden.[11]
For a very long time there were many who counted Bourne as
responsible for this decision, a fact which caused him great
annoyance, and about which he was outspoken. As we have
seen, he was not a member of the assembly, and in point of fact
was definitely opposed to any measure that bound travelling
preachers to any one form of dress.[12]

A further important decision was the appointment of a book
room and printing press for the use of the Connexion; also a
committee consisting of five persons,[13] to receive and examine
all matters to be printed. Bourne was reappointed as editor, and
James Bourne as book-steward.

A decision was also taken regarding the compilation of a new
hymn-book,[14] for which Bourne became responsible. He had
already anticipated this and had himself composed several
original hymns, and had also obtained the copyright of twenty-
five others, written by William Sanders. This explains the
interesting minute of the assembly which reads as follows:

[9] *PMM*, 1821, p. 136.
[10] During the preaching at Burslem, 'chiefly in the street', however, 'a degree of
persecution took place'.
[11] The regulation was re-emphasized as late as 1828, in a quaintly worded
minute: 'That our travelling preachers do not wear trowsers' (*sic*) ((Conf. MS
Jour., 1828, Min. 46), but it was repealed in 1830 (ibid, 1830, Min. 7)).
[12] Walford, II.105.
[13] James Steele, James Bourne, Hugh Bourne, Charles John Abraham, and John
Hancock.
[14] This became known as 'The Small Hymn Book'.

It is resolved that the original hymns now brought be accepted: and that the circuits be requested to forward all the original hymns they can.[15]

In addition to this work upon the hymn-book, Bourne's pen was busy during this year in the preparation of sermons and devotional studies for the magazine, in particular a treatise 'On Worship in the Open-air'.[16]

The only further record of the year 1821 set down by Bourne is of a large camp-meeting held at Mexboro' Common, near Doncaster, on Sunday, 3rd June, when there were sixteen praying-companies; it was believed that more than ten thousand attended, and the conversions numbered several hundreds.[17] This is a further illustration of the triumph of Bourne's policy of evangelism by open-air witness. Bourne adds: 'The general affairs of the Connexion went on as usual.'[18]

The third Annual Meeting was held at Loughborough on 28th May 1822, and remained in session for eight days. An increase of 8,824 members of society was reported.[19]

Whilst we may assume that Bourne was day by day fulfilling his sacrificial labours, we have only an occasional record of his doings during this year. On 19th May he was in charge of a large camp-meeting held at Oakengates, in Shropshire, which lasted two days, and was attended by some thousands of people. It was the first meeting of the kind held in that area:

... yet the praying-companies drew out in as complete order as if they had been accustomed to it. The exercises were with power. The Lord made bare His arm: souls were in distress, and several were brought into liberty . . . how many it could not be ascertained.[20]

On 29th September we find Bourne at Congleton,[21] taking the appointment of a sick preacher. 'To do this I was reluctant, as there was to be a love-feast'—an instance of the lingering survival of his natural timidity. The meeting lasted some seven hours. We find also that in the closing months of the year Bourne became involved in a legal proceeding regarding an infringement of the copyright of the early hymn-book, for at

---

[15] For fuller account see Appendix IV, pp. 195–8,　　[16] See *infra*, pp. 190–3.
[17] *PMM*, 1822, pp. 9–10; Bourne, *HPM* (1823), p. 67.
[18] During the year ten new circuits were formed.
[19] *Gen. Mins.*, 1822, p. 17. The number of circuits in the Connexion was now 26, and the travelling preachers 152.
[20] Walford, II.114–15.　　[21] *PMM*, 1823, pp. 15–16; Walford, II.117–18.

York a printer named Kendrew had printed the book and was selling it for personal profit. A statement of the case was drawn up and submitted to an attorney, with direction to proceed. The offender agreed to relinquish some five hundred copies of the pirated edition still in his possession; it was decided, however, that he should have an allowance for every perfect copy, 'to abate the severity of the thing', there being no desire to injure Kendrew personally, the only concern being the protection of property for the good of the Connexion. The matter was settled in February of the following year.[22]

There is only one remaining glimpse of Bourne during 1821, and this indirectly, through a letter written to John Walford by John Coulson in 1853.[23] In conversation in Leeds in 1822, Bourne had said: 'Brother Coulson, I wish, and would as lief as a one pound note, we had a preacher in London.' Two preachers had been sent there from Leeds in December of that year, and in consequence of the return of one of them, Coulson had gone there in January 1823. He wrote to Bourne [24] intimating his arrival, and almost immediately received a letter from Bourne enclosing two pound notes, one for the assistance of the work and the other for personal needs. It was typical of Bourne's generosity.

The fourth Annual Meeting was held in Leeds, in 1823,[25] when an increase of 4,254 members in society was reported. This meeting directed that 'a large standard hymn book' should be prepared and printed at the Book Room, and that it should contain hymns for the sacrament and for a variety of meetings. It was anticipated that the book might be ready early in 1824. This was not intended to supersede 'The Small Hymn Book', but to be used alongside it. The responsibility of compilation once again rested on Bourne.

During 1823 Bourne's pen was still fully employed, and we find several treatises [26] in the pages of the current magazines.

---

[22] The correspondence may be seen in *PMM*, 1823, pp. 138–41. See also Walford, II.119–21.

[23] Walford, II.126–9.

[24] John Coulson's letter to Bourne is printed in *PMM*, 1823, p. 95. The following is worth recording here: 'If any place in England wants ministers it is London. Some of the inhabitants are the most ignorant, wicked, careless and wretched people I ever saw. . . . We have twenty members in society and on trial: we preach at four places on sabbath days, and eight on week days. It is difficult to get houses here to preach in. A garret lets for five shillings a week, bare walls. We are adding souls and the Lord is opening our way.'

[25] Members 29,472; travelling preachers 202; local preachers 1,435.

[26] *infra*, pp. 190–2.

He wrote *A Treatise on the Duty of Parents*; a *Treatise on Baptism* (afterwards separately printed), and *Advice to Travelling Preachers*.

II

It will be noticed that the increase in membership between 1822 and 1823 was little more than half that for the previous year. This caused Bourne considerable uneasiness, for the missionary labours of the Connexion were always his deepest concern. Although statistics are not available, there is evidence that several circuits were in serious financial difficulty. It was doubtless at the Annual Meeting of 1823 that the situation became apparent, and shortly afterwards Bourne addressed a confidential letter [27] to the travelling preachers, appealing for assistance for the embarrassed circuits. He wrote:

DEAR BRETHREN,

I take the liberty to call your attention to the peculiar situation of our Connexion. A number of our Yorkshire circuits, with one in Derbyshire and some of the Lancashire circuits, are considerably embarrassed. . . . By these embarrassments I mean simply the circuit debts incurred chiefly by raising us support. I would advise for us travelling preachers in this instance to act as parents, taking the burden entirely upon ourselves without troubling any one else, and to pursue the following means:

1. Let every travelling preacher make a point of praying expressly for this thing. 2. Each one to be still more diligent to teach as the Apostles did; Acts v: 42. Also to study earnestly the converting gift and the art of management, to practise more than ordinary frugality and industry, taking due care that the outgo of a circuit do not exceed its income. 3. For every one of us travelling preachers to make a voluntary quarterly subscription, and continue it till we have subscribed £1 each: and this, by strict frugality, most of us may accomplish in twelve months: and by this means the embarrassment will be cleared away. . . . At the same time it should be recommended to such circuits immediately to take up a more proper, frugal line of management, so that their outgo should not afterwards exceed their income.

The Lord may have permitted these embarrassments to try our hearts, and prove our love to His cause: and it will be a noble sacrifice. Also the converting gift and the proper line of management may be more diligently studied. . . .

I remain, Your brother and servant in the Lord,

HUGH BOURNE.

BEMERSLEY, *June 6th, 1823.*

[27] Walford, II.131–2.

Bourne's appeal, however, met with slender response, as the whole fund raised amounted only to £4, including Bourne's own subscription![28]

There were several reasons for this embarrassment,[29] which continued for some three years at least. One was the existence of deep social distress, particularly in the manufacturing districts, where many thousands were thrown out of employment, and there was much mob violence, following Luddite disturbances and other radical attempts at reform.[30] These things affected the infant societies; preachers could not be maintained, and the rent of rooms could not be raised. So many preaching-places had to be relinquished, and the more feeble societies disappeared.

But there were also internal reasons for this decline. The extension of the Connexion had been amazingly rapid; societies arose and speedily became self-sustaining and self-governing, but often they were composed of those whose experience in church affairs was small and their view of discipline rudimentary. Moreover, the demand for missionaries was so great that unsuitable persons gained admission to the ministry, and so proved a burden. The societies often languished under their inefficient labours. A further reason for the decline was the introduction into the societies of 'ambitious, turbulent persons', in some cases previously connected with other communities, and these became sources of dissension and disruption.[31]

With characteristic foresight, Bourne realized the impending crisis and drew up a document entitled, 'A Private Communication',[32] which was published early in 1824, prior to the Annual Meeting to be held at Halifax in June. Its preamble was a solemn warning and call to action.

It is evident that the Lord has, in an extraordinary manner, prospered the labours of the Primitive Methodist Connexion, which proves that the preachers have in their hands a great power in the ministry. But a few things have been complained of, and they will come before the next Annual Meeting. It was therefore thought

---

[28] A statement of account (*Gen. Mins.*, 1824, p. 4) shows that only six preachers responded, and there was a gift of £1 from the North Shields Circuit. The money raised was applied to the York and Brompton Circuits.

[29] cf. Petty, pp. 204-5.

[30] See R. F. Wearmouth, *Methodism and the Working Class Movements of England 1800-1850*, ch. 1.

[31] This explains the section (in the *Gen. Mins.*, 1824) entitled 'Improper Persons to be guarded against'. In *Gen. Mins.*, 1827, the term 'imposter' is used.

[32] The document is printed in Walford, II.132-5.

best, by this private communication, to make them known to the travelling preachers in general, and to the official people in the respective circuits, in order that at the Annual Meeting delegates may be prepared beforehand with proper instruction, and as the cases are but few, the travelling preachers are requested to weigh them over, and, if possible, to devise the best means to correct them. If they be not corrected the reproach of them will be attached to the whole of the travelling preachers.

Bourne then proceeds to list cases in general terms, avoiding risk of exact identification; he names cases of neglect of duty, participation in worldly business, refusal to accept appointments, unpunctuality, injudicious female companionship, and allowing of unsuitable persons to preach. Bourne adds peremptorily:

All these cases will come before the Annual Meeting, when the names of all preachers referred to will be given in, if required: and the Annual Meeting will be called upon to lay down a line of proceedings for the circuits in future, in all similar cases. These circuit embarrassments are becoming serious, and will require the united wisdom of the Connexion.

Bourne ends the document by requesting each embarrassed circuit to send to the meeting a statement in writing, giving full account of the situation and the causes for it, in particular, 'stating distinctly what travelling preachers laboured in such circuit when the embarrassment was first brought on'.

The document bore no signature, but it was soon known to be from Bourne, upon whose head bitter opposition descended as a result. At the Halifax meeting the debate was heated, and much personal feeling against Bourne was engendered.

The seriousness of the situation was evident when it was discovered on examination of returns that the Connexion was more than a thousand pounds in debt—and this discovery still further set the spirit of Bourne on fire. Moreover, in remembrance of earlier progress Bourne viewed the matter in the light of what might have been achieved and therefore he measured the situation in terms of serious spiritual loss in missionary enterprise. His speeches in the assembly were without restraint. Never before had he faced so severe a storm, and part of it seemed to have come from those whom he had long counted as friends. The warmth of temper which characterized Bourne's challenge may be open to question, but there can be no doubt as to the purity of his motive: he believed that only the

exercise of sound discipline could save the Connexion. In this
critical period [33] he rendered outstanding service, and his
energy and determination undoubtedly enabled the connexional crisis to be overcome. In many of the new rules [34]
made at this meeting, his influence is apparent. If the regulations now became more stringent, it was for the purpose of
cleansing the ministry from inefficiency, and the laity from
despotism; in application, they were carried out by him without
partiality. It was a great and distinguished service at a time of
the severest testing for the community.

At this meeting it was agreed that an allowance of the usual
£4 per quarter, plus a weekly sum of ten shillings for maintenance, should be made to Bourne, as editor. Hitherto, indeed
from the beginning, Bourne had supported himself, without
assistance from the Connexion; he had further given liberally
to the support of others, and the proceeds of his publications—
amounting to some hundreds of pounds—had been given to the
circuits and to connexional funds. At the end of 1822 the balance
of profits in the Book Room account amounted to £157,[35] and
Bourne's circumstances were such that he found it necessary to
ask for an allowance.

III

During the year 1824 Bourne was busy as hitherto with his
pen, and we find him producing *A Treatise on Sunday Schools* and
A Treatise on the Cultivation of the Spiritual Gifts. This year also
saw the issue of a Magazine for children, which quickly reached
a circulation of seven thousand copies per month. The first
number was issued in October; [36] it was a project dear to the

[33] The Annual Meeting of 1825 showed 33,582 members in society, an increase of
only 75. The *Gen. Mins.* for the two following years do not record any membership
statistics, but in 1828 the number reported was 31,610, being 1,897 fewer than that
for 1824. Walford (II.137) states that the number had fallen in 1827 to 30,000, a
decrease in three years of 3,507. The reason for no published returns for 1826 and
1827 was the erroneous returns made by inefficient travelling preachers (*Gen. Mins.*,
1828, p. 53).

[34] e.g. Travelling preachers were requested to visit not less than five families
daily; there should be a fine for every appointment neglected; local preachers, for
such neglect, should be lowered in status on the plan; none must be members of
secret orders (e.g. Freemasons, Orangemen, Oddfellows, etc.); none must preach
without proper credentials; for continued neglect financial allowance for travelling preachers should be reduced. Also in 1825 a General Missionary Committee
was formed to have oversight of missionary enterprise through the Connexion.

[35] When the Book Room was established the money for purchase of the plant—
some £370—was laid out by James Bourne.

[36] *PMM*, 1825, pp. 94–5; Walford, II.157; Kendall II.11 gives facsimile of title-
page.

heart of Bourne, though it added materially to his manifold labours.

The following year saw the enlargement of the connexional magazine, and in the first number there appeared the beginning of Bourne's *Ecclesiastical History*, which continued in instalments until 1842, being later published as a considerable volume.[37] In addition we find a new and interesting development in a series of short articles on 'Biblical Criticism', illustrating very clearly the extent of Bourne's linguistical studies, and indicating the value which he placed on Biblical scholarship in the cause of evangelical religion. We may note also a small document of advice regarding the building of chapels, which he drew up for connexional use. Details of construction are set forth, and the document shows how valuable was his early training as a carpenter, and how practical was his common sense.[38]

Of outstanding importance at the Annual Meeting of 1825 at Sunderland was the question of a 'Deed of Settlement' for the legal security of the Connexion: a committee of four persons [39] was appointed to prepare the document, and once more the foresight and common sense of Bourne were to prove invaluable.

The Annual Meeting of 1826 was held at Nottingham, and, as we have already noted, it was faced with a serious situation, many of the circuits being financially involved. At this meeting a stern regulation was passed,[40] probably due to the influence of Clowes, who had been troubled in the Hull Circuit with inefficient preachers and had resorted to severe measures. This policy seems to have commended itself strongly to Bourne's judgement, and it was now resolved that no circuit should be allowed to run into debt, and the travelling preachers should not be entitled to more allowance than the circuit could raise; any deficiency should be accepted by the preachers in equal

[37] See Appendix IV, p. 193.
[38] *PMM*, 1825, pp. 101–3. In a footnote Bourne makes the following observation when speaking of the importance of adequate ventilation: 'Some years ago I was in our chapel at Boyleston. . . . The chapel was unusually full. The window shutters were all closed. In a short time the candles burnt very dim that I was aware if something was not done, they would go out, and the air would be so bad as to injure the people. With great exertions I opened some of the shutters and casements. The candles immediately burned bright and clear.'
[39] Hugh Bourne, James Bourne, William Clowes, and James Steele. It was also resolved that twelve persons, four of whom should be travelling preachers, should be appointed 'permanent members' of the Annual Meeting (*Gen. Mins.*, 1825, p. 9).
[40] *Gen. Mins.*, 1826, p. 6.

shares. 'This being the state of things, there was no way left but to give every preacher an opportunity to make proof of his ministry.'[41] The result was that some thirty preachers, whose labours were inefficient, were induced to leave the Connexion. It was a desperate measure indeed, but the situation was desperate, even as Bourne had foreseen, though he had been unable to convince others of its seriousness. Had his counsel been taken earlier this extreme position might never have arisen. The action brought upon him both scorn and contempt, and the old insinuation that he was against the travelling preachers was renewed. But despite such 'a flood of sorrow', nothing counted in comparison with the prosperity of the work so near to his heart. If he sought the removal of those who were indolent and inefficient, at least his own labours bore witness to his right to demand their removal. The undivided loyalty which he required for the sake of the cause, he himself undeniably gave in fullest measure. To the unworthy or idle, Bourne was 'like a lion in the way'. Suffice it to say that this year formed the turning-point in the crisis, for at the Annual Meeting of 1827, held in Manchester, there were signs of returning health: the sifting process had begun to take effect. To safeguard the interests of circuits and to assist those still in difficult circumstances, it was agreed [42] to appoint Bourne as a special messenger to visit the circuits and 'to try to beg from the goodwill of the people', in order 'to alleviate the ruin from impostors'. Sterner rules were also enforced upon the preachers 'to preserve stricter propriety and to prevent slander'.[43]

A further matter determined by this meeting has reference to Bourne. A year earlier the issue of a 'Preachers' Magazine' had been decided upon, but the opportunity for its publication had not been found possible. The matter was now undertaken,[44] and with typical self-effacement Bourne agreed to suffer any loss if it should prove a failure; if successful, the profits should go to connexional funds. Only one volume was produced,[45] probably because the sale did not justify the cost involved.

[41] In 1828 'a charitable fund' was raised to assist in provision of allowances for those preachers appointed to circuits suffering from the unsatisfactory labours of those who had preceded them in these stations.

[42] *Gen. Mins.*, 1827, p. 6.

[43] ibid, p. 4: 'No preacher shall be allowed to take any female alone with him nor to suffer any so to accompany him (his own wife excepted) in going to or returning from any of his appointments; and the female preachers shall be under a similar regulation.'

[44] ibid, p. 10.

[45] September 1827 to April 1832.

One further item is of some interest, namely, a resolution [46] that throughout the Connexion one day per quarter should be set aside to be observed as a day of fasting; it is more than likely that in his deep anxiety for the spiritual welfare of the societies, Bourne was the one responsible for this decision.

In May 1827 Bourne experienced a great sorrow in the death of his esteemed friend, James Steele, who died at Tunstall, on 8th May. Bourne was with him on the day of his departure: 'His faith was steadfast; he had a zeal for the prosperity of Zion.' [47]

The year 1828 brought encouragement to Bourne, as there were distinct signs of an upward trend in the denomination, both numerically and financially. He writes of the Annual Meeting at Tunstall: 'The Connexion wore a prosperous aspect both in temporal and spiritual . . . the work has been powerful in many places.' Arising out of the request that he should visit the circuits to ascertain the condition and observe how far the rules of discipline were being fulfilled, his engagements became more numerous; furthermore, the preliminary arrangements for the 'Deed of Settlement' occupied much time and thought. The magazine for this year contains much less contribution from his pen, but this may be partly accounted for by the work of the new *Preachers' Magazine*, for the content of which he was almost entirely responsible.

IV

It is now that we are able to take up the thread of Bourne's private journals, and in October 1828 [48] we find him journeying from Shrewsbury southwards, across the Welsh border.

Tuesday, October 7. I walked 29 miles to Ludlow. . . . I found them in a strait. . . .

Thursday, 9. I was very lame: my left foot on Tuesday was not only severely blistered but inflamed, and now it is exceedingly ill: and my right foot sore. I set off very early into Herefordshire, and went to Aymstrey, and at night preached at Coverhope. . . .

Friday, 10. Preached at Presteigne, in Radnorshire. This is a newly formed circuit . . . it has good prospect.

Saturday, 11. I was very lame and scarcely knew what to do, expecting to be obliged to give up and try by some means to get

---

[46] Conf. MS Jour., 1827, Min. 127. There is no earlier MS Journal than this date.
[47] *PMM*, 1827, p. 249.
[48] Occasional printed extracts (from the MS now lost) begin on 3rd October 1828 (*PMM*, 1829, pp. 21–5).

home again. However, these things caused me to pray earnestly. And I set off, intending to go, if I could, to Llanbauhowery. When I arrived I was thankful to find that, after walking eighteen miles, my feet were no worse than when I started, but rather better: they had actually improved on this journey whilst walking. This is what never happened to me before, and I was thankful to the God of all mercies. This is the most uneven country . . . but the land is good.

Monday, 13. At Painscastle. This is a country village and here our people have built a valuable chapel. . . . I set off after dinner, six miles to the Hay, a market-town in Breconshire, situated on the banks of the fine river Wye. I went a few miles farther, to Llangain, . . . and preached in the chapel. After this about three miles farther to the Park, a large farm, where was a kind and pious family.

Wednesday, 15. I, with some difficulty, went to the top of the Black Mountain. Our travellers have compared some parts of the Holy Land to the mountains of Wales, and on this account I wished to ascend the Black Mountain. It commands an extensive prospect of mountains, hills and valleys. . . . At night spoke to a large congregation in the chapel at Cwm, in Herefordshire.

Friday, 17. I walked 20 miles in most uneven country to Blaenavon, in Monmouthshire. I was much fatigued, but I preached in the evening. The land here is poor, but the country populous, the people being chiefly employed in the iron-works and collieries.

Sunday, 19. I preached at Nantyglo, and in the evening at Beaufort. Religion is prospering.

Monday, 20. I got to Abergavenny.

Tuesday, 21. I walked fourteen miles to Monmouth; then about 12 to Pillawell, in the Forest of Dean, in Gloucestershire. I went seven miles to Lydbrook and preached. It was a powerful time. But I was much exhausted and found that, having walked 33 miles, the preaching was rather too heavy for me. But I afterwards recovered. . . . This is one of the King's Forests: and the people are chiefly employed in iron-works and collieries: but employment is low and the people distressed.

From here Bourne came to Purton-passage, and crossed the River Severn, and went on to Stroud. The next day he took coach for Worcester—'the first time of my being on a coach all this journey'—and then came to Birmingham, and in the evening to Darlaston. Two days later he reached Bemersley. He had travelled nearly three hundred miles, and four-fifths of it on foot.

One of the important responsibilities set upon Bourne by the Annual Meeting of 1829 was the 'consolidation' of the rules and regulations, covering the period from the first assembly in 1820; for this work none was more fitted, and it is marked by great clarity and simplicity.

We have no indication of the travels of Bourne during the

first half of 1829, but there is evidence that he was particularly
engaged on the final stages of the draft of the new 'Deed of
Settlement': it seems that several times he had visited London
in connexion with this work. Early in the year he wrote to
George Tetley, who was stationed there:

BEMERSLEY, *Febry. 13th 1829.*
DEAR BROTHER TETLEY,
  The draft of the settlement deed is now completed to full
satisfaction, and we request you to wait upon Mr Wilks [49] and get
him to put it upon parchment, and deliver it to you at farthest
within a fortnight. And you must manage to get it done by that
time, if possible, without fail, and send it direct to James Bourne, by
the express coach, which starts, I believe, from the Saracen's Head,
Snow Hill, London.

         Yours in the Lord,
          HUGH BOURNE.

The above-named attorney had requested Bourne to draw up
an outline of the intended deed, so that the matter might be
expedited, and when it was presented to him he spoke warmly
of Bourne's 'great legislative talents'. Mr Wilks was much
pressed, however, with parliamentary affairs, and this delayed
the work, which was eventually completed by another London
attorney. The final draft was presented to the Conference at
Scotter, in May 1829, and the document was completed and
signed under the seals of Hugh Bourne, James Bourne, William
Clowes on 5th February, 1830, and enrolled in Chancery five
days later. The work had taken some five years to complete,
and it was an outstanding testimony to Bourne's skill, insight,
and patience.[50]

  The Scotter Conference of 1829 was a source of great joy to
Bourne, for there was clear evidence that an upward trend had
now taken place in the fortunes of the Connexion.[51] Bourne
writes:

  The union, harmony and zeal were of a high order. The unction
that attended the doing of business and the meetings for worship

[49] John Wilks, an eminent London solicitor, had been recommended as suitable
for the execution of the deed, and both Bourne and Clowes had had personal inter-
views with him. On one of these occasions he had observed to Clowes: 'Mr Hugh
Bourne makes me think of George Fox, the Quaker' (Walford, II.178).

[50] Walford is in error in stating that it was presented in its complete form to the
Conference at Hull in 1830. Bourne states that, owing to delays in London, it was
'presented, read and approved' at the Leicester Conference of 1831 (Conf. MS
Jour., 1813, Min. 13).

[51] The membership return was 33,720, an increase of 2,110 on the previous year.
Travelling preachers numbered 228; chapels 403.

was great . . . many precious souls were set at liberty. . . . The Conference camp-meeting will long be remembered . . . and the lovefeast much approved.[52]

Bourne was requested to prepare an 'Address to the Societies', [53] the first formal document ever issued in the Connexion. One short extract will suffice to indicate its quality:

Grace and peace be multiplied to you, from God the Father and the Lord Jesus Christ: and this we wish that your souls may prosper, and the saving health of our God may be amongst you, and that ye may abound in all grace.

First of all we thank Almighty God, through our Lord Jesus Christ, for His mercy bestowed upon our Connexion, He has truly called us a people, who were not a people when we look at our Connexion in its exceedingly small beginning, when humanly speaking, it had no prospect of standing its ground or making its way: and when we consider the difficulties which it has had to encounter, and with which it still has to struggle, and look at the extent to which it has spread, and the height to which the Lord in His providence has raised it, we may well be surprised, as well as humbled, and may say, 'Not unto us, O Lord, not unto us, but to Thy name be the praise!'

The decision of outstanding importance at this Conference was the appointment of missionaries to America, the first overseas enterprise of the Connexion. The matter had been under consideration for some time, prompted by the fact that many members of the societies had emigrated; this was now regarded as 'a providential opening'.[54]

---

[52] *PMM*, 1829, pp. 289–90.

[53] Conf. MS Jour., 1829, Min. 155. The Address is printed in *PMM*, 1829, pp. 291–5. See also Walford, II.174–5.

[54] The responsibility was undertaken by the Tunstall and Hull Circuits. From the former, William Knowles and Ruth Watkin were sent, the sum of £25 being allocated to assist this circuit in the enterprise; from the latter, William Summerside and Thomas Morris, a similar sum being given to this circuit. They left Liverpool on 17th June, Clowes witnessing their departure. Before leaving the country the missionaries visited Mow Cop, with Bourne as their guide (*PMM*, 1829, p. 322; Kendall, I.436–8).

CHAPTER NINE

'IN JOURNEYINGS OFTEN' (1829-44)

I

HAVING PROMISED the Conference to visit some of the northern societies, Bourne came to Manchester on 9th July 1829, moving the next day to Bolton, and on the following day to Preston, in Lancashire, where he preached 'with much enlargement'. It was the occasion of the race-week, and he observed that the children of the Sunday school, together with others, made procession through the streets—'followed by a frugal feast—to preserve them from the vanities of the race-course'.[1] Three days later he moved north to Lancaster, and the following day went on to Carlisle, 'to find the work on the rise'. On 20th July he came to Hexham—'they intend to send out a missionary as soon as providence shall open the way'. The next day he reached the hospitable home of Robert Ingram Shafto, Esq., of Bavington Hall,[2] in Northumberland, and from thence by gig to Newcastle-upon-Tyne, twenty-two miles farther on his journey. For some days he visited in the region of North and South Shields, and on the 27th came to Sunderland; then onwards through Morpeth to Alnwick, where he 'saw the preacher and some others, and stayed about an hour', and then set off for Berwick-on-Tweed, reaching there late at night. 'The cause is going on well and they intend to build a chapel; I examined the ground and the plans and pointed out some improvements; at night preached in the open air, with extraordinary liberty.'

On 1st August he came to Edinburgh, an outpost of the Sunderland Circuit, where there had been serious division in

[1] The society appears to have suffered to some extent from the proselytizing of the 'Protestant Methodists' in this part.

[2] Robert Ingram Shafto (1770–1848) was the third son of Sir Cuthbert Shafto, Kt., of Bavington Hall. He had succeeded to the estate in 1826, about which time some of the preachers were holding services in a cottage, and to whom he gave the privilege of preaching in the kitchen of the Hall. Having previously belonged to the Independent Chapel, he now joined the Connexion, and formed the design of erecting buildings for worship and for day and Sunday schools. He became exceedingly generous both in hospitality and gift to the new cause (*PMM* (1848), pp. 513–16; Clowes *Jour.* (1844), p. 364). Bourne makes several references to his kindness.

the society.[3] 'I preached in the open-air, in the grass-market, with good liberty; and then in the preaching room, where I was a little strait.' Two days afterwards Bourne came to Glasgow, where he found the circuit 'going on well'; the next day, 'at three in the afternoon', he set sail for Liverpool, reaching there 'between nine and ten o'clock the next evening'. The following afternoon he came to Preston Brook, and two days later reached Bemersley.

Of Bourne's labours during 1830 we have no account. The fact, however, that the Conference decided that the Magazine should be enlarged suggests an increase of his editorial labours, and we may also assume that his numerous travels continued in oversight of the stations. May we not also suspect his influence behind the following quaint minute regarding the conduct of the conference camp-meetings, which occurs in the Conference MS Journal for this year:

That there be two preachers in each service, and that they be allowed to speak each 20 minutes and not to exceed. . . . The conductor to give each preacher a signal by pressing the point of an umbrella or some other matter against his foot . . . and to repeat the signal, if need be, the instant the time expires. . . .

Bourne was certainly the enemy of long preaching![4] We may note further: 'That no frivolous apologies be used, nor trash talk about "My time is short".'

Through printed excerpts [5] from Bourne's Journal we have some account of his activities during 1831. In June there was a remarkable series of services, in the chapel and lanes around St Martin's Moor, near Whitchurch. 'Some lost their burdens on that day' In July he came to the Congleton camp-meeting, and then to Macclesfield and on to Manchester the day following, from whence he travelled to Liverpool.

At half-past two I set off on the railway. I think there were more than a hundred persons drawn by one engine. We have many stoppages, but arrived at Liverpool 36 miles, in about two hours and a quarter.[6]

[3] This disruption had caused Clowes great concern. 'What shall we do with Edenbrough' (MS letter: W. Clowes to John Flesher, 7th May 1830).
[4] The rule made at the following Conference was even more rigid, when it was decided that every travelling preacher 'trespassing by long preaching' should have ten shillings taken from his quarterly allowance, and this to be given to the 'charitable fund'.
[5] *PMM*, 1831, pp. 407–13.
[6] The Liverpool to Manchester railway was opened in 1830.

The next morning, about half-past six, Bourne left by steamer for Whitehaven.

It was a calm day and we had a good voyage. There were a great many passengers, some of whom were unsteady: and between two and three o'clock, the music-players came to our end of the vessel. I sat on the foredeck, which was raised upwards of a yard higher than the main deck. . . . Some instigated a young woman to ask me if I would come down and dance with her. I rose up and strongly reproved her . . . and exhorted her to leave off all her improper courses, and to think of serving the Lord and saving her soul. This drew the attention of all the multitude: and one set on me on one side and another on another. But I went on with a strong, steady voice showing the propriety of serving the Lord. . . . The music people attempted to play me down, but my voice was too strong for them, and after wearying themselves, they gave it up and went to the other end of the vessel. Soon all the people on the foredeck went down and left me . . . but I continued, as I knew they would hear my voice . . . with all my might. I preached salvation free for all, declaring that Christ had died for all and the promises of God were open to all, even to those who had been making game. . . . We landed at Whitehaven about 20 minutes past six.

For five days Bourne remained, preaching in the neighbour-hood, and then, on 9th August, took coach for Penrith, a journey of forty miles, passing through Cockermouth and Keswick, 'where we stopped one hour . . . a place of resort for the gentry, who come to view the lakes of Cumberland and the mountain scenery: the views here are fine'. After preaching at Penrith, he walked twenty miles across Melberby Fell [7] to Alston, where in the evening he preached in the chapel. 'The inhabitants are chiefly lead-miners, and many have been obliged to leave for want of employment and some have emigrated to America.'

The next day he preached at Nanthead. [8] Three days later he journeyed down Weardale to Frosterley, where he 'led a class', and in the afternoon and evening preached in the chapel at Stanhope. Thence he travelled to Allenhead, where he 'visited and prayed with more than forty families'. Then he moved north some seven miles to Allendale Town, and spoke

---

[7] Bourne makes mention of 'The Helm Wind', the peculiar feature of the Fells in this region.

[8] Here Bourne discovered a new type of cheap fuel for house-fires: 'Many in these parts burn balls rather smaller in size than a man's hand, and made of small coal and soft clay, mixed together by treating. These are laid on the fire in their wet, soft state . . . they yield but little smoke, but they burn a long time and throw out a great deal of heat.'

'with unexpected liberty'; the next day south to Wearhead, where he preached 'to a great multitude', and also found 'a travelling prayer-meeting', the intention of which was to touch every home in turn throughout the neighbourhood. 'It was very powerful.'

The day following he walked ten miles to Middleton-in-Teesdale, there to learn that more than twenty members, including seven local preachers, had some time previously emigrated to America, one of the latter having become a travelling preacher there. The day after, 'assisted part of the way with a horse', Bourne came to Brough, in Westmorland, in order to attend the quarterly meeting of the Barnard Castle branch of the Hull Circuit, returning two days later to Barnard Castle. 'In this branch there is a spirit of prayer and the work is in a good state.' From thence he moved on to Darlington, and on 29th August took coach to Thirsk; he then walked eleven miles to Ripon, and the next day on to Leeds, and through Manchester home again. Such was his continuous labour in the care of the churches.

II

The year 1832 laid specially weighty burdens upon Bourne in the matter of editorial work. As in 1828, he was again commissioned by the Bradford Conference to prepare a new 'consolidated Minutes', and once more his ability in this direction is illustrated. Of further importance was the creation of a Board of Trustees, thirty-three in number, for the control of the affairs of the Book Room, and Bourne was entrusted with the task of preparing a draft deed for the settlement of these.[9] We find also that in this year the Bemersley Book Room undertook the publication of several classical works of Christian devotion, the responsibility of which rested heavily upon Bourne, but which he readily undertook, believing this would be of great value for the spiritual advance of the societies.[10]

[9] At the establishment of the Book Room in 1821, trustees had been appointed, and were to have provided financial means for setting it on foot, but they had failed; so James Bourne had been left to struggle with the difficulties alone. Seeing no prospect of settlement upon trustees, James Bourne settled it, by will, on the Connexion. The new decision was in order to relieve the burden (*Gen. Mins.*, 1832, p. 3).

[10] See 'A Catalogue of Books . . .' (*Gen. Mins.*, 1832, pp. 22–3). The following works are listed: Wesley's *Life of Fletcher*; Bunyan's *Pilgrim's Progress*, *Grace Abounding*, and *The Holy War*; Alleine's *Alarm to the Unconverted*; Baxter's *Saints' Everlasting Rest* and *Call to the Unconverted*; Doddridge's *Rise and Progress of Religion in the Soul*; Fénelon's *Pious Reflections*.

During part of this year Bourne spent much time in visiting the respective District Meetings, by request of the Conference. Thus towards the end of March he set off to Lynn, where the meeting of the Norwich District was to be held. He walked to Ramsor and on to Derby, took coach to Nottingham, and then, similarly, to Lincoln, from whence he went by steamer to Boston. The following day, setting off in a sailing-packet at 5 a.m., he reached Lynn in the afternoon. During the days before the meeting began on 7th April he preached in Lynn, and took a tour of the neighbouring Norfolk villages. At Swaffham, on 3rd April, he spent his sixtieth birthday. It was on that day that he wrote the 'Preface' of his book on *Studies of Language*, which was printed at Bemersley during the year. At the Lynn meeting an increase of 1,020 members was reported: the services for worship were crowded. On 11th April he took coach to Fossdyke, in the Boston Circuit, and the next day went to Spalding, where he preached in the chapel of the Particular Baptists, the ministers of this and the General Baptist Chapel assisting. A service was held in the latter chapel at five o'clock the following morning, and then Bourne set off to walk the sixteen miles to Boston. Thence he took steamer up the Witham to Lincoln, and on by coach to Nottingham, where, on Sunday, 15th April, he preached no less than six times. The following day he returned home.

Yet two days later Bourne left Bemersley again in order to attend the Tunstall District Meeting at Burton-on-Trent, which he reached on Good Friday, 20th April, having walked thirty-five miles. The meeting over, he made his return journey, calling at Tutbury, Church Broughton, and Sapperton; the next day he went part of the way by horse to Wootton, and then walked the remaining eighteen miles to Bemersley. 'Besides having luggage to carry it rained without intermission the whole of the way.'

Again, two days after reaching home he set off for the Manchester District Meeting, to be held at Preston. On his return journey through Bolton he reopened a chapel, 'when a powerful spirit of prayer was poured out'.

During May, Bourne was at Bradford for the Conference, where he rejoiced in the increase of membership,[11] and in particular at the immense camp-meeting at which it was

[11] The increase was 4,105, the total membership having now reached 41,301—at the thirteenth Conference.

estimated not less than ten thousand were present. Preachings were held at an early hour each morning, and Bourne toiled incessantly. 'Though I had gone through much labour . . . weariness was suspended.'

Bourne spent the early days of July in the Black Country—during a period when cholera was widespread and rampant—around Darlaston and Wolverhampton, from whence he came to Shrewsbury, thence to Oswestry and St Martin's Moor, where, because the company was so large, he stood in the doorway and preached at the same time to one congregation inside the chapel and to one outside, despite the unfavourableness of the weather. The rest of the month was given over to labours in North Cheshire.

The month of September brought Bourne into the Midlands, where he began his work at Birmingham. Then he travelled twenty-six miles by cart to Worcester, returning the next day to Birmingham, where for the first time he saw a steam-coach in the street. The day afterwards he came to Stratford-on-Avon—'a good society but straitened for a place of worship'. From there he went to Oxford and on to Witney; then he moved on some fifteen miles to Chilton in Buckinghamshire, and the following day he travelled ten miles farther to Shefford, in Bedfordshire, to find that, despite much previous persecution, the work was progressing.

On the 15th, 'with kind assistance part of the way, and with walking eleven miles', he came to Salisbury; then, after preaching for two days, he went on to Martin Motcomb, Kingston Magna, and to Shaftesbury, reaching Frome, in Somersetshire, on the 22nd, where he preached three times. Then on to Bath—'where in the evening I preached in the street'—and the following day to Bristol. The next morning he set off by steamer to Hayle in Cornwall, and on landing walked ten miles to Redruth, where 'with much liberty' he preached in the open-air; then on to St Ives, where he preached twice in the chapel, and reached Penzance in the evening. At nine o'clock the following morning he spoke at an open-air service in Newquay, and again at Penzance in the evening. In these parts also he found a severe outbreak of cholera. On 3rd October he came to St Day, making also a visit to Gwenapp Pit, recollecting the preaching of Wesley, and also recording that 'our people have held two powerful camp-meetings in it'. On the next day he preached at Falmouth, and in the evening at

Penrhyn. On Sunday, 7th October, he was again at Redruth:
'This evening I preached on judgement, and during the night
there was exceedingly loud thunder; this deepened the impression.' The next day he came to St Austell, where he stayed
some days, preaching and visiting families in the neighbourhood. He also saw the getting of china-clay, much of which was
sent to the Staffordshire potteries: he preached at one of the
mines, where he found a noon prayer-meeting made up of
different religious communities. On Monday, the 15th, he
moved east to Devonport and Plymouth. He took coach to
Exeter two days later, and on the 19th travelled by coach to
Bristol, and the day following to Birmingham. On the 21st he
preached 'in a club-room' at Darlaston: 'There has been a great
turning to religion in those parts since the cholera began its
ravages.' The next day he returned home, having been away
from Bemersley seven weeks. He wrote in his Journal:

With ministerial family visiting, travelling from place to place,
and writing for the magazines, I have been closely employed and
scarcely ever laboured harder in my life. But through the mercy of
God, my health has been good. To His name be the glory!

III

During the year 1833 Bourne pursued his customary itineraries
throughout the circuits. In late January he was in Yorkshire,
around Bradford and Leeds [12] and Halifax. Early in February
he moved across to Manchester, by way of Todmorden. He had
no sooner returned to Bemersley than he set out almost immediately for Oldham, where he found immense congregations. 'I
scarcely ever saw people so closely thronged together.' Working southwards, he came to the home of R. Waller, at Mellor
Moor End, and preached at New Mills and at Marple in
Cheshire. The next day he was at Stockport.

At the end of March Bourne began his journey southwards
in order to attend the London District Meeting. He reached
Birmingham on the 29th—'the circuit has more than one hundred increase for the year and is still rising'—and came to
Coventry. He arrived in London on his sixty-first birthday.
The days were filled with preaching, indoors and out, and the
survey of the work was encouraging.

[12] On 31st January, at Rawdon, near Leeds, Bourne was employed in family
visitation. 'We commenced soon after eleven o'clock and visited upwards of fifty
families. I myself prayed in fifty-one houses in Rawdon, besides discoursing with
the people' (PMM, 1833, p. 111).

From the MS Journal of John Hallam we have also a glimpse of Bourne while attending the Tunstall District Meeting held at Kidderminster in April of this year.

Friday, April 25. . . . In the afternoon we walked on to Stourbridge, and while waiting for the coach, Brother Hugh Bourne came into the town. When the coach came in, the Oswestry and Birmingham delegates were upon it. We joined them and went singing the greater part of the way to Kidderminster. The other people who were on the coach were greatly surprised to hear us sing the praises of God. We got into Kidderminster about eight o'clock. . . . Hugh Bourne gave an account from the pulpit of the work of God in different parts of the Connexion, and a good feeling rested upon us.

During the stay in the town Hallam visited the parish church, the scene of Richard Baxter's ministry, and he also went to the Unitarian Chapel, where he saw Baxter's pulpit. Remembering that Bourne was reading Baxter at this time, it is difficult to think that he did not make a similar pilgrimage before leaving Kidderminster.

An interesting excursion arose out of a letter from the Preston Brook Circuit. On 23rd July Bourne came to Runcorn and then by steamer to Liverpool. The next day, along with Thomas Sugden, of Manchester, he took steamer to Ireland in order to be present at the Newry camp-meeting.[13] They reached Kingstown the next morning, and, coming to Dublin, Bourne was much impressed by the city. The next day they went by car—'fifty Irish miles'—to Newry, passing through Drogheda and Dundalk. The camp-meeting was held on Sunday, 28th July. The day was hot, but the company sang through the streets, stopping occasionally for testimony and prayer. 'The brethren and sisters in Ireland laboured beyond my expectations.' Two days later he attended another camp-meeting at Rathfillan, where 'the meeting took well'. The day after he came some eighteen miles farther north to Banbridge, and then 'walked five Irish miles to Dromore', through 'country uneven and exceedingly bare of trees'.[14] On 1st August he reached Lisburn, and in the course of visitation went to

[13] The Irish mission had begun by the sending of missionaries from the Shrewsbury Circuit to Belfast, early in April 1832: before the end of the same month, Preston Brook Circuit had sent Francis N. Jersey to Dublin, and he began his work at Newry on 27th April. In October the Oswestry Circuit missioned Lisburn (Petty, pp. 45–8). At the time of Bourne's visit the Irish mission had probably about 300 members.

[14] Bourne observed that 'the Irish roads were extremely good and well-made', and adds: 'The ploughs and gates are for the most parts made of iron.'

Maragall, on the White Mountain, where he saw the lime-kilns, and noted the extreme hardness of the limestone, in which he found lumps of flint embedded. He came to Belfast [15] for Sunday, 4th August; the next day he went to Newton Breada, some three miles distant, for an open-air preaching. On the early afternoon of the following day Bourne left by steamer and reached Liverpool about eight o'clock the following morning. In the forenoon of that same day he went by steamer up the Mersey to Runcorn, and on to Preston Brook, where he gave an account of the Irish work. Two days later he was again at Bemersley, 'thankful to God for all His mercies'.

We have a further glimpse of Bourne in a visit to Shropshire in October. The first day he walked to Newcastle-under-Lyme, hoping for conveyance to Oswestry, but, finding it was not available, he walked twenty-six miles to a point south of Whitchurch, and arrived 'grievously foot-sore'. The next day he went a further nine miles to Shrewsbury for the circuit meeting, going on the day after by coach, eighteen miles, to Oswestry. He stayed three days, and on the Sunday, at Treflach Wood, preached to children and to a large congregation both in the new chapel and outside. 'Praying and singing were both in English and Welsh.' On the 16th he came to Rhosymedre, in Denbighshire; five days afterwards to Ellesmere, and then he returned home through Wem.

Before leaving the record of 1833, we have to notice the Sunderland Conference, which began on 24th May, and which, unhappily, was overshadowed by serious tension between Bourne and Clowes. The issue seems to have arisen mainly from the 'particularism' which sprang out of district administration, there being little co-ordination. Bourne appears to have spoken harshly, and at length, in criticism of Clowes and the Hull Circuit, and the wounds went deep.[16] Still more serious was the appearance, shortly after the Conference, of an anonymous pamphlet, bearing the imprint of the Bemersley

[15] The first camp-meeting in Ireland was held at Belfast on Sunday, 19th May 1833 (*PMM*, 1833, p. 418).

[16] Clowes MSS (D), ff. 7–42. The issue had also been raised, though less severely, two years before, at the Leicester Conference of 1831. cf. MS Journal of John Hallam: '1833 *Monday May 27*. The Conference business opened at six o'clock, but oh! what a change. Unpleasant things arose between B[ourn]e and C[lowe]s. They occupied the greater part of the day. Every member of the Conference was deeply affected, and many, with myself, wept much. Oh! Lord, do Thou interpose, and then all things work together for good.' For a fuller discussion of the relations between Bourne and Clowes, see J. T. Wilkinson, *William Clowes 1780–1851*, Appendix B.

Book Room. It was entitled: *A Few Plain Facts: Faith and Industry superior to High Popularity, as manifested in the Primitive Methodist Connexion, between the Conference of the year 1824 and that of 1833—nine years.*[17] It was a further illustration of the evil of 'particularism'. The pamphlet set one group of districts against another, stating that, despite their prestige, the districts of 'high popularity'—Nottingham, Hull, and Sunderland—had only added a small number of members to the Connexion whilst the other group—Tunstall, Norwich, and Manchester—of 'low popularity', had, 'through faith and industry', contributed many thousands. Regrettable as it is, it has to be admitted that Bourne appears to have been responsible for the unfortunate pamphlet. Copies eventually reached Hull, and the preachers there resolved upon an examination of the Hull Circuit, with the result that it was shown that between January 1819 and 1835 the circuit had raised up 14,116 souls.[18]

The whole episode was a sad misunderstanding. It may well be that in it we find the first signs of increasing age which, intensified by long hardships in earlier years, sometimes suspended sober judgement and self-control.

IV

Of the labours of Bourne in 1834 there is little to record. The sole excerpt from his Journal gives a brief account of a sojourn in South Staffordshire and Shropshire. At Birmingham he advised a scheme of 're-missioning', similar to that adopted at Manchester,[19]

... where a number meeting, at nine o'clock in the Sabbath mornings, sing along a street, stop and make a ring, one or two pray about two minutes, borrow a chair, speak six or eight minutes: sing on again in procession: stop and act as before, holding several such meetings, and singing in procession to the chapel at half-past ten.

Bourne found great delight in visiting 'the first infant-school established by the Primitive Methodists', which was at Wolverhampton, in charge of a governess. 'It was delightful to see

[17] So far as we know, no copy of the circular is extant (Kendall, II.361–2).
[18] William Garner, who was there at the time, makes the following comment (*Life of William Clowes* (1868), pp. 366–7): 'It was no doubt aimed at Clowes, and it hit the mark. It wounded his spirit. . . . He expressed his astonishment at the unprovoked and needless attack; but he did not allow it to do much harm.'
[19] *PMM*, 1835, pp. 114–16. The scheme was begun in Manchester on account of the cholera epidemic in 1832, when there seemed to be a deepened spiritual need and new sensitiveness to appeal.

amusement and instruction so beautifully united.' At Wellington Bourne spoke at a large missionary meeting in the Independent Chapel.

We have also some account of an unfortunate happening at Bemersley, when, on the night of 27th March, the Book Room was destroyed by fire, about £2,000 worth of property and material being consumed. The fire appears to have originated from the flue of the stove [20] used to dry the papers. About one-half of the property belonged to James Bourne,[21] and the remainder to the Connexion. An immediate appeal was made to the societies to contribute towards covering the loss.[22]

We have little information as to Bourne's activities during 1835.[23] All we know is that during March of this year he visited Nottingham, and was deeply distressed on account of the situation in that circuit. Some time earlier it had suffered serious division; some members had withdrawn, and certain social functions had become contaminated by intemperance, and the matter had got into the public press. All this gave him 'much trial of mind and deep thought'. But by this time the situation was improving, and 'this was looked upon as a miracle of mercy'. Bourne was able to write: 'I have had to endure much grief and sorrow of heart in the afflictions of this beloved circuit; but the Lord has made all amends.' [24]

Bourne's journey thither was an arduous one. His brother James, having driven him from Bemersley to Leek, Bourne found the coach had departed before its time, and so he walked fifteen miles to Ashbourne.

There was a very strong wind with rain occasionally: and the wet having blown into my shoes, the skin got off my heels; but I still

---

[20] *Gen. Mins.*, 1834, p. 8. cf. J. Hallam, MS Journal, 1st April 1834. We venture the suggestion that some, if not all, of that portion of Bourne's MS Journal for the years 1821–34 was probably destroyed by this fire; against this suggestion there is the fact that Walford makes no mention of any such reason, and if they had thus perished, one might reasonably expect him to have known about it. As we have already seen (*supra*, p. 121), no MSS for this period were in his possession when he compiled the *Memoirs*.

[21] 'Mr James Bourne desires nothing for that portion of the loss which belonged to him; but hopeth that in time, by the kind providence of God, he shall be able to surmount it' (*Gen. Mins.*, 1834, p. 8).

[22] During the first year the response to the appeal amounted to nearly £100 (*Gen. Mins.*, 1835, p. 7). By 1837 it reached almost £500. One penny per member had been asked for.

[23] Perhaps we may discern the foresight of Bourne in a resolution of the Tunstall Conference of 1835, stating that no travelling preacher should 'be allowed to make speeches at political meetings nor at parliamentary elections'. The Reform Bill of 1832 had provided new political opportunities.

[24] *PMM*, 1835, pp. 198–200.

walked on; when I had walked nearly five miles more, the mail took me and brought me to Derby, where I took coach to Nottingham. My heels had bled considerably, but I got my feet washed and hoped they were not much worse.[25]

Two days later, on the Sunday, we find him in the Sunday school hearing the spelling lessons of the children in the alphabet class! Then he preached three times that day. We find this significant note, following the account of evening service:

The congregation was great, and at the conclusion, being much exhausted, I retired; but I was informed that, in the prayer-meeting after, several found peace.

Bourne's labours during the years were now beginning to take their toll.

There is only the most meagre account of Bourne's work during 1836. We find that in February he visited Oldham, where the following incident occurred after the forenoon service.

At half-past one we assembled in the street before the chapel door. . . . We then moved in procession through several streets, and through both market-places. There was by far the greatest number of people I ever saw in a procession. . . .

When we had been moving some time, I happened to turn my head, and was aware of a little girl, about three or four years of age, having hold of my coat and walking by my side in an orderly manner. This a little surprised me. I put her on the footpath to walk with some other girls, but she was immediately at my side again as before. And however dirty the streets or difficult, she kept her place. After we had stopped to pray or speak, she was at once at her place again: and when the street was very dirty I occasionally took her by the hand. I felt a little anxiety lest the little creature should be hurt. But all went well. . . . I afterwards found that this little girl's conduct had drawn the attention of many.[26]

The very recording of this incident by Bourne is illustration of his deep love for little children—a glimpse into the heart of the man. In the afternoon and evening Bourne again preached. Including his short discourses during the procession, he had preached ten sermons on this occasion, besides visiting the schools and leading the class—extraordinary labours indeed for one who was in his sixty-fourth year.[27]

During April he attended the Hull District Meeting at

[25] *PMM*, 1835, p. 196.   [26] ibid., 1836, p. 189.
[27] See letter from Samuel Atterby, 14th February 1836 (*PMM*, 1836, pp. 271-2): 'Hugh Bourne's visit to Oldham has been productive of much good.'

Pocklington,[28] that of the Sunderland District at Westgate,[29] and that of the Manchester District at Liverpool.[30]

Following the Conference at Lynn, in May, Bourne visited Chester in July. He walked a distance of twenty-seven miles, of which he made the following note in his Journal:

> Being now turned three-score and four years of age, and being sensible of much bodily failure through the decays of age, and in particular in regard of walking, I never expected to be again able to walk twenty-seven miles in a day. But the Lord has been gracious to me.

Three days later on his return journey he covered twenty-eight:

> Though I was very footsore, I suffered no material inconvenience. . . . I now see that a person cannot tell what he may be enabled to do, if he trusts in the Lord, and applies himself fully to the work.

For the year 1837 information is even more scanty. From scattered references we know that, after attending the Sheffield Conference in the middle of May, he came into the Norwich District, and then on to Nottingham—'the Divine glory rested upon the services'. He was at Motcomb, near Shaftesbury, probably early in June. During the closing days of the year he visited the Burland Circuit, and then came to Chester, from whence he passed to Runcorn and Liverpool, returning home through Northwich. Beyond these passing notices we have no further record of his labours for 1837.

The year 1838 was marked by bodily distress. A significant resolution of the Conference at Darlaston (where he had been taken suddenly ill, and had to remain in bed during the sessions) records that if, through indisposition, Bourne was unable to fulfil the office of editor, John Flesher should be called in to assist.[31] Nevertheless, Bourne appears to have travelled considerably, though at time under affliction. In April he was at Reading.[32] Two tours are recorded in the printed extracts from his Journal. In July he came into Herefordshire.[33] He preached in the new chapel at Hereford, though 'under much anxiety, doubtful whether I should be able to preach more than twice'; the next day he preached at 'the Cottage chapel' in Cwm Circuit, and the day afterwards at Bromyard. From there he went

---

[28] *PMM*, 1836, p. 307.   [29] ibid., p. 310.
[30] ibid, p. 348.   [31] Conf. MS Jour., 1838.
[32] *PMM*, 1840, p. 131. Bourne preached from Numbers xiv : 21. One who heard records: 'The Lord made that sermon a blessing to many.'
[33] ibid, 1839, pp. 25–6.

to Leominster, Dilwyn, and Weobly, returning to Hereford for a camp-meeting some miles out of the city, 'on a common, the name of which I have forgot', and coming back to his lodgings 'between ten and eleven at night'. On 30th July he took coach to Birmingham, stayed the night, and then set out by railway for home. He notes that a passenger put into his hands a copy of Osborne's *Guide to the Grand Junction Railway*, in which was a description of Darlaston, and a note about the chapel there: 'It is one of the largest and best constructed edifices of its kind in the country.' It brought more than passing pleasure to him.

On 27th September he came to Liverpool, 'so very ill that I expected to be obliged to return'; at five o'clock, however, he boarded steamer, and the next day reached Glasgow, where he preached 'but in much pain'. At night he was at Paisley; then to Edinburgh and on to Alloa—'an ancient town, newly visited by our people', where he found some thirty members in society. Returning to Edinburgh—'the people in Scotland have much zeal for the Lord and to me they showed great kindness'—he took steamer to Newcastle, and had a rough voyage. He saw the new Nelson Street chapel, and then came to Hexham and stayed once more at Bavington Hall, where 'their kindness to me was very great'.[34] Three days later he crossed country to Carlisle, where he 'found all well'; the next morning, at eight o'clock, he went 'by the swift canal boat' to the port, and came on board steamer for Liverpool, which he reached at midnight. 'The wind being strong we were much tossed about and had much sea-sickness.' He came home by railway, and adds an unusual entry:

I called on the doctor. . . . The journey has been in much affliction: but the friends have been very kind. I have gone through the business, and other labours tolerably well, and have providentially got on well with my editing. To this I have been able to apply myself both by sea and land.[35]

v

During 1839 Bourne went to London by way of Birmingham and Coventry, reaching there on 19th April. After staying three days, he came down the Thames by steamer to Sheerness, where he preached under difficulty, having a severe pain

[34] Bourne remarks on the temperance zeal in the Shafto household. 'The public house in the village of Bavington is done away, and a coffee house established for the accommodation of travellers.'

[35] *PMM*, 1839, p. 26.

in the head. He spent two days here on editorial work, and on the 28th went twelve miles to Sittingbourne, in Kent, to a camp-meeting. Two days later he came to the home of John Flesher, in London. The next day he travelled to Reading, from which he made an excursion 'for the opening of the city of Windsor. . . . Our people are taking it up as a mission, and this was their first day.' From Reading he came to Newbury, where he preached in the burying-ground, and then he moved on to Stratton, in Wiltshire, and from there to Wootton Bassett for the meeting of the Brinkworth District.[36] The meeting over—'the business went on well'—Bourne came north through Ashton Keynes to Cheltenham, where he preached in the chapel. The next day, 16th May, he travelled to Staffordshire to attend the Tunstall District Meeting at Brierley Hill, near Dudley. There was a camp-meeting—'very powerful'—at which he preached to the children who had marched to the ground.

We find Bourne next at Runcorn, early in August, and a week later he is in the Isle of Man, at Douglas, attending a large camp-meeting: '. . . many souls were made happy in the field. . . . When the meeting was near its close, I had a manifestation of Jesus Christ which affected the body.' By this he overcame his exhaustion, and gained sufficient strength to preach in the chapel at night. 'There was a breaking out among the children. . . . He turns His hand upon the little ones.' Bourne returned to the mainland on Tuesday, 13th August.[37] We have no further record of his visit to the island.

Towards the end of September—'my low state of health appearing to require a change of air'—he spent a few days in the house of Francis Horobin, at Ramsor, where he worked at editing. But on 1st October he journeyed through Leek to Ashbourne, and on to Derby. Then he went by rail to Nottingham, and two days later to Leicester, where he spent a whole week preaching and lecturing.[38] From there he moved to

[36] It is doubtless due to the suggestion of Bourne that this District Meeting passed a resolution that preachers should address part of their discourses to children in every service, and this was adopted connexionally at the Bradford Conference the following June. It is interesting to record that at this Brinkworth meeting five children were brought to Bourne for baptism (*PMM*, 1840, p. 29).

[37] 'His coming to us was unexpected but seasonable and highly acceptable to all. . . . He scarcely spent one moment unemployed, although much indisposed in body, he was all life.'—Letter from Samuel Atterby to James Bourne, 15th October 1839 (*PMM*, 1840, pp. 115–16).

[38] For some time Bourne had lectured on the origins of the Connexion as well as as upon the growth of Christianity and the principles of religious revival, the last-named subject probably being prompted by Finney's book *Lectures on Revival of Religion* (1835), a book which he had recentlyr ead.

Loughborough and back again to Nottingham, returning to Bemersley on 22nd October, with a heart filled with gratitude for the kindness of many friends. Early in November we find him in the Buckinghamshire mission.[39]

Our final glimpse of Bourne during 1839 is on a brief excursion to Blackburn, in December, to preach anniversary sermons in the new chapel. Three days later he had a similar engagement at Preston.

Sometimes his days were almost beyond his strength. He writes:

If I live till the third of April, 1840, I shall have numbered sixty-eight years; and as it hath pleased Almighty God to visit me with affliction and infirmity, my time in the world may not be long.[40]

During 1840 Bourne tried an experiment in preaching. At some of the large gatherings many people remained for tea between the meetings, and this had to be taken in the chapel, as no other buildings were available. Bourne perceived an opportunity and, as at Leeds, on 1st March he preached from the pulpit whilst the people took tea. 'All this went on well.'

Being appointed to attend the Brinkworth District Meeting, to be held at Newbury, in Berkshire, Bourne came to London early in May, where he stayed for more than a week. On the 13th he visited Silchester, in Hampshire, and the next day came to Newbury. The work completed, he returned by rail to London, coming through Reading on the 20th, the next day coming north to Staffordshire, where his brother met him and conveyed him home.

Early in June he went to Stockport, where he rejoiced in the success of the large Sunday school and gave lectures to the teachers. The day following he came by rail to Manchester—'six miles in about fifteen minutes'—to prepare for the Conference. At five o'clock the following morning he preached 'with good liberty in the Mersey Street chapel'; the next day he administered the sacrament to a large company; the day after was a great camp-meeting, followed by three love-feasts in the evening. Through the labours of the day some sixty souls found liberty.

Most of September was given to the Brinkworth Circuit, in Wiltshire, 'in an agricultural part where the working people earn about eight or ten shillings a week and find their own board'. Some sixteen appointments were planned for him, and whilst there he saw at first hand the financial scheme for debt-reduction on chapel property, which had originated some two years before in 1838, at Wootton Bassett. It came to be known as 'The Golden System',[41] and consisted of the securing at one anniversary promises of friends to collect or give certain sums of money towards the collections of the next. Bourne found the system being tried out at many places, and he heartily espoused it. In illustration of his enthusiasm we may note that when he came to Stroud, after leaving Wiltshire, he spoke of the system and

...with great delight in the evening service I introduced two donations I had brought from Wootton Bassett. These amounted to five-pence. At Wootton Bassett a number of children gave in their names to raise five shillings each for the chapel: and one of these, not eight years of age, presented me with a donation for Stroud chapel, of three pence: the sister, of two pence for the same. The presenting of these donations in our Stroud chapel went well.

On his return to Bemersley, Bourne won over his brother James to the advocacy of the system, and in October it was introduced to societies in the Tunstall District. Bourne also gained the consent of his brother to the publication of an explanatory circular [42] to be sent to the circuits. This was printed and posted, on 21st October, by Bourne at his own expense. A reprint was made a month later, and applications for it became so numerous that a third edition, of more than three thousand copies, was prepared. The widespread adoption of the scheme and the joy of finding chapel debts reduced amply repaid Bourne for his personal outlay and his frequent journeying to secure its adoption in various parts of the Connexion.

VI

We have only fragmentary information concerning Bourne's travels in 1841, there being no journal record. All that is dis-

---

[41] It is sometimes referred to as the 'Wootton Bassett System' because of its place of origin (*PMM*, 1841, p. 36). The name 'Golden System' originated with Bourne, who said he thought it 'worthy of being written in letters of gold'; not, as sometimes has been suggested, because golden sovereigns were asked for as donations (Walford, II.278).

[42] For reprint see *PMM*, 1841, pp. 450 ff. Details of management of the scheme are set forth on pp. 59–60. An outcome of the system was the suggestion of a General Chapel Fund for the Connexion, made by Bourne in 1842 (*PMM*, 1842, p. 417).

coverable in scattered references tells us that he came to Swansea [43] in Glamorganshire, for the meeting of the Brinkworth District, travelling with about fifteen others from Bristol on 6th May. Permission was given to hold service on board ship, and through this preaching one passenger found salvation. The roughness of the sea caused distress, but 'after this we had a stiller sea and another preaching'.

In June he came to the Conference at Reading, and the most notable feature is that in addition to the usual preachings, camp-meetings, and love-feasts, a specially appointed service was that of 'The Holy Sacrament of the Supper of the Lord'. 'This proved to be one of the crowning ordinances, and its celebration will long be remembered.' It was administered by Bourne and his brother James, and William Clowes. So far as we are aware, this was the first occasion on which a service of Holy Communion was appointed in connexion with the annual Conference, and it is worth while noting the details of the occasion as recorded by Bourne.[44]

It was administered in the large Sunday-school room on Saturday evening, June 12, 1841. . . . The room was well set out. At one end stood a table on which the elements were placed; and on either side, and at the end of the table, were placed several forms at a suitable distance, for the people to kneel while partaking the sacrament. . . . There was so great an attendance that, large as the place was, it was nearly filled.

After singing and prayer, one of the brethren [45] stood up and spoke of the first institution of the feast of the passover. . . . He next spoke of our Lord continuing it in the Christian Church. . . . He then took up a plate from the table, which had on it a number of unleavened cakes, and held it up in the presence of the people. . . . Then, setting down the plate, he took up a cake and broke it in the presence of the people, using the words of the apostle, where he speaks of the body of Christ being broken for us. This made a deep impression.

He then took up a bottle (there were four on the table) and he poured out into a cup, and spoke of the blood of Christ which was

---

[43] *PMM*, 1841, p. 382.

[44] *PMM*, 1841, pp. 353–5. In this issue there are explanatory accounts of the sacrament, which would suggest that this was a new development. Hitherto the love-feast had been the custom, and for many years (until the end of the nineteenth century), as in the early centuries of the Christian Church, the love-feast and the communion continued side by side as the usage of the Connexion. Only occasional references to the holding of the service of the supper occur in Bourne's Journal prior to 1841.

[45] That this was almost certainly Bourne himself is suggested by details of the account, because it is likely that he was originally responsible for the holding of the service.

shed for us. . . . He observed that it was prepared in a way similar to that which the Jews prepared their passover wine. . . . So nearly following the footsteps of our Lord in His instituting the sacrament gave great satisfaction.

A quantity of bread was immediately broken into small pieces on one of the plates: and the three appointed to minister took the sacrament. A number then came forward and kneeled at the forms placed there for that purpose: and one administered the unleavened bread and another the unleavened wine, the cup of blessing. The other, during this, broke an additional quantity of bread to be in readiness; and gave other needful assistance. When these had partaken, a verse was given out: and whilst it was singing they rose from their knees and returned: and a number more took their places. In this way they proceeded until all had partaken in obedience to the order of our Blessed Lord.

It was a great satisfaction to all, it being the first time that many of them had taken the sacrament with unleavened bread in a cup of blessing which was the fruit of the vine. . . .

At the close, many of the delegates wished for and obtained each a piece of the bread that remained, to take with them, to their respective circuits; and others obtained pieces also.[46]

Certain resolutions [47] passed at the Reading Conference of 1841 suggest that there was complaint in the minds of some regarding the work of Bourne as editor, notwithstanding the fact that the magazine seemed still to maintain its former efficiency. The reason for this criticism seems to have been that Bourne had taken John Hallam into the Bemersley household,[48] partly because the latter's health was such that circuit work was too exacting, and partly because his being there would relieve Bourne for other duties. Bourne had agreed to pay one-half of Hallam's allowance, and James Bourne the other. The arrangement continued for some two years, at a cost to Hugh Bourne of nearly £50. But the experiment proved disappointing.

Whether this is the explanation or not, at the end of 1841 Bourne laid down the task of editorship which he had diligently fulfilled since 1820. In a carefully written word,[49] 'as the next volume enters on a new arrangement', Bourne thinks 'it

[46] In *PMM*, 1841, pp. 34–5, Bourne gives detailed instructions for the making of unleavened bread and of 'pure wine from raisins, after the manner of the Jews for the Passover'.

[47] Conf. MS Jour.: 'A small committee was formed to draw up regulations for editorship.'

[48] This was probably in 1836, when Hallam had been appointed to assistant-editorship by the Conference. See letter from Hugh Bourne, dated 5th July 1841, in Walford, pp. 289–90.

[49] Entitled 'Preface', December 1841.

may not be amiss' to review the origin and progress of the magazine under his editorship. He summarizes its features and concludes with reference to his own responsibilities for it:

Promoting these great and extensive benefits has cost the editor abundance of authoring and a large outlay of money for necessary books. . . . But he has endeavoured to serve his own generation by the will of God.

At the following Conference at Newcastle, in 1842, it was resolved [50] that Bourne 'be relieved from the anxiety and toil of the editorship', and for the following reasons: that he had 'long borne the burden in this department'; that he might be 'more unfettered in the evening of his life, so that, when his help or counsels are sought for, he may be at liberty to attend to the solicitation of his friends, if agreeable to himself'; and that probably 'under the editorship of some popular man the sale of our magazine might be considerably extended'. He was requested to complete the work until the end of 1842, the new editor, John Flesher, to begin his duties in the September of that year.

It is more than likely that Bourne felt keenly the suggestion that he should retire from the post, and there was more than a hint that another would be welcomed, but he seems to have accepted with grace and goodwill, the more so as it was soon to open other doors of new service for the church.

At this Conference Bourne was placed on the list of super-annuated preachers, and a grant was made to him of an annuity of £25 a year.[51] William Clowes also became a supernumerary, and received a similar allowance. The Conference resolution was as follows:

That the Conference records its thanks to Almighty God for the very great service rendered by Bros Hugh Bourne and William Clowes to the Primitive Methodist Connexion, which under God they have been the chief agents in raising or founding, and whose services are still blest by the Lord: and furthermore we unite in fervent prayer for their future welfare.[52]

[50] Conf. MS Jour., 1842.

[51] As there was no superannuation fund then in existence, the amount was shared equally between the funds of the Book Room, the Conference, and the Assistant Sick-Preachers' Fund. Bourne also received a similar sum from the Preachers' Friendly Society—so that his annual income was about £50 per annum. Unfortu-nately, he had soon to devote a considerable portion of his resources to aid his brother, who had become financially embarrassed; also to contribute to the relief of the Burslem chapel, of which he was a trustee.

[52] Conf. MS Jour., 1842.

As a testimony to the regard in which they were both held, Bourne's name was to remain at the head of the Tunstall station, and that of Clowes similarly for the Hull Circuit. Each was given 'inalienable right to be a member of successive Conferences'.

VII

Bourne had now reached seventy years of age, and it was a great gratification to him that the Conference gave him liberty to collect subscriptions on behalf of a new chapel at Mow Cop —a project dear to his heart.

We know little of his journeying throughout this year. He attended the meeting of the Norwich District at a village, Rockland St Peter, in Norfolk,[53] where he conducted a sacramental service similar to that already recorded. 'Great was the Holy One of Israel in the midst of us.'

In November [54] he visited the societies in Manchester and Oldham, returning home through Stockport and Poynton and Macclesfield. From there he walked to Congleton and on to Bemersley, covering 'a full twenty-one miles on foot for the day'. 'I was very footsore and much tired.'

In the middle of December, Bourne set off to Derbyshire, where he laboured in and around Chesterfield until the turn of the year. On 3rd January 1843, he set off by train to York, in order to be present at a 'teetotal meeting' in the Merchant's Hall, at which he spoke. This theme had steadily mounted in his mind, and shortly after his superannuation we find him energetically entering into the temperance movement, and journeying throughout the country to preach temperance sermons or give lectures, or to preside at temperance meetings. Whilst at York he had 'great liberty in all the preachings' round about, and after a fortnight he moved northwards to Thirsk, a week later going on to Northallerton. On 3rd February he came to Darlington, when he preached to immense congregations and also met the preachers in conference. Eight days later he went by rail to Shildon, in county Durham, where he touched an interesting fact about himself: 'One of the brethren said he had fixed my portrait up at St Petersburg, in Russia.' Thence he moved on to Bishop Auckland, Stockton, and

---

[53] *PMM*, 1842, p. 395.
[54] The extant MS Journal begins again 9th November 1842, and continues without break for the next ten years.

Middlesbrough, 'quite a new town lately sprung up', from whence he passed on, after some days, to Hartlepool. On 1st March he came to Durham. 'I had good liberty but expected to fail in the pulpit, through bodily weakness.' He found that the circuit had increased by one thousand during the year, and he preached at many of the surrounding colliery villages. 'Multitudes in these collieries have been converted to God.' Thence he came north to Sunderland and, much in need of rest, went twenty miles on to Knitsley Grange, the hospitable home of John Gordon Black,[55] where he stayed for some days.

From here he came south-east into Weardale, where he laboured for a week, and then moved up into Allendale. But the work was heavy:

> I was much worn out. I have for twelve weeks had people at almost every place to give out hymns and pray, otherwise I could not have stood the labours. . . . I am aware of failing much.

He had now reached seventy-one years of age. Crossing over the fell he came into Cumberland to the region round Alston, and then on to Penrith, and by coach to Kendal. On 12th April he travelled by boat and rail to Preston, and the next day on to Manchester, reaching home on 21st April.[56]

Yet he stayed only one day, and spent most of it preparing the books for the Norwich District Meeting, which he was to attend in place of his brother, James. The next day, therefore, he set off to Ashbourne, and then on to Derby and Nottingham. On the 28th he travelled by coach to Lincoln, then by steamer to Boston, and from there by coach to Lynn, to be 'welcomed at the house of my old friend, Mr Sainty, butcher, Norfolk Street'. Two days afterwards he reached Norwich for the meeting. This being concluded, he hastened on to the meeting of the Hull District, and on 16th May was again in Bemersley. 'The Lord has given me journeying mercies.'

On Sunday, 21st May, he preached at a camp-meeting on Mow Cop, but the next day was 'extremely ill with

---

[55] cf. Clowes *Jour.* (1844), p. 362: 'I preached a short discourse in the house of Mr Black to his family and servants. I was greatly pleased with the order and management of this Christian household, on which the blessing of God eminently rested.' John Gordon Black (1791–1851) was one of the original signatories to the Deed Poll. 'His home became a rallying point for evangelical nonconformity in the borough' (*PMM*, 1852, pp. 129–34. See also Kendall, II.204).

[56] For 16th April there is an interesting item: 'I signed the petition to Parliament against the Education Bill.'

over-labouring'. Yet four days later he was on the road again, moving in the direction of Nottingham, to attend the Conference.

The latter half of July was given to South Staffordshire, in and around Walsall and Wolverhampton, whence he moved into the Dudley Circuit, preaching there at a large camp-meeting 'to hosts of children'. He then came through Stour-bridge and Halesowen to Birmingham, on by rail to Coventry, where he administered the sacrament. Leaving there, he travelled through Leamington to Banbury and the surrounding villages. An interesting scene is recorded: it took place in an Oxfordshire lane, on a September afternoon.

By the way, in a stubble, were many women and children glean-ing: some were our members. A number of children were in the lane, as if just come out of the field. I engaged them and many of the women and children flocked near; quite a congregation. It was a time of liberty and then we prayed. I was much blessed.[57]

On 9th September Bourne came to Oxford, and in the evening went on to Witney, returning a week later to Oxford, and, going on by carrier, to Wallingford. On the 23rd he reached New-bury, and then went on to Hungerford, where he found that the society had been disturbed by the influence of the Latter-Day Saints. From there he came to Marlborough, and made his way northwards through Broad Town—where, with the Rechabites, he joined in his first 'teetotal procession', and also preached on this theme in the open-air—on to Wootton Bassett. At the beginning of October he returned to Oxford, again to Wallingford, and then by train some fifty miles to Chippenham. On the 30th he came south to Trowbridge, where he preached at the opening of what had formerly been an Irvingite Chapel. On 8th November he was at Yatesbury, where with great interest he saw the White Horse on the Downs. Two days later he came by rail to Reading, and on to Great Marlow and High Wycombe, where he preached in the Independent Chapel, and spent several days in the Thames Valley, returning to Reading at the end of the month, going then to Newbury, and south to Andover, in Hampshire. He stayed in this region until January, preaching daily in the villages all around.

On 19th January he travelled to Southampton, and a week later crossed to the Isle of Wight, where he stayed twelve days, then returning to Southampton, four days later taking train

[57] Bourne MSS (Jour.), 5th September 1843.

for London. After two days' preaching—and a visit to the
Thames Tunnel—he came by rail to Birmingham, and reached
Bemersley on 16th February, after being absent for nearly seven
months. But it was a sad homecoming. 'All in desolation and
distress. Lord undertake for us: no arm but Thine can do it.'
It was now that he learnt of his brother's serious financial
condition.

This discovery on the part of Bourne seems somewhat surprising, until we remember that, though deeply attached to
James, he had never been accustomed to make inquiry into
financial matters, and had trusted his brother's commercial
insight. The latter's refusal of compensation from the Conference
after the Bemersley fire had confirmed Bourne in the opinion of
his brother's security. Unfortunately, James had become en-
tangled in financial enterprise with certain potters, to whom he
had loaned money, in one case to a sum of £6,000, and all had
been lost.[58]

The month of March was spent in visiting the Cheshire
societies, and working northward to Manchester, where he
spent his seventy-second birthday. 'I have been a professor of
religion forty-five years: I trust the Lord will keep me to the
end.' That night he preached in the Oxford Road chapel. The
next day he came to Oldham, and then by rail to Wakefield,
and after nearly a fortnight he went on to Pontefract. He visited
the potteries, near Castleford, and came back to Bemersley,
early in May.

The next day he set off to Market Drayton, and the day
following he walked nineteen miles to Shrewsbury, to attend
the District Meeting, at which there was a large camp-meeting
and love-feast held in the Town Hall. He returned home on the
20th. During his travels he had endeavoured to secure donations towards the Burslem chapel, and he rejoiced to be able to
pay over some £18.

A week later he was on trek again for Derby, and on to
Nottingham, from thence to Lincoln, and by steamer to
Boston, reaching Lynn, for the Conference, on 4th June.
Especially noteworthy was the camp-meeting held upon a
piece of land some two acres in extent. 'It appeared to be filled
with people: such a sight I have seldom seen. I am of the
opinion that there was about twenty thousand.'

For Friday, 11th June 1844, there is a significant entry:

[58] Walford, II.304.

Much was spoken relative to our cause in Canada; and this day I agreed to go to America, and to take up the superintendency as far as necessary in Canada. This came into my mind, and at the same time into the minds of several of the brethren. We thought it was the will of the Lord. . . . O Lord, Thy will be done.

On the 14th Bourne left Lynn by steamer for Hull. He had time for reflection upon his recent decision.[59]

The trouble of mind relative to America remained, but in reading the lives of some pious women who lived in suffering times, the clouds broke, and I gave myself up to God, to be cast into the waves on the voyage, or, if I arrived safe, in Canada, then to do and suffer all the will of God whatever it might be.

From Hull he crossed to Lincolnshire and then returned, to find the preparation of his outfit for the American journey progressing. On the 22nd he went by rail to Leeds; [60] two days later he travelled to Manchester, and returned home. On 27th June he wrote: 'Preparing for America. My feelings were keen. I made my will.' [61]

The Journal continues:

Friday morning, June 28, 1844. I left Bemersley. The Lord knoweth whether I shall ever see it again. So I leave my brother James and all. My feelings were keen. O Lord, I beseech Thee, save him and save us all. He has been unfortunate, but the Lord will be with him and save him. O Lord, have mercy on us all.

I came to Manchester. . . . My feelings about Bemersley are still keen. O Lord, be with me.

So began his journey to America—in his seventy-third year!

[59] Bourne MSS (Jour.), in loc. cit.
[60] It was whilst here that Bourne resolved to write an account of his life. This is almost certainly the A Text of the Bourne MSS (Auto.).
[61] See Appendix III. Amongst Bourne's papers, Walford discovered a document, dated 'Lynn Regis. June 12th 1844'; it is a remarkable illustration of his Christian charity. It contained his proposals to the Conference: (1) that the missionary committee should pay annually his subscription to the Friendly Society and deduct the amount from the payment due from this annuity, the balance to be paid to his brother, James Bourne, to relieve his distress; (2) that the annuities due from Conference funds should be devoted to the liquidation of the Burslem Chapel debt; (3) that the money contributed under a proposal by John Garner, made in the Conference for Bourne's assistance in America, be devoted to the same cause, and when all debts were paid, the balance to be put into the missionary funds (Walford, II.309–11).

CHAPTER TEN

MISSION TO AMERICA (1844–6)

O<small>N TUESDAY</small>, 2nd July 1844, Bourne went on board the *Oberon*, in the King's Dock, Liverpool, to begin his voyage to Montreal. Friends from Manchester and others were with him to bid him farewell. 'We prayed in the cabin and departed.'[1] 'The leave-taking was tender indeed.' Finding the vessel would not sail until the next day, Bourne crossed over into Cheshire, to the home of his friend, George Horbury, of Poulton. 'Our parting in his house was tender: he accompanied me a little way, and strengthened my hands in the Lord.' The next day the vessel set sail 'with a fair wind'. On the Saturday Ireland was 'fully in sight'; the day following, though unwell, Bourne attended Divine service twice. Things began to improve and we find him 'much engaged with scripture and A[dam] Clark[e]'s *Commentary*'. The vessel was making four knots. The days following brought a strong wind: 'the vessel pitches much and makes me very ill'. Yet Bourne 'was blest in exhorting and praying with the sailors on deck'. They had now been at sea a fortnight. On Sunday, 21st July, he preached in the afternoon. 'I thought of a night service, but was too unwell: but had the great satisfaction to hear them employed in a religious service among themselves: this is excellent!' An unfavourable wind brought stormy weather and for the next ten days Bourne was again ill. On Sunday, 11th August, though weak in body, he preached in the afternoon and at night read and prayed. 'I am of opinion the Lord is at work with every man we have on board.' The next day, with a fine morning and little wind, they got beyond Newfoundland, and the day afterwards sighted Cape Breton. They came into the St Lawrence on Saturday, the 17th; a week later the ship arrived at Quebec, at midnight on Saturday, 24th August.

[1] A letter from Samuel Longdin, of Manchester, describes the scene. 'It was affecting to see the venerable sire surrounded by friends, all deeply solicitous for his comfort. . . . Before we left him we entered the cabin, and joined our supplications to the God of all grace on his behalf: surely we were in the house of God. . . . Having closed our devotions, we bade him adieu in the name of the Lord. . . . He was perfectly happy' (*PMM*, 1844, p. 318).

The next day Bourne attended the Methodist chapel in the forenoon, and the Scotch church in the afternoon. The day following he disembarked from the *Oberon*, and boarded another vessel for the remainder of the journey. He reached Montreal on 27th August, where he was welcomed by James and Phœbe Cooper, his nephew and niece. For a few days he was compelled to rest, having had his foot damaged by a plank during the storm, but he seized the opportunity: 'I began to write out my hymns.' The following Sunday he worshipped in the morning at the Kilhamite chapel, and at the Methodist in the evening.

Twelve days later he left Montreal for the journey of 390 miles by steamer to Toronto. The passage through locks and canals made the progress slow. One evening he witnessed a sunset, which he describes:

The face of the sun was in appearance of a most beautiful red: and below it there appeared a glory coming from it, of an equally rich, deep and beautiful red. It was equal to the sun in width, and reached down to about three times the breadth of the sun in its length. . . . It continued more or less till the sun sank below the horizon. At the same time the western sky had but few clouds, and made a fine appearance of a faint red, or rather of an amber colour, and after the sun setting, it appeared for some time to tinge the water by its reflection. Glorious are Thy works, O Lord!

Many passengers were on board, and the following day Bourne gained permission to conduct Divine service: he expounded the third chapter of St John's Gospel. The captain requested him to hold a second service in the afternoon. The day after, whilst the ship was passing through the Rideau Lake, a little girl was lost overboard, just before they reached Kingston, on Lake Ontario. On 20th September Bourne landed at Toronto and was met by Mr William Lawson, one of the lay pioneers of the Canadian mission.

The work began immediately: appointments were planned and visitations arranged, with Toronto as centre; preaching continued almost daily without intermission, though entries in the Journal indicate that he spent much time in reading and writing.[2] Throughout his stay in America, his Journal chiefly consists of little more than a catalogue of the places he visited, with the usual routine of preaching, visitation, administration

---

[2] It was whilst in America that Bourne wrote the MS of his autobiography, B and (possibly) C Texts.

of affairs, and an occasional glimpse at some place of unusual interest to which he turned aside in the course of his travels. He makes reference to incidental things which he saw: the structure of a log-house; a new type of threshing-machine (about which he wrote an account for a farming journal); the brilliance of the sunlight on the snow; his first ride upon a sleigh on a journey of several miles; his first sight of some Indians, a few miles from Toronto; a Canadian saw-mill; the collecting of sap from the maple-trees and the boiling of maple-syrup; a woodpecker; a meal of Indian corn, eaten with milk, which he greatly liked.

Having spent the intervening weeks in Toronto and the neighbourhood, on 13th November Bourne attended his first quarterly meeting there—'a tolerable time'.

Beyond Toronto the Canadian mission had four circuits, and on 1st December Bourne moved into the Markham Circuit and remained there till the end of the month. On Christmas Day he came into the Etobicoke Circuit. 'A noble missionary meeting: the collection liberal.' A few days later he travelled into the Brampton Circuit: 'We held a missionary meeting and closed the labours of the year 1844.'[3] On the following day he walked twenty miles back to Toronto, to find a letter awaiting him, sent from the preachers of the society in New York, asking him to visit them on his return to England, whenever that might be. 'We believe it would be to the glory of God, and the good of our cause in this city.'

On 8th January he took a twenty-five-mile journey in a waggon through the snow, and had his first glimpse of a northern water, Lake Simcoe. Ten days later he preached at the opening of a new chapel in the Etobicoke Circuit, and a week later went farther, to the Brampton Circuit again, where he preached at a child's funeral. Snow fell heavily during February, and for some days travel proved impossible. He experienced the rigours of a Canadian winter. The quarterly meeting at Brampton was difficult, because of a case of ministerial discipline, a matter which gave him considerable anxiety for some time. One morning in the middle of February, having returned to Toronto, he went several miles on a sleigh over the frozen waters of Lake Ontario, and found some thrill in the experience.

[3] In 1844, including Toronto, the membership was just over 1,000, and there were 10 travelling preachers and 12 chapels; many small meetings were held in farmsteads and other houses (*PMM*, 1844, p. 300).

With improvement in the weather we find him journeying
on foot, twenty-five miles out of Toronto to Keyworth's
chapel, where he commenced a Sunday school, after gathering
some fifty children. 'I never saw a better school on the first
day.' The following day, in visitation, he came 'to the sugar
bush and helped in making molasses'. Here he spent his
seventy-third birthday. By the middle of May the Sunday
school had come to number more than a hundred scholars:
'This is wonderful: it is the Lord's doing.' This month brought
the usual quarterly conferences over which Bourne presided:
financial concerns caused him some anxiety for the Canadian
enterprise: 'this deprived me of sleep during the night.'

On 17th May Bourne went southwards by steamer to
Niagara Falls, in the region of which a new circuit had recently
been opened. He described his impressions:

I went much under the great sheet of water in the great Horse
Shoe Fall; I only went under the edge of it, but in doing that the
spray made me wet, running from my hat like a spout. I also went
through the museum . . . upwards of five thousand interesting
specimens.

At night he preached in the Falls chapel.

On 31st May Bourne crossed the border into the American
State, and came to Buffalo, where he preached in the open air
'with good liberty': in the forenoon he went to the service at
the Methodist Episcopal church. He stayed for some days in
this region, and one morning he went into the woods, where he
saw the felling of a hemlock tree and the peeling of the bark for
tanning. He travelled back to Buffalo 'on the top of a load of
timber'. A few days later he preached at the Methodist Episcopal church at Lancaster, some ten miles from Buffalo;
shortly afterwards he was at a camp-meeting at Niagara: a
similar meeting, though larger, was held at Buffalo, on 20th
July. He remained in these parts until early in August. Whilst
at Niagara he visited a farmer, helped in the harvest field, and
'learned the art of "cradling" wheat'. After the Niagara
quarterly meeting, he took steamer to Toronto in order to
attend the corresponding meeting there. For some days he had
suffered from an affection of the eye: he found relief by the
following remedy: 'My eyes were dressed with cold tea, the
best eye-water I ever had!' On his arrival at Toronto he found
sad news awaiting him, for letters informed him of a decrease

of some eight hundred members in the English work: 'strange news' it was to him.

On Tuesday, 26th August, he set off on his journey of some six hundred miles to New York. He came the first ninety miles by steam-boat on Lake Ontario to Rochester, then day and night, on three different boats drawn by horses, to Schenectady, which he reached on Friday afternoon, proceeding then by rail to Albany, and by steamer down the Hudson River to New York.

The decision to go to New York caused some concern to the missionary committee in England,[4] for whilst Bourne had gone out with a considerable measure of personal freedom, it had been understood that, 'as an adviser from the English Conference', he had gone to superintend the mission in British North America, and certain arrangements were in hand for sending out William Towler to assist in the States mission. Therefore, Bourne's decision meant the disapproval of the committee, but they accepted it and gave confirmation to the new enterprise.

There was also some disappointment at the scanty reports sent in by Bourne for publication in the magazine,[5] but there is evidence that such reports were written and despatched to England. On the other hand, Bourne himself declared that he did not receive any official communication from England during his months in British North America[6]; it was afterwards discovered that documents had been addressed to William Lawson and Bourne jointly; the former had received and opened them, but had not passed them on to Bourne, as intended.[7]

The day after his arrival at New York, Bourne preached three times, 'with gracious liberty'. So the work began immediately and went on without interruption as in the Canadian enterprise. A few days afterwards, Bourne engaged to be the New York preacher for a quarter, and on 13th October he presided over his first quarterly meeting of the American mission as a whole.[8] On the same day he called upon his

[4] MS Minute Book of American Mission, 1844.
[5] The committee instructed him to draw up a code of rules for the better government of the American societies, as he had done for the Canadian work. 'I got the power of attorney complete . . . and sent it by post to Manchester, Old England' (Bourne MSS (Jour.), 22nd July, 1845).
[6] MS Minute Book of American Mission, 1844, Min. 252.
[7] ibid., 1846.
[8] The American mission had societies in New York, Brooklyn, Pottsville, Philadelphia, and Paterson. In 1845 the membership was 433; travelling preachers 5, in addition to Bourne.

nephew, Joseph Bourne, but found his domestic circumstances difficult, it would seem, due to his intemperate habits.[9] During these early weeks Bourne was in regular correspondence with the friends of the Canadian mission, acting as Father-in-God to them, giving further counsel and direction though absent from them. Until the month of November Bourne was occupied with labours in New York and Brooklyn: on the 20th he went to Paterson, in New Jersey. Whilst there he went to view the Passaic Falls.

The rocks are great and appear to be strangely rent by convulsions of nature . . . to a great depth. These appear to be rather more than a yard wide, and in others less than a foot: the waters of the Passaic river fall into one of these remarkable chasms. These falls are of great service to the country; the river is turned out of its bed a short distance above the falls, and it turns cotton mills, linen mills, a woollen manufactory, foundry and machinery mills and a grist mill—in all thirty-five mills.

On the 23rd was the opening of a new chapel—an evening congregation of some seven hundred people.

A week later Bourne returned to New York, to prepare for his journey to Philadelphia. A day or two before his departure, whilst at the quay side, he saw a ship due to sail for Liverpool: it stirred in him a desire for the homeland, to which for some time he had turned with wistfulness. 'This gave me satisfaction: O Lord, direct me in this matter and preserve me and my means of going. The Lord Jesus grant it.'

On 16th December he came to Philadelphia, some ninety-six miles, and the next day he was taken round the city.

In this, one wish of my heart was gratified. I had long had a peculiar wish and desire to see Sir William Penn's city, and now the Lord in His mercy has granted me this. . . . I saw much to admire. . . . I do not remember seeing any city or town that has its streets so well and beautifully laid out.

Bourne found the work proceeding well, but the travelling preacher was sorely afflicted: Bourne counted his visit 'a gracious opening'. Three days later he went a further hundred miles to Pottsville, situated in a mountainous region, in order to attend the quarterly meeting at St Clair, some three miles to the north

---

[9] 'I gave him a letter I had written on Temperance, and it had weight with him. I trust the Lord will apply it to his heart' (Bourne MSS (Jour.), 20th October 1845). Bourne seems to have given him much paternal care, and was able later on to write: 'He is a new man'.

of the city. On Christmas Day he preached 'with good liberty' and during the love-feast in the afternoon 'there was a breaking through'.

> I received an extraordinary blessing, a manifestation; a hope that the Lord would look on my affliction,[10] and in His mercy would raise up the work afresh. I shall not forget this season.

In the evening he preached on 'The Birth of Christ', and the services closed with 'a protracted meeting', which continued for five days.

The next day Bourne came sixteen miles through the snow to Tamaqua for a chapel opening, where, in preaching, he had 'unusual liberty'. At a watchnight service in this new chapel he saw the breaking of the year 1846. 'Glory be to God for all His mercies.' The day following he returned to Pottsville, and visited Port Carbon, a railway centre, with its great works, at the head of the Philadelphia canal.

On 19th January he returned eighty miles by rail to Norristown on the Schuylkill River, where he found serious criticism of religion on account of the relation of the Episcopal Methodist church to the slave-trade, 'grievous indeed'. He stayed here just over a week, returning to Philadelphia on 28th January, preaching on that day in the Protestant Methodist church. 'I did not know but that it had been our own church.' One evening he attended an 'exhibition' and saw Scripture pictures displayed 'by magic lantern'—a new experience! On 10th February he went by steam-car sixty miles to South Amboy, and then by water back to New York, where he met the new missionary, William Towler, who had just arrived from England. Learning more of affairs in the homeland, by letter sent from the missionary committee, he felt a strong urge to return to England immediately. Three days afterwards he went to see an American ship, the *Montezuma*, and arranged for a passage to England, the fare to be ten dollars. Sixteen days later, on Sunday, 1st March, Bourne met the New York friends for the last time.

> W. Towler preached; sacrament followed with unleavened bread and unfermented cup; it was a solemn time and I gave a sovereign towards the rent of the church there.

[10] For some time he had suffered from inflammation of the left eye, and severe pains in the head, which at times became prostrating.

The next day he went to the ship and that night slept on board. As the wind was contrary, setting out was deferred, so he crossed to Brooklyn and preached; in remembrance of their kindness also, he left a little money for the work.

On the following day, 4th March, the ship sailed and the work of Bourne for the American mission came to an end. That evening the ship sailed through the river-ice and past Sandy Hook; the voyage across the Atlantic had begun. 'I am now once more on the ocean: the Lord's will be done.' Six days afterwards the ship passed the banks of Newfoundland; two days later serious trouble arose, as water began to enter the ship's hold and reached a depth of more than six feet, so that the position became dangerous, but the hole was stopped and the water pumped clear. The wind continued unfavourable, but on the fourteenth day a fine morning broke, and there was hope that within a week the shores of Ireland might be sighted. Much of the time Bourne spent in prayer and reading the Scriptures. 'I read much in A[dam] Clarke on the Acts.' There seemed little desire amongst the crew and passengers for any religious ministrations, though Bourne did conduct a religious service on board: 'I could only plead through mercy.'

The voyage appears to have brought new vigour to Bourne.

When I left New York I felt a general weakness throughout my whole frame; I thought it a general sinking of old age. But by the blessing of God it has left me. I had also an affliction in my eyes, and this was the worst; but it is gone, and I have recovered a portion of my former vigour. . . . Now I can praise God for returning health. To Him be glory for ever! [11]

On Tuesday, 24th March, in the evening, Cape Clear, in the south of Ireland, was sighted: 'the sight was cheering.' The ship reached Liverpool on Thursday, 26th March, after a voyage of twenty-two days. Bourne had endured amazingly, and apart from an injury to his right leg, due to a fall over a box shortly after the voyage began, he returned in good health. That same evening he attended a fellowship meeting in the Maguire Street chapel, Liverpool. The next day he wrote a long letter to his American friends.

[11] Bourne MSS (Jour.), 20th March 1846.

CHAPTER ELEVEN

CONFIRMING THE CHURCHES (1846-51

I

FOR SEVERAL days after his arrival in England Bourne spent much time writing letters to old friends, telling them of his safe return. On the afternoon of his seventy-fourth birthday, 3rd April, he set off from Liverpool, intending to walk through the Wirral to Preston Brook, but on account of the injury to his leg he had to change his plans. For some days he had to rest completely, but by the kindness of a friend he was able to visit Parkgate, in order to see the place where Wesley had often embarked for Ireland.[1] Under advice he abandoned his journey on foot, and, returning to Birkenhead by rail, he took steamer up the Mersey to Runcorn, and then came by canal to Preston Brook two days later. He reached Bemersley on 18th April, after an absence of nearly two years.

After a little more than a week at home he set off on foot for Derby and Nottingham. On 1st May he was at the District Meeting at Loughborough, and attended the camp-meeting. 'The work was powerful; but I was much overdone, much exhausted.' Two days later he went by rail to Birmingham, and then on to West Bromwich, proceeding by coach to Rubery, at the foot of the Lickey Hills, going on to Redditch, where he saw 'the manner of pointing needles'. On the 22nd he came to Dudley, on to Brierley Hill and Oldbury, and from there by canal-boat to Wolverhampton, and then by 'the penny-a-mile train' to the border of the Potteries, reaching Bemersley in time for the Conference at Tunstall on 3rd June

This Conference was a trying one for Bourne in consequence of the financial position regarding the Burslem old chapel, of which he was a trustee.[2] 'Troubles were on me not of my own

---

[1] Parkgate, some sixteen miles up the Dee from Chester, was the port for Irish traffic, prior to the silting up of the estuary.
[2] When the cause at Burslem had become established, Bourne had wished to be free from the burden of trusteeship, and so far as possible he pursued a plan of non-interference, but his name had remained to the old securities, even though the chapel had become connexional property. Negligence and mismanagement by some in whom he had placed confidence brought the financial crisis, and payment

causing.' The Conference sought inquiry as to the exact position, so as 'to take an equitable view of it, and the mode of free-
ing him therefrom',[3] stating also its willingness, if the case were
fully proved, to borrow connexional moneys and to authorize
an appeal to the Connexion, 'to effect Hugh Bourne's own
safety'. But Bourne felt the responsibility was his own, as a legal
trustee, and the position was therefore embarrassing for him.

Immediately after the Conference Bourne journeyed to
Manchester for the yearly meeting of the Friendly Society, from
whence he moved on to Blackburn, Bolton, and Oldham, after
which he spent most of a month preaching at places near his
own home. In the middle of August he set out upon a lengthy
sojourn in Yorkshire, and came to Rochdale, then walked
northwards to Hebden Bridge and Keighley—where, uncon-
cerned at his own danger, he called upon a preacher who was
afflicted with cholera, and where also he found a thousand wool-
combers out of work 'having turned out for wages'—and then
came to Skipton-in-Craven.

Coming south again into Lancashire, he reached Rochdale
in order to be present at a large teetotal meeting under the
auspices of the Rochdale Total Abstinence Society.[4] He comments: 'I set teetotalism forth as a branch of Christian temperance.' Afterwards he returned over the Pennines to Keighley,
and went across the moor to Otley, and north to Pateley Bridge,
in Nidderdale, where he stayed ten days preaching in the dale
chapels. Then, moving southwards to Ilkley, he reached
Bradford early in November, whence he came to Hudders-
field, and stayed in the region for more than three weeks, his
movements severely hampered by snow and frost. He reached
Dewsbury on 7th December, and two days later he was at
Birstall, where he visited the grave of John Nelson.[5] 'I saw also
the Wesleyan chapel in building on his grounds: old John built
it first: it was then rebuilt, and now splendidly building afresh.'
A few days afterwards he went to Shipley, where he spoke 'of
the Christian course from our Lord's time, in a brief way, until

due on promissory notes could not be met. The amount of debt had reached £100,
and Bourne was held legally responsible: also his brother's financial embarrassment caused his own difficulty for payment.

[3] Conf. MS. Jour., 1846, Mins. 195–201.

[4] The bills announcing Bourne's visit had the following comment: 'The religious
and moral portion of the country are specially requested to attend and hear this
veteran in the cause of Christianity and the people' (Bourne MSS (Jour.), 17th
September 1846).

[5] John Nelson, 1707–74. See *Journal of John Wesley*, Std. ed., III.11n., 136n., etc.

now'; on 18th December he came by train to Manchester, and on to Bolton, and back through Stockport and Macclesfield, to be home again in time for Christmas Day. He was greatly moved by preaching a sermon in the chapel at Mow Cop two days later: 'the congregations are large, so that in the spring they think to enlarge the chapel! Glory be to God!'

On the first day of 1847 Bourne came to Ramsor to preach the funeral sermon of his old friend, Joseph Buxton: he stayed in the area till nearly the end of the month, and then moved on to Burton-on-Trent, returning early in February to the Weaver Hills, but finding travel heavy. 'It was hilly and I had luggage. I was much tired.' He was home again at the end of the month.

Early March saw him setting out on an excursion into Shropshire, where he remained several weeks. During this time he was suffering again from the affliction of the eye,[6] and this time he tried a strange remedy, which he remembered from his boyhood, namely, a pounded mixture of 'bole armoniac', the white of an egg, bound round the wrist or arm, on the left if the right eye is affected, and on the right if the left eye.

Towards the end of April he came into the Burland Circuit, in Cheshire, and reached Chester on 8th May, where he remained for more than a week, then moving north-west through the Wirral to Liverpool, from whence he came to Manchester. He went on to Oldham, then across by train to Halifax, for the Conference on 1st June. This Conference was important for Bourne, in that it decided to undertake the case of the Burslem chapel and release him from further responsibility. This was a profound relief, because one of those who had loaned money to the chapel appears to have threatened legal proceedings, and Bourne had envisaged a possible imprisonment, as such was the penalty for debt in those days.[7]

II

But there was still a more serious matter which arose at the Halifax Conference of 1847. There is no precise record of what occurred, but there was occasion of serious tension between Bourne and Clowes. A sense of integrity in historical narrative

---

[6] The trouble appears to have been severe conjunctivitis, for Bourne speaks of the remedy being used for 'pearls in our eyes'. See *Family Recipes collected by H. Bourne*, p. 2. Sometimes hemlock was used in place of the white of an egg. The recipe was widely known at the time.

[7] This seems to be the implication of a letter written by Bourne on 24th February 1847 (Walford, II.307–8).

compels us to take notice of it, however reluctantly. So far as
can be discerned, the cause of the conflict seems to have been
the publication of Clowes's *Journals* in 1844, probably only a
short time before Bourne's departure for America. Bourne
makes no reference to it until September 1845, though he may
have seen a copy before leaving England. Bourne's references
to it in his American Journal are in the context of the recently
received news of the connexional decrease of 800 members
reported at the Conference of 1845, and, in what seems to us
a strange judgement, Bourne relates the two things as cause and
effect. Amazing as it may seem, Bourne characterizes Clowes's
Journals as 'mis-representation and deceit mixed with some
truths'. It was a blind judgement indeed; one in which the only
element of justification is the fact that the *Journals* do contain
inaccuracies and mis-statements, though without any intention
whatever of 'mis-representation or deceit'.[8] The fact was that
Clowes was writing from memory, without a manuscript
record of events before him, and dates and names in particular
not seldom became wrongly recorded. Also it may have been
that Bourne felt that in the record of Clowes, Bourne's own
significant place in the early history of the Connexion had not
received its just proportions—the very thing which Clowes
himself had experienced in regard to his share in the beginnings,
when he first read Bourne's *History of the Primitive Methodists*
twenty years before.[9]

It seems that Bourne had brooded upon these things, and on
his return to England had been severe in his criticism of Clowes,
an attitude which had naturally been resented by many. The
issue appears to have reached its climax in the Halifax Conference, for on that occasion Bourne freely and frankly made
public apology for his action. The document, which is extant
under Bourne's signature [10] is as follows:

I hereby give this Conference held at Halifax, 1847, a Pledge in
the sight of God and my brethren that I will, from this time, cease
from the course I have persued [*sic*] in speaking disrespectfully of
Mr William Clowes, whether publicly or privately, throughout the
Primitive Methodist Connexion or elsewhere.

Signed by me in the presence of my brethren in open Conference this eleventh day of June, one thousand eight hundred
and forty-seven.

HUGH BOURNE.

[8] For full discussion of this, see J. T. Wilkinson, *William Clowes 1780–1851* (1951).
[9] ibid, pp. 89.   [10] Conf. MS Jour., 1847.

The whole incident makes painful reading; but that is not the only aspect of the matter. We venture to assert that this document stands forth as witness to the strength and greatness of Bourne's personality, and is a record of a profound contrition of heart such as only a Christian soul could express. It should call forth our admiration for a man who, amidst the growing infirmities of old age, had been responsible for a tragic misunderstanding of one who for long years had been his colleague and friend. Suffice to say that the whole thing was a strange distortion of judgement in one whose discernment was usually so wise, but it was redeemed by this noble act of open admission that he had been wrong.

III

Immediately after the Conference of 1847 Bourne returned to Manchester, where he listened to James Caughey,[11] with deep satisfaction.

He preached with power and effect. Every stroke appeared to be aimed at the root; and each sentence appeared to search the heart. It was a common-sense oratory.

Bourne came home next day.[12] Within a couple of days, however, he was on his way north to Lancashire once more, on to Stalybridge and by rail to Sheffield, and thence by coach to Doncaster. 'I introduced the "golden system", and by the Divine blessing the engagements amounted to £10.' He remained in this area for nearly a month, and then moved northwards to Barnsley and Leeds, where he stayed in the house of Mr John Reynard. Thence he went to York, and a week later came to Thirsk, and on to Northallerton, where he preached at the market-cross. From there he came to Darlington, where he stayed ten days before going north to Sunderland—where he saw the launching of a ship, 'a noble and pleasant sight'. Whilst here he was presented with 'a new hat and black handkerchief, a new coat and waist-coat'.[13] He remained three weeks, preaching mainly in the colliery villages round about.

---

[11] James Caughey was a minister of the Methodist Episcopal church who spent several years in England, and by dramatic and sensational methods attracted large congregations. See *A Brief Memoir of the Labours of the Rev. James Caughey* (1847).
[12] Bourne MSS (Jour.), 16th June 1847.
[13] We get a glimpse into Bourne's simple mode of life here: '*Friday, 18.* I was at Tunstall and bought a quart of ink. I washed my coats yesterday and today and dyed them by brushing ink upon them. The ink was good.'

On 14th October he returned to Darlington, and moved westward to the head of Weardale, whence, after a stay of nearly a fortnight, he came to Richmond, then through Stokesley down to Bilsdale, and then north by rail to Newcastle-on-Tyne, which he reached on 13th December, remaining there over Christmas, and inaugurating a great temperance movement in Nelson Street chapel.[14] After visiting villages in the Tyne valley he came to South Shields on 5th January, and stayed several days.[15] Whilst there he visited Jarrow, 'the place of the Venerable Bede: I felt satisfaction in visiting this'. He continued in Northumberland and Durham until the middle of March, when he came back to Bemersley in time for his seventy-sixth birthday.

In April he travelled once more to Manchester for the purpose of attending an important Temperance Conference of some two hundred ministers of various denominations, to which he was appointed to read a paper: this was well-received and it made a deep impression as he presented the subject in the context of Scripture.[16]

From Manchester Bourne travelled up into the Rossendale valley, and on to Blackburn, where for nearly a month he preached and lectured. Returning to Manchester on 22nd May, he went the next day by train to Leeds, in preparation for the Conference. At this assembly Bourne became the acting-president for an important session.[17] He was back again in Bemersley on 20th June, but, as usual, remained only a few days, yet there is an important entry for 26th June: 'Completed my commentary on St John's Gospel. To God be praise and glory.' This work had been undertaken throughout his northern journeys during the previous months, and it is clear that he seized every leisure moment to proceed with this work.

At the end of June he set forth again, this time westwards to Chester and on into Flintshire, moving down to Oswestry,

[14] It should be remembered that as early as 1832 the Conference had committed the Connexion to a temperance policy by its own resolution: 'That we highly approve of Temperance Societies in our Connexion' (Conf. MS Jour., 1832).

[15] Whilst at South Shields Bourne stayed with a Mr Bulmer, boat-builder, and it is probable that whilst here the ship was being built for James Robinson, a ship-owner, which was to bear the name *Hugh Bourne,* and the figure-head of which was a carved model of Bourne's head and shoulders; it sailed the Atlantic and Mediterranean for many years.

[16] William Antliff, though not present, met some who had attended.

[17] Bourne was several times elected Secretary of Conference, but there is nothing to suggest that he was ever elected President, though it should be stated that for several years no records are available.

where he attended a camp-meeting at Cyrny Bwch; but he found the labour exhausting:

... about a thousand attended. I exercised till my body was injured, but the power was great. At night a love-feast at Oswestry ... but I was too much exhausted to join in this.[18]

Yet the following evening he 'went through an extended course of history' for his lecture! He next turned his footsteps north-wards, coming through Bangor-ys-coed to Wrexham, passing still farther north into the Wirral and on to his friend, George Horbury, at Poulton. The next day he took steamer to the Isle of Man, where he remained three weeks, preaching through-out the island no fewer than twenty times. On the day of his arrival he began writing a commentary on the Acts of the Apostles. He returned to Liverpool on the last day of August.

The day following he came to Rizley, a scene of his earlier labours, 'and found all well', and 'talked with the playing children, got up a meeting and preached to the children in the open air'.[19] From there he went up to St Helens, and whilst there visited an iron-foundry.

There is now an ominous entry in the Journal: 'My little toe on the left foot grievously sore.' Ten days later he came as far as Englesea Brook, but had to remain there, for the situation had become more serious. 'Ill indeed: attended the doctor: my toe dangerous: was bled with six leeches.' From a letter written by Mr Salmon, who had married Bourne's niece, and in whose home he stayed at Englesea Brook, we learn that already Bourne had lost part of one toe. The doctor urged him to desist from his labours, but he replied: 'Foot or no foot, I must be about my Master's business.' After a day of great suffering, he himself declared that nothing was now left for him but 'to pack up and die'. But the following morning he said that he had received a revelation that he should not die yet, and added, with a smile: 'My work is not quite finished.'

He was compelled to remain there for five weeks, unable to go out of doors, but spending much time in writing letters and an account of his early experiences.[20] When he was brought to

[18] Bourne MSS (Jour.), 9th July 1848.

[19] On this occasion Bourne preached the opening sermon for the new Rizley chapel from Rev. iii : 4, 'They shall walk with me in white' (A. Mounfield, *A Short History of Independent Methodism*, p. 21).

[20] These reminiscences were printed early in 1849, at Tunstall, in pamphlet form as *Notices of the Life of Hugh Bourne*. They formed a second edition of similar pamphlets printed in 1834.

Bemersley on 21st October, he was again confined to the house, and continued to be bled with leeches, though for a time a new remedy was tried—'Bryony root was grated and applied to my foot'—but there was little effect. Towards the end of November there was some improvement, and he managed to walk abroad —in order to borrow a copy of Wesley's *Journal*. On 3rd December he writes: 'I am still confined; but the Lord is with me in family worship.' On the last day of the year he was at the class at Brown Edge, the first meeting he had attended for some ten weeks.

At the end of January we find Bourne, with indefatigable courage, preparing for another journey, although his foot was still sore. He travelled by train and cart nearly forty miles to Bloxwich, in South Staffordshire, beginning once more to preach, and going from there to Lichfield. He came north to Stafford, took train to Longport, and from there walked the remaining five miles home, declaring 'my foot was better than usual'.

IV

Bourne remained at Bemersley for more than three months and, with an exception of a short period at Ramsor, made no journeys far afield. On 3rd April he wrote: 'Today I am seventy-seven years of age: I have been healthy but am now getting infirm.' On 28th May he attended the funeral of his eldest brother, John, who was buried at Norton-le-Moors, having reached his eighty-seventh year. Two days afterwards Bourne walked to Kidsgrove, and from there travelled by train to Manchester, and the next day on to York, reaching Sunderland on 1st June, in view of the approaching Conference. An interesting entry occurs in his Journal for 3rd June:

> All went on well. At three in the afternoon I and W[illiam] C[lowes] had a great time in prayer. The matter was the Lord in His mercy had returned.

This seems to imply a healing of the former breach; but later in a session of the Conference unhappily the tension arose again, when Clowes and Nixon brought certain charges against Bourne, who 'got in a few remarks', but was not allowed to proceed further. It would seem that despite his pledge to the Halifax Conference, Bourne had spoken in criticism of Clowes's *Journals* whilst in the Isle of Man, and had also written a hurtful letter to Clowes, though the Conference did not regard this as a breach of Bourne's pledge.[21] There is no doubt that the cause of this further outburst was the fact that, under the gathering weakness of old age, Bourne was beginning to lose his mental grip, for which his physical infirmities were responsible. It is essential to judge the matter in this light. His lack of perspective is further illustrated by the fact that when in the Conference John Ride was appointed to go out to the Australian mission, Bourne expressed his wish to accompany him, though he added: 'But this I must leave to the Lord.' In all these matters it is plain that the spirit was willing but the flesh was weakening.

That the conflicts came to be healed seems to be suggested by Bourne's entry in his Journal on his departure from the Conference:

Before this time I did not remember leaving a Conference without heaviness; but on this occasion I not only felt comfort, but joy in the Lord.[22]

From Sunderland Bourne came to Manchester, whence he visited Stockport, New Mills, and Glossop. The month of July was spent at home; early in August he set off for Derby and Nottingham, and on the 25th came to Lincoln, then once more by packet to Boston, and forward through Peterborough to Wisbech, in Cambridgeshire, thence into Norfolk through Downham Market to Lynn, covering many villages in the area, and coming to Swaffham and East Dereham; thence he moved north to Fakenham and Wells, from where he visited numerous villages in the west of the county. On 28th December he came by rail to Norwich, and beyond to the villages in south-east Norfolk, and to Yarmouth on the coast. 'The great chapel was filled, and I spoke with great liberty.' On 5th February 1850 he was in Lowestoft, and went on to the villages scattered amongst the Norfolk Broads and to the south-east. On one of these journeys by carriage the vehicle overturned, owing to the drunkenness of the driver, and Bourne's shoulder was severely hurt.

On 23rd February Bourne went to Ely, 'on the Parliament train', and preached in the Cambridgeshire fenland for the space of six weeks. He moved to Peterborough on 13th April, preached three times on the Sunday, and the next day came by

[21] Conf. MS Jour., 1849.   [22] Bourne MSS (Jour.), 15th June 1849.

H.B.—12

train to Derby. He reached Bemersley the day following. Bourne was now in his seventy-ninth year.

In the middle of May he set off for Derbyshire, preaching at Wirksworth, Cromford, and Ambergate, and reaching Nottingham in time for the Conference of 1850, on 5th June. At the camp-meeting, possibly the largest yet held, Bourne preached seven times; his comment is therefore not surprising: 'I was quite worn out, and was not able to do more, so I retired.' At the Conference the sum of £15 per year was granted to him for house-rent, and a similar sum to his brother, James; also sums were authorized to be paid in liquidation of the debt on Burslem chapel. The assembly proved 'the most agreeable and harmonious Conference we ever had'.

During July he was at Bemersley, preaching and writing and also assisting in the hay harvest, but himself far from well. He writes: 'Weak of body, but quite well in mind! Thank God!' Early in September he came again into Derbyshire, into the region around Bakewell, returning by cart to Buxton, and then, to his own amazement, walking ten miles to Macclesfield on his way home. October was spent in writing his autobiography, and dispatching copies of his publications to London and elsewhere; his right foot was troublesome. Apart from a short visit to the villages in the Weaver Hills, he stayed at home during the remainder of the year.

On 18th January 1851 Bourne came to Derby, and the next day preached in the new Kedleston Street chapel: he then went north to Chesterfield, and through the Sherwood Forest to Ollerton, remaining in that neighbourhood three weeks and then turning westward to Mansfield. After preaching on the Sunday he was seized with severe cramp, but three days later he reached Nottingham, and on 6th March arrived back at Bemersley. He was at home more than a month, much occupied with reading and writing, and occasional preaching. On 11th April he went to Newport, in Shropshire, bound for Oakengates and Wellington; he also touched Madeley and Wrockwardine Wood, Much Wenlock and Ironbridge. He was back again early in May.

v

In anticipation of the Conference at Lynn, in June 1851, Bourne went across to Peterborough and on to Wisbech, spending days in North Norfolk. In the Conference camp-meeting he preached to the children at every stand. The sessions completed, he went to Norwich, then back through Wisbech into Lincolnshire, and up north by way of Spalding and Boston to Lincoln, reaching home again by 10th July. During his three weeks' stay he spent some time in revision of his manuscript of the commentary on St John's Gospel. On the 30th he came to West Bromwich, and thence to Birmingham and Coventry, north to Nuneaton and Stafford, and then home once more. On this journey and after his return he continued the work of revision just referred to, and also worked on his commentary on the Acts of the Apostles: 'chiefly writing' is a frequent entry in his Journal at this time.

During the succeeding weeks he was often unwell, but was taken to the home of his niece at Englesea Brook, and also to that of John Walford, at Hatherton, where he preached, but was taken ill with severe pain. He writes: 'I believe I must preach no more for the present.' He was able to return to Bemersley by the middle of December, and a week later he walked to Leek, to be there for Christmas Day; during several days, he preached in neighbouring villages, but returned home early in January, 'much fatigued and distressed'. Ten days later he wrote a letter stating that he intended to be at the Conference to be held at Yarmouth. During the succeeding days he passed through 'great trial of mind', and could move about only a short distance. Still hopeful of rendering further service, he wrote to Hereford stating his intention to visit there in April, but it could not be. Entries in the Journal now become scanty.

Saturday, February 13. In general unwell.
Sunday 15.[23] So ill of my right foot that I staid at home.
15–20; so ill of my right foot as not to go out.
Thursday, 25. My foot is better.
Friday 26. My foot is worse.
Saturday 28.[23] Not able to go out.
Sunday, 29.[23] . . .

Here the Journal ends. It had been kept almost daily for half a century.

His brother James took him, probably in April, to the North Staffordshire Infirmary at Hanley for surgical treatment of the

[23] The above entries are given as in the MS, but are actually dated incorrectly. The mistakes obviously indicate frailty.

foot, but his return to Bemersley was not long delayed. Day by day he became more enfeebled. He was visited by kind friends who bore testimony to his strong and unshaken faith, and to his unbroken fortitude. The Gospel which he had preached to others so long was now his own comfort.

> During his affliction he grew more and more humble, gentle, meek and resigned . . . his affections became exquisitely tender: their natural character seemed vastly changed: his views, his hopes and his joys were heavenly.[24]

Asked by someone as to his willingness to depart, he replied: 'I cannot say that I have a will of my own; it seems swallowed up in God's will.'

On Monday, 11th October, he arose as usual, and appeared cheerful and content. About four in the afternoon he lay on the sofa and fell asleep, but arousing a little, appeared to be in conversation with someone, though the words were inaudible. Then, beckoning with his hand, as though anxious for a nearer approach, smiling, he said several times: 'Come! Come!' and looking upwards, and pointing as if to something near at hand, he said: 'Old companions! Old companions! My mother!' Then without pain or sigh, and with a shining face, his spirit passed into the hands of God who gave it. The earthly pilgrimage had ended.

VI

Whilst staying at Englesea Brook during his illness in 1849, Bourne had expressed a wish that he should be buried there, although some eleven miles from Bemersley. The funeral took place on Sunday, 17th October.[25] Early that morning many assembled at the home of James Bourne for prayer and singing before the departure. It had been arranged that throughout the whole of the journey, children of the Sunday schools should meet with their teachers, and by the time one school had escorted the cortège to a given point, another school should take its place and so proceed. An eye-witness describes the scene:

> At one particular bend of the road, as we neared Tunstall, the sight was imposing . . . the solemn sound, while the different choirs

---

[24] Thomas Bateman, 'Memoir of Hugh Bourne', *PMM*, 1853, p. 706.
[25] It was estimated that some 20,000 persons witnessed the scene or joined in the procession during its course (*Staffordshire Advertiser*, 23rd October 1852).

chanted in measured time, was carried on the autumn breeze, and the echo, returning from the neighbouring heights, fell in touching accents on the ear: 'Mortals cry—"A man is dead!": Angels sing—"A child is born!" '[26]

When they reached Tunstall a funeral oration was delivered to a vast multitude assembled in the market-square, after which the journey was resumed, and along the road large numbers were gathered. Reaching Englesea Brook the coffin was placed in the chapel, and in an adjoining field an open-air service of worship was held, fitting indeed in remembrance of Bourne's own labours. Afterwards more than a thousand people filed past the bier to take a last look at one whom all had revered. Then the remains were interred in a new vault in the adjoining burial-ground, beneath the slender arms of a willow tree planted for the occasion by the family in whose home Bourne had so often stayed. So he came to rest in the quiet acre of a Cheshire hamlet. The final journey of this 'man of the golden heart' had reached its end. 'Like the morning star, he gently melted away into the cloudless sky and endless day.'

[26] Walford, II.379.

THE BOURNE MANUSCRIPTS

AFTER THE death of Hugh Bourne, in 1852, his personal papers passed into the hands of John Walford, his nephew and literary executor, who made full use of them in the writing of the *Memoirs*, published in 1856–7. In 1858 these papers were purchased by the Conference, for the sum of £150, and thereby became connexional property.[1] Apparently they had suffered much deterioration: 'many of them were torn, dirty and thrown together in confusion, like waste paper, utterly worthless.'[2] The documents were sifted, and some being 'found to reflect on the character of individuals and courts', these were eventually destroyed—perhaps an unfortunate decision from the point of view of historical record. Those manuscripts which have survived are the Journal and an Autobiography, and these documents are now in the Library of Hartley Victoria College, Manchester.

The Journal consists of twenty-two separate sections.[3] Some portions are in ordinary exercise-books; others in smaller notebooks; others are constructed of sheets of paper cut to size and stitched together, bound in paper covers; the later portions are in bound volumes.

The Journal proper[4] begins in 1803 and ends on 28th February 1852, a little more than seven months before Bourne's death. For the period between 18th February 1821 and 9th November 1842—i.e. for just over twenty-one years—no manuscript material exists, so far as we can discover.[5] Occasional extracts from the missing portions, however, appear in the connexional magazines between 1828 and 1841. As already suggested, it is likely that the earlier missing portions were

---

[1] Conf. MS Jour., 1858.

[2] From a letter to the Conference, 1858, written by John Petty and Thomas Bateman, who had been entrusted to deal with the transaction.

[3] One of these, a small book covering the period from 2nd July to 7th December 1808, was probably not included amongst the purchased documents: it was presented to the College Library by the Rev. E. Barrett, M.A., in 1946.

[4] The *Self-review*, dated 17th August 1800 (*supra*, p. 29 n.), though included in the number of sections named above, is separate from the rest, and is not strictly in the form of a journal.

[5] *supra*, p. 121 n.

destroyed in the fire at Bemersley, in March 1834,[6] and it may also be that some were lost in the short period between Bourne's death and the purchase of those which still exist. Against the latter suggestion is the fact that Walford appears to have made use of only those still extant, with very little exception.

The handwriting of the Journal is legible throughout, and mistakes are exceedingly rare. Only a few pages are indecipherable in ordinary reading, but the writing becomes distinct under ultra-violet light. These pages are in one section only, and the deterioration is probably due to damp. Written in many places —by the road-side, on canal-boats, in houses where he stayed— these books for his Journal were carried in the pocket, and the final lines on the pages are sometimes partially erased through wear and tear. Some passages in the Journal are written in shorthand, the key to which we have not yet been able to discover, though the system seems to be a variant of Macaulay (1756). On some of the pages Hebrew and Greek vocabularies for books of the Bible are to be found; here and there we also find medical recipes, probably gathered by Bourne during his travels.[7]

The Journal is a day-to-day record, and in much of the later period is a catalogue of places visited for preaching appointment, the discourses usually being stated. As we might expect, the Journal throughout is preoccupied with religion; it is the record of a man who had only one object—the salvation of his own soul and the souls of others. It is in this that the writer stands revealed. Yet these pages are not without incidental glimpses of persons and places, customs and events, often written in an illuminating way.

The Journal is of supreme importance as a chronicle of the emergence and expansion of Primitive Methodism; without it much of the story must have remained untold.

The MSS of Bourne's Autobiography consist mainly of large sheets, stitched together, some of these being copies of old plans, the blank side being used for the purpose of the record. There are three distinct documents, which we have designated A, B, and C Texts, the two latter being recensions of the first. The A Text must be regarded as the most satisfactory. These belong to the later portion of Bourne's life, and bear the marks of advancing years; they are, however, of considerable value.

[6] *supra*, p. 146.   [7] *infra*, p. 192.

The A Text consists of 313 folios, the writing of which was commenced in Bourne's seventy-third year,[8] was continued during his outward journey to America in 1844, and was completed not long after his arrival.

The B Text is shorter (70 folios), and this was most probably written shortly before Bourne's departure from America, or soon after his arrival in England in the spring of 1845.

The C Text consists of 177 folios, and was written in 1850–1, and has important additions.

Bourne seems to have intended publication, but this was never carried out, probably because the record only covers the years until 1811, and therefore the MSS must be regarded as incomplete.

In the light of his numerous responsibilities and engagements Bourne must have had an extensive correspondence, yet only five MS letters [9] have come to light, although others may still be found. Scattered amongst the pages of his Journal are some fifteen letters, written by Bourne and copied in the text in his own handwriting; in the printed pages of Walford another dozen are to be found, and a similar and additional number are printed by Antliff.[10] It is unfortunate that so little of Bourne's correspondence has survived.

[8] cf. Bourne MSS (Jour.), 24th June 1844: 'I thought in writing an account of my life . . . to write with care, lest any man should think of me above that which he seeth me to be, or that he heareth of me.'

[9] Four of these are in the Library at Hartley Victoria College, Manchester. The fifth (recently traced by the Rev. Frank Baker, B.A., B.D., to whom we are indebted for a copy of it) is in private possession, and is written upon the back of a pamphlet sent by Bourne to 'Mrs Jane Godfrey, Schoolmistress, Eakring, Nottinghamshire' (Bourne MSS (Jour.), 8th March 1851). It reads as follows:

DEAR SISTER GODFREY,

Grace and peace be with you. Today, May 7, 1851, I arrived at Bemersley, that is at home, and my toe is nearly well. Yours in the Lord, HUGH BOURNE.

[10] Of letters written to Bourne, sixteen are to be found printed in Walford and Antliff, and two in the PMM: six others are copied by Bourne in the pages of his Journal.

PORTRAITS OF HUGH BOURNE

1. *Portrait in oils.* 2 ft. 6 in. × 2 ft. (Frontispiece) *æt. c.* 50.
   Artist unknown.
   Presented to Hartley College, Manchester, about 1890,
   by Thomas Buckley, Esq., of Woodley, Cheshire.

2. *Portrait in oils on wood.* 18 in. × 15 in. *æt. c.* 55.
   Painted by Watson Smith,[1] of Leeds, and presented to
   Hartley Victoria College, Manchester, in 1849, by the
   Rev. Samuel Walpole, of Tilehurst, Reading, whose
   wife was a grand-niece of the artist.

3. *Portrait in water-colour.* 4¾ in. × 4 in. *æt. c.* 75.
   Artist unknown. Presented to Hartley College, Man-
   chester, in 1906, by John Hugh Walford,[2] Esq., of
   Sydney, Crewe.

4. *Portrait: half-tone block. æt. c.* 50.
   Reproduced in Kendall, II.2. The original painting has
   so far not been traced, but it may be the portrait in oils
   referred to (*PMW*, 1898, pp. 233, 651), as being purchased by the Connexion to be 'permanently hung in
   the committee-room . . . in Aldersgate Street'.

5. *Portrait and steel-engraving. æt. c.* 60.
   This is the work of John Freeman, of London,[3] and was
   first reproduced in *PMM*, 1836, afterwards as the
   frontispiece in Walford's *Memoirs* (1856), and later in
   Antliff's *Life . . . of Hugh Bourne* (1872). This is the best-
   known portrait of Bourne.

6. *Portrait and steel-engraving. æt. c.* 60.
   The work of C. Laurie, and is to be found in *Methodist
   Worthies*, J. C. Stevenson (London), 1884, Vol V; also
   in *PMW*, 1907. It is probably a reproduction of No. 5.

[1] Watson Smith (1802–62), an early member of the Leeds society, was the
brother of the Rev. Samuel Smith (1796–1877), and also of Mrs Reynard, wife of
John Reynard (d. 1854), an early figure in Leeds Primitive Methodism (*PMM*,
1862, pp. 515–17).

[2] John Hugh Walford was a grandson of James Bourne.

[3] John Freeman was engaged as engraver for portraits of the travelling preachers
by the Conference of 1833 (Conf. MS Jour., 1833), and continued this work until
1854.

7. *Portrait in profile: lithograph.*
   Printed as frontispiece to Bourne's *History of the Primitive Methodists* (1823).

8. *Portrait in profile: wood-block.*
   This silhouette portrait was first printed on the plan of the Winster Circuit, *c.* 1848,[4] and was afterwards reproduced in Kendall, I.8. It was drawn from No. 7.

9. *Plaster-cast mounted on wood.* Life-size. *æt. c.* 67. The work of William Andrews,[5] of Bradford, made in 1839 whilst Bourne was attending the Conference.

10. *Bust of Hugh Bourne.* Staffordshire Pottery. 10 in. high.
    Made by the Royal Crown Pottery Company, Tunstall, in 1908.[6]

[4] *PMM,* 1897, p. 361.

[5] On this occasion Bourne was the guest of the artist, a Bradford architect, on whose death the cast was left to his son, Thomas Andrews, who later gave it to Charles Neal, of Bradford, in whose family it remained until about 1893, when it was handed over to the Connexion, and was later placed in the Library of Hartley College, Manchester.

It is recorded (*PMM,* 1894, pp. 614–15) that Bourne did not relish the experience of the making of the cast, for when it was done, he bluntly inquired: 'Have you got it?' and to the affirmative answer came his rejoinder: 'If you had not, you never would have.'

[6] *PMW,* 1908.

THE WILLS OF HUGH BOURNE

I

IN HIS Journal dated Sunday, 17th January 1819, we find the following from Bourne's pen:

I was taken ill and was under the doctor's hands; overmuch fatigue and labour had brought on an extraordinary weakness; I could not eat solid food. I removed to Loughborough, and then Jas Bourne fetched me home.

It was nine days later that Bourne made the following will:[1]

In the Name of God Amen I Hugh Bourne of Bemersley in the parish of Norton in the Moors in the County of Stafford Licenced Teacher being ill in body but of sound mind and memory do make this my last will and testament as follows first of all my just debts and funeral expences to be paid and satisfied I then give and devise to my brother James Bourne of Bemersley aforesaid all my estate and right in and to a piece of Land in Tunstall in Stafford-shire the same being situated at Wellington place in Tunstall and on which has been built a Chapel for the Primitive Methodists All my right and estate in and to this Chapel and piece of ground I give and devise to the same my brother James Bourne and to his heirs assins for ever Also to the said my brother James Bourne I give and devise all my estate and right to Talk o'th Hill Chapel Also I give to all our Sunday Schools all or any monies they may owe me All the residue of my personal estate I give . . . [to] James Bourne my said brother to . . . follows first to pay and discharge all . . . [a]nd funeral expences and any expence . . . [m]y illness and afterward for the remain[der] . . . [e] his own property. Lastly I nominate . . . said my brother James Bourne to be the sole . . . my last will and testament Hereby . . . [f]ormer and other will by me at any other time . . . [i]s only to be my last will and testa-ment . . . [witne]ss whereof I have hereunto set my hand and seal this twenty sixth day of January one thousand eight hundred and nineteen.

HUGH BOURNE (LS)

Sealed signed published and delivered by the said Testator in the presence of us

JAMES MOON
JOSEPH DURANT
THOMAS THOMPSON

[1] This document is in the Library of Hartley Victoria College, Manchester. No copy of Bourne's will dated 19th October 1809 (*supra*, p. 69) is extant, so far as we have been able to trace.

II

In the Journal dated Thursday, 27th June 1844, there is the following:

Preparing for America. My feelings were keen. I made my will.

A copy is subjoined: [2]

In the Name of God Amen I Hugh Bourne of Bemersley in the parish of Norton in the Moors in the county of Stafford licensed teacher and late editor of the Primitive Methodist magazine being of sound mind memory and understanding and being on the point of setting sail to Canada in North America do make this my last will and testament in manner and form following First that my executor out of my real and personal estate do pay and satisfy all my just debts and funeral expenses. In the next place I give devise and bequeath to my brother James Bourne of Bemersley the aforesaid farmer all my estate real and personal with all the goods chattels commodities appurtenances of which I may be possessed or which may be belonging to me at my decease with all my copyrights and in particular the copyright of and in my large hymnbook for the use of the Primitive Methodists my collection of hymns for camp meetings revival &c for the use of the Primitive Methodists my spellings numbers one two three and four [3] my ecclesiastical history printed in the Primitive Methodist magazine my treatise on chairmaning [4] my publications called Notices of Hugh Bourne's Life with all the copyrights of whatever else I may write or publish either in England or in America And I nominate and appoint the said James Bourne as and to be the sole executor of this my last will and testament And I hereby revoke and make void all former wills by me at any time made declaring this only to be my last will and testament

In witness whereof I have hereunto set my hand and affixed my seal this twenty seventh day of June in the year of our Lord one thousand eight hundred and forty four.

ELIZABETH BEECH ⎫   HUGH BOURNE (LS)
SARAH FOSTER   ⎬ Witnesses
ANN BIRCHENOUGH ⎭

Sealed, signed, published and declared by the said testator as and for his last will and testament written with his own hand and signed by us as his witnesses at his request and in his presence and in the presence of each other.

ELIZABETH BEECH
SARAH FOSTER
ANN BIRCHENOUGH

[2] Walford, II.312. Punctuation is omitted.
[3] Bourne had published graded spelling-books for use in children's classes.
[4] i.e. *Treatise on Discipline* (1820).

THE LITERARY LABOURS OF HUGH BOURNE

THROUGHOUT HIS life, Hugh Bourne had a strong literary interest: his reading was varied and extensive; he possessed a considerable library in his home at Bemersley,[1] and it was his custom to take books with him on his travels; much of his literary work was done away from home, and remembering his constant journeyings, and his daily care of the churches, it is amazing that he achieved so much.

I

Bourne was responsible for the beginnings of the connexional literature. As early as January 1818 he was 'planning a small magazine', and in March had secured an estimate for its printing from John Tregortha, of Burslem. Less than a month later he received 340 copies—he had arranged for 2,000—at Derby; the next day he obtained 800 more. On 18th April he carried 300 to Loughborough. The issue was entitled *A Methodist Magazine . . . conducted by the Society of people called Primitive Methodists*. It was to be produced quarterly. A second number appeared late in July; but the venture was not successful, and Bourne bore the loss.

Bourne seems to have contemplated a monthly issue, and he welcomed the suggestion of 'the friends at Leicester' that such a magazine should be printed, though he insisted that it should not be undertaken unless 500 subscribers could be obtained.[2] On 11th January 1819 he put the proposed magazine into the hands of a Leicester printer; on the following Sunday he was taken ill, and had to be removed to his home. This necessitated someone else undertaking the work, and the first eight

---

[1] Amongst the books there was a complete, well-bound set from the beginning of *Arminian Magazine* and *Methodist Magazine*: the first volume contained a preface neatly written and signed by John Wesley in his own handwriting. . . . Other books were Wesley's and Fletcher's *Works*, Adam Clarke's *Commentary*, Gillie's *Historical Collections*, Finney's *Lectures*, Hebrew and Greek Lexicons, etc. ('Reminiscences of a residence at Bemersley,' *PMM*, 1900, p. 752.)

[2] See facsimile of autograph letter (Kendall, I.330).

numbers [3] were issued under the temporary editorship of William Goodrich,[4] a solicitor's clerk, in Leicester.

This was entirely a private venture, and in no sense the work of a connexionally appointed editor. This new venture was little more successful than the earlier attempt. In 1820, at the first 'Annual Meeting', Bourne was appointed to the editorship, and was asked to complete the first volume; so we find the issue of June 1820, 'intended as a substitute for September 1819': two other numbers were issued similarly,[5] thus completing the first volume.[6] Thus the Magazine struggled into existence.

At the beginning of 1825 it was enlarged, and five years later was printed in octavo size and sold at sixpence per number.[7]

Bourne continued as editor until 1842—nearly twenty-two years. Every volume bears the marks of his ability, and a vast amount of material from his own pen. It was a monumental contribution.

II

Early in his ministry Bourne became convinced as to the value of suitable literature in the form of tracts for distribution.[8] Several came from his own pen, printed at his own expense, and some of these had previously appeared in the pages of the magazines.

Two tracts deal with the subject of the inner life. In 1808 he published *Rules for Holy Living*,[9] of which many thousands were printed, and widely distributed, especially at camp-meetings. Bourne seized every opportunity:

12 February, 1810: On the road I went to Broughton Church, and put in three hand-bills (*Rules for Holy Living*) through the broken panes in the windows. I believe God will direct them.[10]

A Treatise on the Cultivation of the Spiritual Gifts (1824) [11] reveals Bourne's intimate knowledge of the Scriptures and their value for much of his own inner life.

[3] These were printed by 'J. Fowler, High Cross, Leicester'.   [4] Kendall, I.331.
[5] One was printed at Burslem; the other at Derby: some time during 1821, the printing was undertaken by James Bourne, at Bemersley.
[6] The volume bore the quaint title: *A Methodist Magazine for the Year 1819, conducted by the Camp-meeting Methodists, known by the name of Ranters, called also Primitive Methodists.*
[7] In October 1824 *The Primitive Methodist Children's Magazine* was started, under the editorship of Bourne (Kendall II.11). In 1832 came *The Primitive Methodist Preachers' Magazine.*
[8] *supra*, p. 58.   [9] Reprinted in Walford, I.168–70.
[10] Bourne MSS (Jour.), loc. cit.   [11] *PMM*, 1824.

Four tracts have special reference to work amongst children. As early as 1801, at Harriseahead, a Divine word was impressed upon Bourne: 'I will lay My hand upon the little ones.' He had often observed James Bourne talking to his own children, and 'a concern for the souls of the little ones' was awakened in Hugh Bourne, which he never lost. So in preaching it became his habit 'to wait on the Lord, treat them with inward reverence, and speak earnestly' to them.

In 1807 he prepared *The Great Scripture Catechism, compiled for Norton and Harriseahead Sunday Schools, and intended for Schools in General*:[12] he hoped this 'might assist in promoting Bible knowledge and rendering it more lasting and effective'.

In 1824 he published several articles *On Sunday Schools*[13] containing practical instructions for the work, together with some historical account of the labours of Robert Raikes, and he also declared that 'Methodists were pioneers of the voluntary system', through the adoption of 'gratuitous teachers'.

A year earlier, in 1823, he had written *A Treatise on the Duty of Parents*,[14] an extensive survey of parental responsibility as indicated in the Scriptures.

Bourne's most important tract on this subject, however, was entitled *The Early Trumpet: a Treatise on Preaching to Children*, written in 1842, probably the last separate production from his pen, he 'being now advanced in years'. He urged that 'children must not be undervalued' by preachers; the word of the preacher must be in 'home-language' and 'home-voice', and for his message the preacher 'must trust to common observation and to God'. A thousand copies of this tract were printed, once again at Bourne's expense.

A considerable amount of Bourne's writing was given to matters of church administration and affairs. As we have seen, his skill in such matters is reflected in the 'consolidation' of connexional minutes, and the preparation of official documents in general. In 1820 he wrote an important work, *Treatise on Discipline, chiefly as it respects meetings for Business*, a manual of vital significance for the new and rising community,[15] and which was approved officially by the first Annual Meeting.

We quote the prayer with which it ends:

[12] Part I is printed in Walford, I.127–39, and contains sixty questions with Scripture answers. So far as we know Part II is not extant.
[13] *PMM.*, 1824.
[14] ibid., 1823.
[15] ibid., 1820. This was printed separately and widely used by the preachers.

O Thou Great Master of assemblies, grant wisdom to Thy children. Enable them to guide their affairs with discretion, and in the fear of the Lord: and as will be most to Thy glory, and the good of precious souls, for the sake of Jesus Christ our Lord and Saviour. Amen.

In 1808 Bourne wrote two interesting tracts: the first, entitled *Remarks on the Ministry of Women*,[16] written after his attendance at the Conference of the Independent Methodists at Macclesfield in 1807, and completed in the home of Peter Phillips, at Warrington. In it he urges the sanctions of Jesus, the countenancing of the apostles as a warrant for the ministry of women in ministry for the conversion of souls. The second tract was entitled *Advice to Young Women*.[17]

We may note here that in 1823, under the title *Advice to Travelling Preachers*, Bourne wrote an important series of articles marked by spiritual insight and full of practical wisdom.

In the same year Bourne published *A Treatise on Baptism: in Twelve Conversations*, to which he added five hymns, which he himself had composed for use on occasions of infant baptism. The 'conversations' are between minister and parent. Tracing the practice of baptism on its scriptural background, he asserts:

In baptising infants you can make no error, for of such is the kingdom of God . . . their title to the outward baptism is more clear and certain than that of grown-up persons (p. 12); all the baptisms appointed of God promote and increase faith, and lay a foundation for future information and instruction (p. 13). Your lovely infants are the care of the Almighty, and you may bring them heartily to Jesus Christ, and let no one forbid them: you may devote them to Him by baptism in the fulness of faith (p. 14).

Finally, we may note that Bourne published a small four-page tract entitled *Family Receipts*, in which are twenty-one recipes for various complaints! The fly-leaves of his MS Journal were frequently used for recording such recipes for sickness, some of which he collected during his travels. His tracts recall, in miniature, Wesley's *Primitive Physic* (1747), which, indeed, Bourne may have read.

We should also note that the magazines contain some fifty sermons from Bourne's pen, though these were never printed separately.

[16] Reprinted in Walford, I.172–7. In particular, Bourne instances the case of his own mother, and that of Mrs Fletcher, of Madeley.
[17] Bourne MSS (Jour.), 22nd December 1808. See also Walford, I.192. We have not been able to trace an extant copy of this tract.

III

A considerable amount of Bourne's literary work was historical in character.[18]

In 1803 he wrote a small tract entitled *Observations on Camp Meetings, with an account of a Camp Meeting held on Sunday, May the 31st, 1807 at Mow Cop*,[19] which is of particular value as the earliest and chief record of this important occasion, and of an English camp-meeting.

Invaluable for an account of the beginnings of the Connexion is Bourne's work, *History of the Primitive Methodists*. It was written in response to a request of the Preparatory Meeting at Nottingham (1819) for some account of connexional origins, and the MS was read at the Hull Conference of 1820,[20] and was afterwards published in the magazines the following year. It was printed separately in 1823.[21]

An outstanding piece of historical writing is Bourne's *Ecclesiastical History* which was printed in the magazines from 1825 to 1842. In 1865 it was published separately, in a slightly abridged form, edited by William Antliff, in a volume of nearly eight hundred pages. Two thousand copies were printed. Though somewhat out of proportion—one-half of the work is devoted to tracing the development of Christianity up to the Apostolic Age—it is an amazingly detailed summary of the story of the expansion of Christianity, often with quotations from original sources, and reaching up to the end of the eighteenth century. The work implies a vast amount of historical reading and research, and also reflects considerable historical judgement.

IV

The Journal of Hugh Bourne shows that from early days he was interested in linguistic study; there is evidence that in later years he gained considerable knowledge of Hebrew, Greek,

[18] We may note here three autobiographical tracts, entitled *Notices of the Life of Hugh Bourne*, which he wrote in 1834, and a similar revised tract in 1849; also four published *Letters to Mr Aaron Leese, of Tunstall* (1842), who had written an account of the development of Methodism in the area.

[19] Printed by C. C[h]ester, Newcastle-under-Lyme, 1807.

[20] The work caused some dispute, as it seemed to imply that Bourne was to be regarded as the sole founder of the Connexion. It was suggested that Clowes should 'look over it before it was passed'. He writes (Clowes MSS (Auto.), Text D, f. 9): 'I took it to my room and read the greatest part of it, and I must confess . . . I did not approve of it.' Its publication in 1823, with a portrait of Bourne as frontispiece, strengthened this criticism (see J. T. Wilkinson, *William Clowes 1780–1851*, App. I).

[21] A revised edition was printed in 1835.

Latin, and French.[22] In 1832 he published *The Studies of Language*, a volume of some two hundred pages, the intention of which was 'to furnish a family book which might be useful both to parents and children'. There seems also to be an undercurrent of religious purpose, because many, if not most, of his examples for grammatical illustration are in the form of scriptural quotation.[23]

The work is divided into two parts, the first containing a discussion of the origins of language, and the progress of literature to his own day. He makes a rapid survey of Christian writing —from the Apostolic Fathers down to the seventeenth century —and then proceeds to give a brief glance at Greek and Latin [24] literature: then follows an account of the story of writing and the art of printing.

The second part deals with the grammatical aspect; in orthography, Hebrew and Greek comparisons are made; in grammar, the comparison is with Latin formations; the last section is on syntax.

The work indicates the possession of a true scholarly instinct on the part of Bourne.[25]

V

On 18th June 1816 Bourne writes in his Journal:

This morning I began to write a commentary upon the Scriptures, adapted to the capacities of children. I intend to call it 'The Children's Friend; or a Companion for families and Sunday schools' . . . a commentary intended to assist the lovers of the rising generation.

How far Bourne proceeded with this MS is not known: the work was never completed, and what was written was never published.[26] This is also true of his work on a commentary on the Acts of the Apostles, 'which he began when in the Isle of Man', as late as 1847.[27]

---

[22] We may note here that Bourne's linguistic studies prompted his incursions into Biblical textual criticism and exegesis, to which a number of articles in the magazines bear witness.

[23] Bourne speaks of the Scriptures as 'the great monument of literature, a great light and lantern of mankind', op. cit., p. 39.

[24] 'The Latin language may be compared to the struggle of a butterfly: the English to the flight of an eagle,' p. 49.

[25] It may be recorded here that Bourne was well-versed in Dr Johnson's *Dictionary of the English Language* (1755), and in Dr Hugh Blair's *Lectures in Rhetoric* (1783).

[26] Occasional fragments appeared, however, in the magazines.

[27] Bourne MSS (Jour.), 1847, loc. cit.

We find, however, under date 26th June 1848: 'Completed my commentary of Saint John's Gospel. To God be praise and glory.' Much of the MS had been written at places where he stayed on his travels, though its last stages were completed at his home at Bemersley: he was in his seventy-seventh year.

The manuscript came into Walford's possession, along with the rest of Bourne's papers, and was published after his death, prepared for the press by William Antliff, in 1866.

The commentary shows the influence of Wesley's *Notes on the New Testament* and Adam Clarke's *Commentary*, but it has Bourne's own imprint upon it, and is marked by simplicity of style, at times epigrammatic, and with occasional reference to the Greek text of the Gospel. It exemplifies Bourne's devotional spirit and his evangelistic zeal.

VI

Of great importance in the development of the Connexion was Bourne's literary work upon its succession of hymn-books.[28] As early as 1809, in association with the camp-meeting movement, Bourne produced a hymn-book under the title: *General Collection of Hymns and Spiritual Songs for Camp-Meetings, Revivals &c.*, of which, until 1823, edition after edition was published, and so eagerly bought that the revenue from its sale greatly helped to sustain and promote the missionary enterprise of the Connexion.[29] This book contained sixty-three hymns in the 'new and enlarged edition' of 1819.[30]

The book was an adaptation of Lorenzo Dow's *A Collection of Spiritual Songs used at Camp Meetings in the Great Revival in the United States of America*,[31] and of the twenty-three hymns in this

[28] See art. 'Reminiscences of Early Primitive Methodism', T. Bateman, *PMM*, 1883, pp. 542–3.

[29] We have already noted (*supra*, p. 125) that provincial printers sometimes discovered its value, and issued pirated editions—with slight alterations. Kendall (II.2) states that he had seen eight such editions, printed severally at York (2), Leeds, Gainsborough, Selby, Burslem, Bingham, and Nottingham. We are inclined, however, to think that Kendall is mistaken in assuming that the edition printed at Bingham was a pirated one, in the light of the following entry in the Journal, dated 30th April 1818: 'Was at Bingham . . . put hymn-books to the press: was today to have seen a proof.' This is also probably true regarding the copy printed at Burslem (ibid, 15th July 1818): 'Put a small hymn-book to the press.' The edition printed by James Kendrew, of York (1821), became the most famous of these pirated editions, in consequence of the legal action brought against him (*supra*, p. 125).

[30] We have not been able to trace any copy earlier than 1819, but it is reasonable to suppose that the number of hymns in editions before that date was less than that named above.

[31] This was printed in Dublin (1806) and Liverpool (1807).

collection, twenty-two were incorporated by Bourne in his own book.[32] The remainder of the hymns in Bourne's book were selected from other sources, and include hymns by Isaac Watts and John Newton.[33]

In 1821 Bourne resolved to copyright the book, and with this purpose in mind he composed twelve hymns.[34] William Sanders,[35] a young travelling preacher, was asked to do the same. In a curious document, in precise legal form, he makes a contract to furnish twenty-five original hymns for the same number of shillings.[36] Further hymns were contributed by members of the societies, following a request from the Annual Meeting of 1821.[37] About twenty hymns from Wesley's *Collection* were included.[38] This book—afterwards known as 'The Small Hymn Book'—contained 154 hymns in all.

In 1823 there was a feeling that even the improved edition of 1821 was inadequate; a book was called for which 'should contain hymns for sacraments and the general varieties of meeting and worship'. 'The new book is expected to be got ready by the close of the present year or early next year.'[39] It appeared in 1824, printed at Bemersley, by James Bourne, and it bore the title *Large Hymn Book for the use of the Primitive Methodists*. It contained 536 hymns.[40] To this book Bourne contributed twenty hymns of his own composing, and William Sanders the same number. We also find that some 138 hymns are under the joint signatures 'W.S. & H.B.', and these are hymns composed

---

[32] Of these, eighteen were afterwards admitted into 'The Small Hymn Book' (1820).

[33] An edition 'printed for the Editor', by J. Hutchinson, Silver Street, Hull, contains 65 hymns; another edition, 'Printed for the Committee', by John Barr, Briggate, Leeds, contains 66.

[34] Dr Julian, in *A Dictionary of Hymnology* (1892), p. 165, mentions only ten.

[35] Little is known of William Sanders (1795?–1840?), who became a travelling preacher in 1821 (*PML*, 1905, p. 704). In the *PMM* between 1822 and 1840 there are some fifty pieces from his pen: sixteen hymns are in the 'Small Book' and twenty in the 'Large Hymn Book' (1824).

[36] Kendall, II.10. The document is as follows:

Received, Mar 1821, of Hugh Bourne, the sum of twenty-five shillings for twenty-five hymns, which by contract were composed by me for his use, and which I have made over to him in the fullest sense of the word, and which from this time become and are in every sense his own absolute property. . . . I say received by me. WILLIAM SANDERS.

Signed in the presence of C. J. ABRAHAM.

[37] *Gen. Mins.*, 1821: 'That the circuits be requested to forward all the original hymns they can.'

[38] ibid., 1820. Q. What steps shall be taken respecting another collection of hymns? A. Let one be selected from Mr Wesley's.

[39] ibid., 1823.

[40] The 'Small' and 'Large' hymn-books were afterwards issued bound together in one volume, and later editions bear a portrait of Hugh Bourne as frontispiece.

by Sanders and probably corrected by Bourne.[41] Some fourteen others bear the signature 'H.B. & W.S.', which may imply joint authorship. The collection includes 220 hymns of the Wesleys.

Bourne was responsible for the editing and compilation of the three hymn-books named above. It was no mean achievement. Some twenty-six additional hymns written by Bourne may be found in the magazines.[42]

It cannot be said that Bourne's own compositions are of exceptional quality; but all his hymns are marked by true piety and simplicity. There is some evidence of the influence of Watts and Wesley in his work.

We select three examples of hymns written by Bourne:

I

The Lord into His vineyard come,
The blossoms yield a rich perfume,
   The ripening fruits appear;
The sun of righteousness breaks forth,
The showers refresh the teeming earth,
   And glory crowns the year.

Beneath His hand his children rise,
Like cedars tow'ring to the skies,
   And shed perfumes around:
Their roots are by the waters spread,
The heavenly dew rests on their head,
   With grace and glory crown'd.

S.B. 11.

II

O Righteous Father, Lord of all:
When parents for their children call,
   Bow down a gracious ear;
Regard, O Lord, our infant charge,
And all our tender hearts enlarge,
   And fill us with Thy fear.

May we as in thy presence walk,
And with our children daily talk,
   And tell them of Thy name:
That they in righteousness may grow,
And perfect holiness below,
   And all Thy truth proclaim.

[41] Art. 'Reminiscences of Early Primitive Methodism', T. Bateman, *PMM*, 1883, p. 542.
[42] The number of hymns may be larger than this, because it is not possible, with certainty, to identify several hymns in these pages, though comparison suggests that some may be from his pen. Moreover, before setting out for America in 1844 Bourne left several hymns in MS ready for the press, with a view to forming a supplement: these 'were offered to the Connexion after his death, but were returned'. The MS was in Walford's possession in 1855 (Walford, II.107).

Fill all their hearts with living faith,
And guide them in the perfect path,
  That leads to realms on high:
May wisdom crown their rising years,
While passing through this vale of tears,
  To joys that never die.

                                    L.B. 456.

III

We now approach Thy table, Lord,
  O bless the bread and wine,
And feed us richly with Thy word,
  And consecrate us Thine.

Thy meek example may we learn,
  And feast on heavenly food:
And may we now, by faith discern,
  Thy body and Thy blood.

                                    L.B. 427.

INDEX